# Islamic Divorce in the Twenty-First Century

**The Politics of Marriage and Gender:**
**Global Issues in Local Contexts**

*Series Editor: Péter Berta*

The Politics of Marriage and Gender: Global Issues in Local Context series from Rutgers University Press fills a gap in research by examining the politics of marriage and related practices, ideologies, and interpretations, and addresses the key question of how the politics of marriage has affected social, cultural, and political processes, relations, and boundaries. The series looks at the complex relationships between the politics of marriage and gender, ethnic, national, religious, racial, and class identities, and analyzes how these relationships contribute to the development and management of social and political differences, inequalities, and conflicts.

For a list of all the titles in the series, please see the last page of the book.

# Islamic Divorce in the Twenty-First Century

## A Global Perspective

EDITED BY ERIN E. STILES AND
AYANG UTRIZA YAKIN

RUTGERS UNIVERSITY PRESS
NEW BRUNSWICK, CAMDEN, AND NEWARK, NEW JERSEY, AND LONDON

LIBRARY OF CONGRESS CATALOGING-IN-PUBLICATION DATA

Names: Stiles, Erin E., editor. | Yakin, Ayang Utriza, 1978– editor.
Title: Islamic divorce in the twenty-first century : a global perspective / edited by Erin E. Stiles and Ayang Utriza Yakin.
Description: 1. | New Brunswick : Rutgers University Press, 2022. | Series: Politics of marriage and gender: global issues in local contexts | Includes bibliographical references and index.
Identifiers: LCCN 2021058230 | ISBN 9781978829060 (paperback) | ISBN 9781978829077 (hardcover) | ISBN 9781978829084 (epub) | ISBN 9781978829091 (pdf)
Subjects: LCSH: Marriage—Religious aspects—Islam. | Divorce—Religious aspects—Islam. | Husband and wife (Islamic law) | Separation (Islamic law) | Divorce (Islamic law)
Classification: LCC HQ525.I8 I826 2022 | DDC 297.5/77—dc23/eng/20211217
LC record available at https://lccn.loc.gov/2021058230

A British Cataloging-in-Publication record for this book is available from the British Library.



∞ The paper used in this publication meets the requirements of the American National Standard for Information Sciences—Permanence of Paper for Printed Library Materials, ANSI Z39.48-1992.

www.rutgersuniversitypress.org

Manufactured in the United States of America

This book is dedicated to our families.

# CONTENTS

# SERIES FOREWORD

The politics of marriage (and divorce) is an often-used strategic tool in various social, cultural, economic, and political identity projects as well as in symbolic conflicts between ethnic, national, or religious communities. Despite having multiple strategic applicabilities, pervasiveness in everyday life, and huge significance in performing and managing identities, the politics of marriage is surprisingly underrepresented in both the international book-publishing market and the social sciences.

The Politics of Marriage and Gender: Global Issues in Local Contexts is a series from Rutgers University Press examining the politics of marriage as a phenomenon embedded into and intensely interacting with much broader social, cultural, economic, and political processes and practices such as globalization; transnationalization; international migration; human trafficking; vertical social mobility; the creation of symbolic boundaries between ethnic populations, nations, religious denominations, or classes; family formation; or struggles for women's and children's rights. The series primarily aims to analyze practices, ideologies, and interpretations related to the politics of marriage and to outline the dynamics and diversity of relatedness—interplay and interdependence, for instance—between the politics of marriage and the broader processes and practices mentioned here. In other words, most books in the series devote special attention to how the politics of marriage and these processes and practices mutually shape and explain each other.

The series concentrates on, among other things, the complex relationships between the politics of marriage and gender, ethnic, national, religious, racial, and class identities globally, and examines how these relationships contribute to the development and management of social, cultural, and political differences, inequalities, and conflicts.

The series seeks to publish single-authored books and edited volumes that develop a gap-filling and thought-provoking critical perspective, that are well-balanced between a high degree of theoretical sophistication and empirical richness, and that cross or rethink disciplinary, methodological, or theoretical boundaries. The thematic scope of the series is intentionally left broad to encourage creative submissions that fit within the perspectives outlined here.

Among the potential topics closely connected with the problem sensitivity of the series are "honor"-based violence; arranged (forced, child, etc.) marriage;

transnational marriage markets, migration, and brokerage; intersections of marriage and religion, class, or race; the politics of agency and power within marriage; reconfiguration of the family: same-sex marriage or union; the politics of love, intimacy, and desire; marriage and multicultural families; the politics (religious, legal, etc.) of divorce; the causes, forms, and consequences of polygamy in contemporary societies; sport marriage; refusing marriage; and so forth.

*Islamic Divorce in the Twenty-First Century* is a groundbreaking collection of case studies illuminating the complexity of the legal, power, religious, and gender dynamics of the final period of marriage and marital relational work in globalized Muslim contexts. Using analytical perspectives from socio-legal studies, anthropology, and history, the chapters offer a fascinating account, not only of the wide variety of ways in which both laypeople and legal professionals interpret (and reinterpret) and utilize Islamic family law while managing marital disputes and divorce, but also of the continuous, multilevel dialogue and interplay between global social, economic, and political tendencies of the twenty-first century and changing local ideologies, practices, and strategies of divorce. By analyzing legal texts and experiences from ethnographic research, the authors brilliantly demonstrate how state laws and local-level traditions of divorce shape each other; how diverse is the group of techniques and strategies used by Muslims who are seeking divorce, and how flexibly Islamic divorce is being adjusted to new circumstances and challenges in the contexts of social and political upheaval and transnational migration. *Islamic Divorce in the Twenty-First Century* is essential reading for all those who are interested in the significance and manifold practices of Islamic law in the modern world.

Péter Berta
University College London, School of Slavonic and
East European Studies and Budapest Business School,
Faculty of International Management and Business

# PREFACE AND ACKNOWLEDGMENTS

Every book has its own story, and this book is no exception. The book came about at the invitation from the series editor, Péter Berta, to contribute a volume on contemporary practices of Muslim marriage and divorce for the series the Politics of Marriage and Gender: Global Issues in Local Contexts. After meeting at the International Society for Islamic Legal Studies (ISILS) in Finland in 2018, the editors envisioned this collaboration as a way to bring together an international group of scholars doing innovative ethnographic and socio-legal work on Islamic divorce law in very different cultural and political contexts. The resulting volume is the first to take a truly global look at contemporary Muslim processes and practices of divorce disputing, and our contributors hail from Africa, Asia, Europe, and North America. In addition to adding important new lines of inquiry on Islamic divorce practice in the well-studied Middle East and North Africa (MENA) region, South Asia, and Indonesia, the chapters bring much needed attention to Muslim marriage and divorce in parts of sub-Saharan Africa and western China.

OVER THE COURSE OF THE FOUR YEARS during which we have been working on the volume, we have incurred many debts to family, friends, and colleagues. It is a pleasure to extend our gratitude to many people for their support in making the completion of this book possible.

First, we are grateful to our generous authors for agreeing to contribute chapters, and we would like to thank them for their patience during the writing and revision process. Our author team worked together with mutual respect, kindness, and understanding, which immeasurably improved this book in both form and content.

Next, we thank Péter Berta, our series editor, whose interest in the topic of Islamic marriage and divorce inspired this volume. We would like to express our gratitude for his constant encouragement and enthusiasm and for his help in sharpening the project's objectives to meet the goals of the series. In the same vein, we owe much gratitude to Jasper Chang, editor at Rutgers University Press, who introduced us to the world of publication at RUP and has worked with us with generosity and professionalism. We also thank the anonymous reviewers and readers of the book for their constructive comments and invaluable critical insights. We would like to extend our most sincere thanks to His Honor Fahrurrozi Zawawi, a judge in Selong Sharia Court in East Lombok, Nusa Tenggara, Indonesia, who helped us obtain the photo for our book cover, and to Herdyanto Yusuf Pradana, who photographed the divorce case heard by the Honorable Hakim Zawawi.

Last but certainly not least, it is a delight to thank our families for their unconditional love and unbounded moral support.

ERIN E. STILES WANTS TO THANK HER HUSBAND, Edward, and her two children, Anna and Owen, for their love and support. She is grateful for Edward's tireless enthusiam for her projects and his belief in the worth of her academic endeavors. She thanks her children for their joy and energy and for reminding her every day of what is truly important in life. She also thanks her colleagues in the Department of Anthropology at the University of Nevada for their support and extends her gratitude to Associate Dean Daniel Enrique Perez and to the members of her 2020–2021 UNR writing group for their encouragement and advice. Erin would also like to extend a heartfelt thanks to her coeditor, Ayang Utriza Yakin. Without his enthusiasm and excitement for this project and his excellent powers of organization, the volume never would have seen the light of day.

AYANG UTRIZA YAKIN WANTS TO THANK HIS WIFE, Ima, for her boundless patience in letting him work and her encouragement of his academic endeavors. He also thanks his four children: Afra, Akhtar, Ayman, and Alifa, who are a source of endless joy. He thanks them in particular for their understanding of his hectic writing schedule. He is grateful to Louis-Léon Christians and Geert van Oyen of the Research Institute Religions, Spirituality, Cultures, Society (RSCS) of Catholic University of Louvain (UCLouvain), who provided generous fellowships and always supported his research in 2017–2020, and to Baudouin Dupret, who recruited him as a postdoctoral researcher in Sciences-Po Bordeaux, France, for the Agence Nationale de Recherche's project on Equality and Law in Personal Status (ELIPS), 2021–2023. He is thankful to the Section of Arabic and Islamic Studies, Department of Language and Cultures, at Ghent University, which permitted him to continue his research alongside his teaching assignments in 2019–2021. Above all, Riza would like to thank tremendously Erin E. Stiles for inviting him to embark on the project at the end of 2018.

Erin E. Stiles
Ayang Utriza Yakin

# ABBREVIATIONS

| | |
|---|---|
| ACHPR | African Court on Human and Peoples' Rights |
| ADEMA | Alliance pour la Démocratie au Mali |
| AMUPI | Association Malienne pour le Progrès et le Salut de l'Islam |
| APDF | Association pour le Progrès et la Défense des Droits des Femmes Maliennes |
| APWA | All Pakistan Women's Association |
| ASWAJ | Ahlu Sunnah Wal Jama'a |
| BADILAG | Badan Peradilan Agama (religious courts body) |
| CAPMAS | Central Agency for Public Mobilization and Statistics (Egypt) |
| CC | Constitutional Court |
| CCP | Chinese Communist Party |
| CEDAW | Convention on the Eradication of All Forms of Discrimination against Women |
| CEPED | Centre population et développement |
| CII | Council of Islamic Ideology |
| CMA | Coordination des Mouvements de l'Azawad |
| CPCCS | Code de Procédure Civile, Commerciale et Sociale |
| DMMA | Dissolution of Muslim Marriage Act |
| FSC | Federal Shariat Court |
| GCC | Gulf Cooperation Countries |
| GDP | gross domestic product |
| HCIM | Haut Conseil Islamique du Mali |
| HSIC | Higher Shi'i Islamic Council |
| IHRDA | Institute for Human Rights and Development in Africa |
| IRD | Institut de recherche pour le développement |
| IT | information technology |
| KHI | Kompilasi Hukum Islam (Compilation of Islamic Law) |
| LE | Egyptian pounds |
| MARI | Mahkamah Agung Republik Indonesia (Supreme Court of the Republic of Indonesia) |
| MFLO | Muslim Family Law Ordinance |
| MJC | Muslim Judicial Council |

| | |
|---|---|
| MMB | Muslim Marriags Bill |
| MORA | Ministry of Religious Affairs |
| MPL | Muslim Personal Law |
| NGOs | nongovernmental organizations |
| OLFR | Ottoman Law of Family Rights |
| PP | Peraturan Pemerintah (government regulation) |
| PRC | People's Republic of China |
| PRODEJ | Programme Décennal de Développement de la Justice |
| RSA | Republic of South Africa |
| SCA | Supreme Court of Appeal |
| SCC | Supreme Constitutional Court |
| SDD | Social Development Department |
| UCT | University of Cape Town |
| UDPM | Union Démocratique du Peuple du Mali |
| UUP | Undang-Undang Perkawinan (marriage law) |
| UU PA | Undang-Undang Peradilan Agama (religious court law) |
| XUAR | Xinjiang Uyghur Autonomous Region |

# NOTE ON TRANSLITERATION

For Arabic transliteration, we followed the *International Journal of Middle East Studies* (IJMES) system and wordlist, except for Islamic legal schools (e.g., Ḥanafī, Mālikī, Shāfiʿī) and Arabic names of Islamic scholars (e.g., Aḥmad Ibn Ḥanbal). Dates are given in CE format or in the Hijri Islamic calendar followed by the Common Era date (AH/CE format).

# Islamic Divorce in the Twenty-First Century

# Introduction

## Muslim Marital Disputes and Islamic Divorce Law in Twenty-First-Century Practice

ERIN E. STILES AND AYANG UTRIZA YAKIN

In a state religious court in Central Java, Indonesia, a young Muslim woman filed for divorce because her husband could not satisfy her sexually. She explained that she and her husband had never had proper sexual relations due to his premature ejaculation. Her husband denied this, but a witness testified to their ongoing marital problems and claimed that the young woman's husband sent a text message to his wife inviting her to "use a cucumber" if she was not happy with their sexual relationship. The three-judge panel granted the wife the divorce she requested.

A Muslim woman in Accra, Ghana, approached a community Islamic authority figure known as a *malam* to ask for his help in saving her marriage. She explained that her husband had divorced her unilaterally out-of-court through the Islamic procedure known as *ṭalaq*, but she did not know why he had done so and she did not want the divorce. The malam tried to reconcile the couple by asking the husband to rescind his repudiation but he refused. As a malam plays only an advisory role and does not have any official capacity to rule on divorce, the repudiation became binding.

In Patna, India, a Muslim woman twice found herself negotiating her marriage in a nonstate shari'a court, *dar ul-qaza*. The first time, her husband sued for her return to the marital home after she had temporarily migrated to the Gulf for employment. In her view, the first court session resulted in a successful negotiation of household economics, and so she later returned with her own suit for divorce, hoping to renegotiate household roles. The young woman was shocked when the *qazi*, the Islamic judge, granted her the divorce.

A Muslim man in Beirut, Lebanon, argued with his wife on the phone and then told her not to come home because he was going to divorce her. This prompted the wife to file a claim for maintenance against her husband in a state Shi'a court. He retaliated by refusing to divorce her unless she compensated him with a large sum. She refused. After many months in court, the Shi'a judged gently urged the couple toward an Islamic divorce known as *khul'*, in which a wife compensates her husband for the divorce.

In Cape Town, South Africa, a professional Muslim woman requested a divorce from a nongovernmental Muslim Judicial Council (MJC) on the grounds of emotional abuse. South African law does not recognize Islamic marriages contracted only through religious ceremonies, so she could not apply for divorce in a state court. The woman's husband failed to show up for the many scheduled hearings at the MJC. After a year of waiting and a great deal of frustration, the imams leading the council finally granted her a religious divorce through *faskh*, an Islamic dissolution of marriage in which little or no property changes hands.

THESE FIVE VIGNETTES, which are drawn from this volume, show the wide range of Muslim experience in marital disputing and in seeking Islamic divorces. The chapters span the globe from Ghana to Indonesia, and each chapter explores aspects of the everyday realities of disputing and divorcing Muslim couples in the twenty-first century. Most of the chapters focus on Muslims who are seeking an Islamic divorce of one kind or another. When we use the term *Islamic divorce*, we refer to situations in which Muslims seek to end their marriages in accordance with Islamic law, regardless of whether the state issues or recognizes the divorce.[1] Today, many Muslims around the world marry and divorce with reference to Islamic law, a dynamic and flexible legal tradition that covers every aspect of Muslim life, including matters of personal status. For many Muslims, the ability to marry and divorce in accordance with Islamic law is of paramount importance. However, as we see from these brief snapshots of divorce practice, their experiences differ tremendously. Together, the chapters consider variations in the lived practice of Muslim marriage and divorce in light of twenty-first-century challenges and developments. The chapters take a close look at the ways in which Muslims around the world—both lay people and legal professionals—engage with and navigate Islamic law and other relevant norms in times of marital breakdown.

The volume takes a truly global approach, and the chapters discuss Islamic divorce in nine different countries in Africa, the Middle East, and Asia. Some of the countries have large Muslim majorities, such as Indonesia and Pakistan, and others have small Muslim minorities, such as South Africa and China. Some countries make provisions for state-supported Islamic courts, such as Lebanon; some recognize different marriage and divorce laws for different communities, such as India; and still others do not recognize the legitimacy of any religious marriage or divorce, such as China. Despite these differences, we see that Muslim men and women in all these countries actively seek out religiously appropriate ways to end marriages. As we will see, there is great variation in how Muslims access Islamic legal options in divorce. In states that incorporate Islamic personal-status law into the state legal system, Muslims may have the option of taking their marital disputes to state-supported courts that apply Islamic law or may be required to do so.

Elsewhere, Muslims who desire a religiously valid divorce must seek authorization outside the state legal system.

All the chapters consider divorce as a mode of Islamic law in practice, and together, the chapters show us that the Islamic legal tradition is flexible, malleable, and context-dependent. What is often referred to as "classical" Islamic law of personal status establishes several types of divorce, most of which are widely recognized by Muslim scholars and lay people. However, as numerous works of scholarship from the last two decades have shown, Islamic law in practice—including practices of divorce—is not and has never been static or monolithic, and institutions like Islamic courts and judiciaries do not exist in a vacuum (Tucker 1998; Haeri 1989; Bowen 1998, 2003; Peirce 2003; Zubaida 2005; Dupret 2007b; Osanloo 2009; Stiles 2009; Otto 2010; Mehdi, Menski, and Nielsen 2012; Giunchi 2014; Clarke 2018; Peletz 2020). Rather, the Islamic legal tradition is flexible and the ways in which divorce laws are interpreted, implemented, and utilized vary significantly over time and across cultures. In practice, people engage with Islamic legal principles in conjunction with other legal rules, local norms, and "legally relevant ideas" (Bowen 1998). As a result, most socio-legal scholars today argue that Islamic law should be studied as it is practiced in the household, in the community, and in the courtroom.

The chapters in this volume consider divorce in two primary ways. First, many chapters examine processes of disputing to understand why and how divorces happen in particular Muslim communities. These chapters examine changing expectations in marriage involving aspects such as household roles, economic arrangements, labor migration, sexual relationships, and affinal relationships and how the failure to meet these expectations may lead to divorce. Second, many of the chapters consider resolution, arbitration, and adjudication processes in divorce with particular attention to how religious leaders, elders, and judges and other authority figures handle divorce disputes. Although a number of these chapters engage with state-level legislation on divorce, they do not take a strictly law-on-the-books approach to understanding divorce but rather turn an eye to the ways in which legal practitioners like judges understand, interpret, and utilize these laws vis-à-vis their interactions with lay people.[2]

The chapters thus highlight how lay people and legal professionals navigate complex legal landscapes in pursuing and arbitrating divorce and how lay and professional legal reasoning can be understood in part as a product of their interactions. Together, the chapters show that despite widely varying cultural contexts and differences in the "formal" status of shariʿa, in everyday practice at the ground level, Muslims—both lay people and legal professionals—develop similarly pragmatic strategies for navigating plural legal landscapes to achieve favorable outcomes in marital dissolution. The construct of *legal pluralism* was formulated by John Griffiths (1986), who defined it as "the legal organization of society which is congruent with its social organization." In other words, it is "the presence in social field of more than one legal order," or "normative heterogeneity." In their book *Legal*

*Pluralism in the Arab World*, Dupret, Berger, and al-Zwaini (1999) describe legal pluralism from two different perspectives. From the lawyerly perspective, legal pluralism is the state's recognition of the existence of various legal sources (religious law, customary law, international treaties, etc.) in legislation or secondary sources in the case of legal absence or uncertainty. From the socio-legal scholar's point of view, legal pluralism is the parallel existence of a plurality of interacting legal norms that are produced by different and autonomous social fields (see also Moore 1973). Many African and Asian states—including those discussed in this volume—recognize a plurality of personal-status laws, and Muslims also draw on various normative and legal resources that are not recognized by the state. The literature on legal pluralism in Islamic contexts is growing (Benda-Beckmann 1981; Caplan 1995; Bowen 2003; Dupret 2007a; Shahar 2008, 2015; Stiles 2018), and nearly all the contexts described in this book are examples of legal pluralism in that different legal orders and sets of rules are in play. Many of the chapters explore pluralism from the point of view of everyday people in their focus on strategies that men and women pursue when seeking divorce. What is notable about this volume is that we get a sense of how Muslims in various contexts perceive of, understand, and navigate plural legal landscapes "from the ground up" (Stiles 2018: 106). A number of chapters also explore pluralism from the institutional side by investigating how judges and other legal authorities utilize different kinds of legal sources and norms in adjudicating or arbitrating disputes.

Furthermore, the book's cross-cultural, comparative look at Islamic divorce indicates that local-level Muslim practices must always be considered in the global context. The chapters discuss Muslims seeking Islamic divorce from Ghana to China, thus moving far beyond the well-studied Middle East and North Africa region. The chapters show that from Mali to Indonesia, Muslim marriages and divorces are impacted by global discourses on Islamic authority and authenticity, global discourses on human rights and gender equity, global patterns of and approaches to secularity, and global economic inequalities and attendant patterns of urbanization and migration. The chapters indicate that their influence is particularly evident in debates over authority in divorce processing and in changing expectations of marital relationships.

Certainly, as Peletz recently argued, Islamic judiciaries might be thought of as "global assemblages" in that they draw on various global resources (2020). In his examination of the Malaysian shari'a judiciary over the last three decades, Peletz conceptualized the "sharia judiciary as global assemblage"—or a creative human agency in the process of assembling, constructing, and creating a heterogeneous repertoire as it is forged in relationship with a wide array of global discourses, practices, incentives, and constraints (2020). We find this application of the concept of global assemblage useful in that it provides a shorthand for the way in which Islamic judicial practice has drawn, and continues to draw, on global influences. While Peletz looks particularly at the "rebranding" of the shari'a judiciary and its incorporation of procedural elements of the civil courts (drawing on common law due to its colonial history) and Japanese auditing procedures, the chapters in this volume consider this idea from the perspective of disputants.

The topics of the chapters vary significantly in focus, yet each takes a socio-legal approach in that the law is studied in context and in practice and most chapters draw on ethnographic research to some extent. We view socio-legal studies as "a way of seeing and recognizing the mutually constitutive relationship between law and society, which emphasizes the importance of understanding the context of the law and the exploration of social context" (Creutzfeldt, Mason, and McConnachie 2019, 3–4). As Baudouin Dupret argued, socio-legal studies seeks to explain law in terms of relationships of force, power, and domination; in terms of modernity and rationalization; or as a symbolic translation of an internalized culture (Dupret 2006, 97). The socio-legal approach is used to study, research, describe, analyze, and evaluate "real law"—or law in practice—based on either quantitative or qualitative social sciences. The approach "focuses on understanding not only what law is, but what it can and cannot do" (Menkel-Meadow, 2020, 35–44). In short, *socio-legal studies* is a generic term that covers all approaches to the law that considers its social dimension.

## Types of Islamic Divorce

Nearly all the chapters in this volume look at how Muslims understand and use different forms of Islamic divorce. The essential regulations and principles of marriage dissolution in Islam are laid down in the shari'a; namely, in the Qur'an and the *hadith*. What is often referred to as the "classical" Islamic legal tradition refers to the development of legal scholarship over a few centuries after the death of the Prophet Muhammad, which led to the emergence of several legal schools of thought, known in Arabic as *madhhabs*. The Qur'an authorizes a couple who legally contracted an Islamic marriage to end their marriage if necessary (2:227, 2:231), although this is not encouraged. Indeed, according to the Prophetic tradition, Abū Dāwūd reported a hadith in which the Prophet Muhammad declared that "the most detestable of all permitted matter to Allah the Exalted is divorce" (Sunan Abu Dawud no. 2178, 2008, 1:20). Although the dissolution of the marriage is permitted, according to the classical tradition it should be exercised only under strict circumstances. The guidelines of the separation between the spouses are explained thoroughly in *fiqh* (Islamic jurisprudence), including a wide variety of opinions from the different madhhabs across time and place. In Islamic law, the separation between the spouses can be done in many ways; here we address three primary ways: *ṭalāq*, *khul'*, and *faskh*.

### *Ṭalāq*

Ṭalāq is a divorce through a husband's unilateral repudiation of his wife. The term *ṭalāq* means "dissolution." and etymologically it means an elimination or removal of the bond (*al-ḥall wa raf' al-qayd*). The classical Islamic jurists (*fuqahā'*) define ṭalāq as the removal or elimination the bond of the marriage (*raf' al-qayd al-nikāḥ/ izāla al-nikāḥ*) that occurs immediately following specific words (such as "I divorce you") or similar expressions (such as "go to your parents' home"). Ṭalāq is the exclusive right of the man because, according to the fiqh, he paid the marriage gift (*mahr*, or dower) to his wife and provided her with accommodation and maintenance (*nafaqa*). Consequently, ṭalāq is often referred to as the "man's divorce." The Qur'an permits a man to divorce his wife in verse 2:231 and Ibn Mājah reported the following hadith: "Divorce belongs to the one who takes hold of the calf (i.e., her husband)" (no. 2081, 1952, 672). Referencing the legal scale in the Islamic tradition that designates actions on a scale from obligatory (*wājib*) to prohibited (*ḥarām*), the majority of the classical jurists opined that divorce is allowed (*jā'iz*) and permissible (*ḥalāl*). However, it could become obligatory (*wājib*) if the husband fears he cannot fulfil his duties as a husband or prohibited (*ḥarām*) if after a divorce his wife would face great trouble (such as committing adultery or living in misery). Accordingly, although ṭalāq is in the hands of a husband, the jurists agreed that this right could only be used under specific conditions.

The divorced wife must observe a waiting period (*'idda*) of three months (Q. 2:228, Q. 65:4). If the husband changes his mind during this period, he can return to the wife without a new marriage contract. The possibility of reuniting during the waiting period is what fiqh terms *ṭalāq raj'iy*, a revocable divorce. When the waiting period expires, the ṭalāq becomes an irrevocable divorce (*ṭalāq bā'in baynūna shugrā*). In this case, the ex-husband must give a *mut'a* (amenity payment or consolation gift) to his ex-wife (Q. 2:241). If a man eventually wants to return to his wife, he must renew his marriage contract with a new mahr (dower). A husband can divorce his wife two times, and he has the right to remarry her (Q. 2:229). If the husband divorces his wife for the third time, the divorce become an irrevocable divorce (*ṭalāq bā'in baynūna kubrā*) and the couple can remarry only if two conditions are met: the ex-wife must get married to another man and her new husband must then divorce her (Q. 2:230) (see Ibn 'Abidīn 2003, 4:423–424; *al-Mawsū'a al-Fiqhiyya*, 1414/1993, 29:5; al-Zuḥaylī 1985, 7:356–363; al-Jazīrī 1423/2003, 4:248–281; *Encyclopaedia of Islam* 2000, 10:151–155).

Ṭalāq is a right that is only available to the husband, and there is no similar unilateral repudiation available to women. Given this inequity in the law, many contemporary states have statutorily attenuated or circumscribed a man's right to ṭalāq by banning it, requiring judicial approval, or limiting the circumstances under which it is permissible. In Tunisia, men and women have equal legal access to divorce. However in most states, "the formal target of such legislation is not the husband's power of talaq itself, but the arbitrary and unreflective use of this power" (Welchman 2007, 109). For example, numerous contemporary states that were part of the Ottoman Empire limit a man's abilities in ṭalāq by not recognizing the legality of a ṭalāq uttered in inebriation (Welchman 2007; Landry, this volume). Moreover, in many states, legal action has focused on limiting a man's ability to enact a "triple-ṭalāq," or three ṭalāqs pronounced at once, which is in essence an instant irrevocable divorce. In 2017 the Indian Supreme Court determined ṭalāq to be unconstitutional and even deemed pronouncing ṭalāq a criminal offense. Six of the chapters in this volume address practices of ṭalāq in the twenty-first century.

### *Khul'*

Another Islamic dissolution of marriage is referred to as khul'. Etymologically, the Arabic word *khul'* means to "take off" and to "eliminate." The Qur'an considers a couple as a garment to each other (2:187) and, therefore, through khul' a wife is permitted to "take off" her garment by separating from her husband. Khul' is the separation of spouses with compensation (*'iwaḍ*) paid by the wife or her family to her husband from the dower or other financial compensation. A khul' can be initiated by the wife or her legal guardian, and specific words might be used (such as khul' or ṭalāq) to release the wife from the bond of the marriage. In the classical sources, khul' is an extrajudicial divorce, like ṭalāq.

Khul' is permissible according to the Qur'an, which says, "There is no blame on them for what she gives up to become free thereby" (2:229). It is also permissible according to a well-established hadith concerning a woman named either Jamila or Habiba, the wife of Thābit Ibn Qayyis, who returned the garden her husband gave her as a marriage gift in exchange for her divorce (as reported by al-Bukhari no. 5276, Ibn Hajar al-'Asqalānī, 1421/2001, 9:312). The classical jurists explained that a woman could request khul' on many grounds: the irregularity of marriage, the apostasy of her husband, harmful acts of her husband (*ḍarar*), disputes between spouses (*shiqāq*), the absence of a harmonious relationship between spouses, lack of maintenance from her husband (*nafaqa*), a husband's poor morals, the husband's health, and so forth. In short, the jurists agreed that if a woman fears that she will not be able to fulfil God's rules (*ḥudūd Allāh*) and if there are any causes considered ḍarar (harmful acts), then she can request the khul' to prevent her from suffering more acts of violence and abuse, both physical and emotional. Once khul' is issued, it counts as one irrevocable divorce. According to the classical sources, khul' does not require the intervention of a judge. After khul', the majority of jurists agree that the waiting period before remarriage for the woman is three months; a minority opinion requires one month (al-Zuḥaylī, 1985, 7:480–508; *al-Mawsū'a al-Fiqhiyya* 1410/1990, 19:234–259).

Today the potential of khul' as an equalizer in divorce rights is widely acknowledged. Indeed, numerous states in the late twentieth and early twenty-first centuries have sought to expand women's options in khul'; first Pakistan, followed by Egypt, Algeria, Jordan, Morocco, and Gaza (Welchman 2007; Sonneveld and Stiles 2019). Most often, states did this by permitting unilateral khul', with a judge's approval, at the demand of the wife and without the consent of the husband. Lynn Welchman has referred to this as the "third wave" of Islamic reform of divorce law (2007; see also Sonneveld and Stiles 2019). Because it may be initiated by a woman, khul' has sometimes been referred to as "the woman's divorce." However, research has shown that characterizing khul' simply as a woman's divorce is somewhat simplistic, as in some cases, khul' can be both costly and stigmatizing to women (Carroll 1996; Vatuk 2008). Furthermore, in some contemporary contexts, such as southern India and Zanzibar, men may seek khul' and woman may strive to avoid it (Vatuk 2019; Stiles 2019). Moreover, in some cases, religious or even secular judges may impose khul' (Moors 1995; Stiles 2019; van Eijk 2019). Thus, even though Muslims around the world agree on the scriptural basis for khul', the way that it is used and understood differs significantly across cultures (Sonneveld and Stiles 2019). Many of the chapters in this volume address local manifestations of khul'.

### *Faskh: Judicial Divorce*

In Islamic classical law, the judicial dissolution of marriage is referred to as faskh. Etymologically, *faskh* means "annulment" or "separation" and by definition it is the annulment of a contract; thus the *faskh al-nikāḥ* is the annulment of the marriage contract. It should be emphasized that through the faskh, the marriage contract becomes void as if it never happened. Classical sources define the grounds for dissolution of marriage through faskh for two conditions. First are the contingency conditions (*asbāb ṭār'ia*) that contradict the marriage, such as the apostasy of spouse (*ridda*), a spouse's negligence in practicing Islamic obligations, or if a family relationship by blood or marriage prohibits intermarriage, such as the wife and her father-in-law or the husband and his mother-in-law. Second, the comparative conditions (*asbāb muqārana*) include grounds for faskh such as the marriage of children before reaching the age of maturity, the marriage of unequal conditions between spouses, the marriage with the lowest dower according to the norms of the community, unusual or irregular contracts, and so forth. Illness or disease are also grounds for faskh according to jurists from the four Sunni madhhabs, who explained such conditions at length. A disease might affect either spouse, such as mental illness, leprosy, elephantiasis; only the man, such as impotence or lack of a genital organ; or only the woman, such as abnormalities of the genitalia that would prevent intercourse. In Islamic classical law, faskh can only be obtained through a judicial process or by the decree of an Islamic judge; if grounds for faskh are not present, a spouse can file through ṭalāq or khul' (al-Zuḥaylī 1985, 7:348–356; al-Jazīrī 1423/2003, 4:161–177; *al-Mawsū'a al-Fiqhiyya* 1415/1995, 32:131–139).

As with khul', in the contemporary context there is much variation in how and when judges or other religious and legal authority figures use faskh in dissolving a marriage. In this volume, faskh is addressed in the chapters on South Africa, Indonesia, India, and Pakistan.

## Thematic Organization of the Volume

We have divided the chapters in this volume into three broad parts, each of which attends to a particular set of contemporary circumstances that affect Islamic divorce practices on the local level. One of the aims of this volume is to show how Muslims use Islamic law in divorce practice even if shari'a is not formally recognized by the state: the law is thus more than what is mandated by the state. In many of the countries addressed in this book the state has incorporated Islamic legal rules into the national legal system to some degree. However, in others there is no formal recognition of Islamic law, and Muslims seeking religiously valid divorces must approach nonstate actors and institutions. It is important to note, as many others have done, that for centuries, Islamic law has always coexisted with other legal norms and other sources of law and has frequently been "subordinate to other norms" (Otto 2010, 616; see also Zubaida 2005). The chapters in the first part consider the relationship between shariʿa and state law and questions of the politicization of divorce law in Pakistan, Egypt, and South Africa.[3] The second part includes chapters on Indonesia, Ghana, and Lebanon, which address how varying forms of legal pluralism impact Muslim possibilities in enacting and arbitrating divorce by considering gendered strategies of pursuing divorce and judicial responses to them. The chapters in the final part explore the impact of large-scale global movements such as urbanization, labor migration, and Islamic renewal on divorce practices in Mali, China, and India.

### *State Politics and Divorce Law: Reform and Recommendations*

The chapters in part I addresses the impact of state level legislation or codification—and the lack thereof—on the practice of divorce. In the growing body of socio-legal scholarship on Islamic law, many scholars have examined late-twentieth- and early twenty-first-century state-level reforms in family law in Muslim-majority countries (Carroll 1996; Bowen 2003; Buskens 2003; Moors 2003; Welchman 2003, 2007; Würth 2003; Osanloo 2009; Nurlaelawati 2010, 2013; Schulz 2010; Sonneveld 2012; Holden 2012; Voorhoeve 2012; van Huis 2019; Al-Sharmani 2017; Clarke 2018; Sonneveld and Stiles 2019; Peletz 2002, 2020). Lynn Welchman identifies three broad waves of legal reform beginning in the nineteenth century, all ostensibly with the intention of improving women's status in divorce (2007). She describes the third phase of reform as state-level efforts to make gender rights in divorce more equitable. A number of states have attempted to balance a man's right to unilateral ṭalāq by introducing nonconsensual khulʿ on the initiative of the wife (2007, 109). Pakistan did so in the late twentieth century, and others states, most notably Egypt, followed suit early in the twenty-first; the impact of khulʿ reforms has been explored by numerous scholars (Carroll 1996; Zantout 2006; Sonneveld 2012; Al-Sharmani 2017; Sonneveld and Stiles 2019).

Related scholarship focuses on the politicization of divorce rights and family-law reform in contemporary states (e.g., Osanloo 2009; Sonneveld 2012; Al-Sharmani 2017). A key example of this approach comes from Arzoo Osanloo (2009), who explored how the postrevolutionary Iranian government deliberately politicized women's rights to meet international trends and standards concerning gender issues. Osanloo argues that understanding women's rights in any one locale requires understanding the political history and cultural and social practices in question. The ideas, meanings, discourses, and practices of "rights" are social, cultural, and historical constructions. Osanloo shows how Iranian courts can be considered "dialogical sites" where women can mobilize "rights talks" to win their demands. The first two chapters in this part follow in this vein by critically examining the aftermath of state-level legal reforms of khulʿ and ṭalāq in changing political climates in Pakistan and Egypt; in both cases, the reforms were aimed at improving women's status in divorce. The third chapter, on South Africa, considers the consequences of state law that fails to recognize the validity of Islamic religious marriage and divorce.

In chapter 1, Elisa Giunchi examines legislation and recent decisions concerning khulʿ in light of the changing political climate of Pakistan and questions whether khulʿ actually limits women's possibilities in divorce. Pakistan has a large Muslim majority of over 96 percent. Starting from the advent of independence in 1947, Pakistan continued the colonial policy of combining English common law and Islamic law for matters of family and personal status. Women's rights in the domestic sphere were expanded in the 1960s. In the late 1970s and 1980s, under General Zia ul-Haq, there was a concerted attempt at Islamizing Pakistani criminal law, with the effect of penalizing women and contradicting legislation on family law. Increasingly, however, the judiciary has referred to Islamic ideas in an effort to enhance women's rights. Today, all matters of personal status—including marriage and divorce—are heard in the family courts. The Federal Shariat Court (FSC) was established in 1980 to hear appeals of *ḥudūd* (criminal cases with prescribed punishments) and to review whether laws are contrary to the principles of Islam.

Giunchi combines an analysis of Pakistani legislation with an examination of recent court decisions and interviews with judges to show how laws regarding khulʿ are applied and utilized in the courts. An intriguing aspect of the chapter is Giunchi's consideration of politicized debates between modernists and traditionalists over the use of *ijtihād* (independent legal reasoning): who has the authority to perform ijtihād and how does this affect the application of khulʿ? Giunchi finds that in a number of rulings, Pakistani judges and their courts reasoned that it is more appropriate to return to the Qurʾan and hadith rather than rely on generations of Islamic legal scholarship (fiqh). Through this reasoning, courts have determined that in some cases, a husband's consent is not necessary in khulʿ. Giunchi argues that secular higher-court judges have thus turned what might be considered "medieval legal tools" like *talfīq* (patching together legal principles from different legal schools) and *takhayyur* (privileging the position of one legal school) into something new, and have often done so to keep decisions in line with global discourses on human rights. In some ways, this has enhanced women's capacity for ending their marriages, particularly in cases appealed from the lower courts. However, like others who have researched the possibilities and pitfalls of khulʿ (Carroll 1996; Vatuk 2008; Holden 2012; Sonneveld and Stiles 2019; Stiles 2019; Al-Sharmani 2017; Sonneveld 2010), Giunchi finds that the potential of khulʿ is limited. Unlike men, women still need to approach the court for divorce; women may also be at significant financial disadvantage in seeking khulʿ and may be stigmatized for doing so. Giunchi's chapter also shows that judicial divorce practice is shaped by changing political climates: "the rise of militant groups may induce judges, whatever their outlook, to exercise greater caution or may pressure the legislative and the executive to abrogate or amend progressive legislation on divorce" (40).

In chapter 2, Nathalie Bernard-Maugiron considers how recent attempts by the Egyptian state to circumscribe men's options in ṭalāq play out in courts when judges try to validate it. After the establishment of the Arab Republic of Egypt in 1952, the Egyptian state turned toward socialism and nationalism and unified the legal system, which eliminated separate shari'a courts. However, the national courts continued to utilize Islamic law for matters of personal status (Sonneveld and Berger 2010). The principles of shari'a have been nominally recognized as the primary source of law since passage of the amended 1980 constitution, but in practice this has never expanded beyond the realm of personal status to include civil or criminal law. Personal-status law was partially codified over the last century, and where there is no relevant legal provision, judges in state courts utilize Ḥanafī jurisprudence (Sonneveld and Berger 2010, 74). Muslim women have been able to file for many types of divorce in Egypt's courts since the 1920s, and since 2000 women have been able to request no-fault khul' in courts, the political consequences of which have been profound (Sonneveld 2012; Al-Sharmani 2017).

Muslim men in Egypt have maintained the right to unilateral divorce through ṭalāq, but by law they must register the divorce. In 2017, President Abdel Fattah al-Sisi tried to further curtail men's ability to pronounce divorce unilaterally by declaring that ṭalāq would only be valid if pronounced in front of a registrar. Bernard-Maugiron shows the highly charged nature of the relationship between politics and religion in the domain of family law in Egypt as political and Islamic authorities struggle for "control of the religious sphere." Although Sisi's declaration received a great deal of support from women's rights groups and other progressive bodies, al-Azhar University criticized it on the grounds that men's rights to ṭalāq have a long history in the Islamic tradition. Bernard-Maugiron's chapter combines an analysis of decisions of Egypt's two supreme courts with decisions made by family judges. Similarly to Giunchi, she looks at the judicial response to ṭalāq laws, and particularly how decisions from higher courts impact what happens in the lower-level family courts. She finds that the lower courts do not contest precedents set by the higher courts even if they might appear to conflict with fiqh, for example, by requiring a man to register his ṭalāq. However, judges also specifically reference shari'a in their legal reasoning, "but only to legitimize the legislative reforms by emphasizing that they conform to shari'a or Ḥanafī fiqh" (59).

Fatima Essop's chapter on South Africa provides an excellent counterpoint to the chapters on Egypt and Pakistan because the South African state does not recognize Islamic marriages. Only about 2 percent of South Africa's population is Muslim, and Muslims have historically handled matters of personal status within their own communities (Allie 2010). Although the 1996 Constitution of South Africa makes provisions for the recognition of multiple family-law systems based on different religions and cultures, no formal legislation has yet recognized Islamic marriage and thus there is no formal provision for Islamic divorces, although Muslims have called for the recognition of religious marriages (see also Amien 2020). Muslims thus seek out religious divorces in nonstate Muslim judicial bodies.

One such body is the focus of chapter 3. Based on her extensive ethnographic research in the nonstate MJC in Cape Town, Essop argues that the formal recognition of Islamic personal-status law in South Africa would lead to positive change for Muslim women. At present, South African Muslims handle matters of marriage and divorce in nonstate institutions such as the MJC and there is no state option for Islamic divorce. Essop argues that this presents a particular challenge to Muslim women, and her chapter contributes to a growing literature on how Muslims seek out religious marriages and divorces in states that do not formally recognize Islamic law (Fournier 2006, 2016; Bano 2012; Berger 2013; Moors 2013; Bowen 2016; Jaraba 2019; van Eijk 2019). She writes that while South African Muslims generally acknowledge the validity of ṭalāq among themselves, Muslim women who want to initiate divorce must take other means—usually by approaching one of the shariʿa courts run by organizations such as the MJC. Essop argues that although the MJC and similar institutions fill a much-needed gap in legal accessibility for women, they have a number of shortcomings and Muslim women are generally not satisfied with the assistance they receive from them. Essop's chapter takes a policy-oriented advisory approach, and she outlines several steps that the MJC and similar bodies could take to improve outcomes for women who seek a divorce. She recommends that there should be more female judges, better training for the judges, clearly defined court procedures, and the adoption of the more lenient grounds for faskh from the Mālikī school. In sum, Essop argues, the state recognition of Islamic law and courts would do much to enhance women's standing and options in divorce.

### *Gendered Strategies and Judicial Responses in Marital Disputing*

Part II considers the perspectives and strategies of Muslim women and men who are seeking divorce and how legal authorities (both state and nonstate) respond to their claims and strategies. Recent decades have seen the emergence of an extensive body of literature on gendered practices of disputing in Islamic legal contexts, both past and present (Caplan 1995; Würth 1995; Tucker 1998; Sonbol 1996; Hirsch 1998; Mir-Hosseini 2000; Peirce 2003; Agmon 2006; Osanloo 2006; Vatuk 2008; Osanloo 2009; Stiles 2009; Sonneveld 2012; Stockreiter 2015; McMahon 2015; van Eijk 2016; Al-Sharmani 2017; Lemons 2019; Peletz 2002, 2020). The chapters in part II build on this rich body of work by adding new dimensions, both geographically (Ghana and Lebanon) and topically (sexual dissatisfaction as grounds for divorce in Indonesia). Each chapter considers how changing social conditions and cultural meanings in the twenty-first century can lead to new litigant strategies in seeking marriage dissolution. The chapters all examine legal pluralism from the standpoint of everyday people navigating changing legal options and the ways in which different kinds of religious and legal authority figures—both within and outside the state—respond to these changing strategies.

In chapter 4, Ayang Utriza Yakin considers the increasing number of men and women in Indonesia who petition for divorce on the grounds of a wife's dissatisfaction with the marital sexual relationship. Today, Indonesian Muslims handle family-law cases in religious courts that are presided over by judges (*hakim*) with training in Islamic law. Indonesia's legal system has incorporated religious courts for decades, and the twentieth century saw a number political upheavals resulting from controversy over the place of shari'a in the constitution. In 1966, the National Assembly issued a decree stipulating that the Pancasila (the five principles of Indonesian political philosophy) should be the sole source of law.[4] However, the state accommodated Muslim aspirations in legislation by recognizing elements of the shari'a, especially in civil matters. The Islamic courts were centralized by legislation in 1989 and a number of shari'a-referred laws relevant to marriage and divorce have been promulgated since then, such as the Law of Marriage in 1974 and the Compilation of Islamic Laws in 1991 (Hosen 2007; Hefner 2011).

Yakin's chapter considers a fascinating set of cases to explain why both men and women file for divorce on the grounds of female sexual dissatisfaction and how religious courts deal with these claims, given that the lack of sexual fulfilment is not a legitimate reason for divorce according to Indonesian law. The chapter is based on ethnographic work in the religious court of South Jakarta and an analysis of religious court judgments from the Indonesian Supreme Court database. Yakin suggests that the recent increase in divorce petitions on grounds of sexual dissatisfaction may reflect broad social changes, as recent research finds an increasingly widespread belief among Indonesian women that they have the right to a satisfying sexual life in marriage (Riyani 2020). Although sexual dissatisfaction is not grounds for divorce in Indonesia law, Yakin finds that judges usually grant these divorce requests and support their rulings by adapting existing Indonesian law to the needs of the case. Yakin proposes that these religious courts thus redefine what constitutes "continuous and irreconcilable discord" according to Indonesian law: they argue that sexual dissatisfaction can be interpreted as a form of "irreconcilable discord" (*syiqaq*). To address uncertainty in the Indonesian legislation, the courts indirectly refer to sources beyond Indonesian law on the books, such as contemporary fiqh books and even Egyptian family law. In a thought-provoking take on legal pluralism and Peletz's notion of the Islamic judiciary as "global assemblage," Yakin shows that when dealing with uncertainty in the law, Indonesian judges accommodate litigant requests through a creative jurisprudence that adheres to the letter of Indonesian law but also draws on a range of legally relevant sources external to this law. Recently, De Hart, Sonneveld, and Sportel observed that studies of Islamic law have generally neglected men's perspectives and experiences, which may result in overlooking important aspects of family law and modalities of masculinity

(2017, 44); Yakin's chapter remedies this shortcoming by taking into account of men's strategies in divorce negotiations.

In chapter 5, Fulera Issaka-Toure considers how Muslim women strategize to achieve divorce arrangements to their benefit in Ghana's pluralistic legal environment. Muslims make up about 18 percent of Ghana's population. The Ghanaian Constitution does not establish an official religion and does not make specific provisions for Islamic law, although it is included as a form of "customary law," which may be applied in customary courts and is therefore not formally overseen by the state. Muslims may pursue divorce either through customary measures or English common law.

One of the most important contributions of Issaka-Toure's chapter is her finding that although Muslim women's everyday practices and understandings of divorce may differ from "classical" Islamic law, they are upheld by the community and by Islamic authority figures as legitimate Islamic divorce practices. Although in theory the law is more favorable toward men, Issaka-Toure shows that Ghanaian women find ways of applying it to their advantage. Drawing on ethnographic research conducted in Accra, Issaka-Toure argues that although Muslim women in Accra articulate gendered inequities in classical Islamic laws on divorce in cases of ṭalāq (known locally as *saki*), they maintain confidence in the abilities of an Islamic religious authority known as a *malam* (plural, *malamai*) to bring about marital reconciliation. When initiating divorce themselves, most Muslim women tend to seek a divorce in one of two different ways, only one of which involves a legal authority figure. First, some women separate from their husbands and go through a judicial process with the malam to obtain a divorce. Other women separate from their husbands on their own initiative, maintain they are divorced, and then remarry. In some cases this results in what is known colloquially as "marriage on top of marriage." Women who pursue this option do not perceive their actions as unlawful, but rather as a legitimate marriage following a legitimate divorce. Issaka-Toure's findings show that Islamic law on divorce is malleable, and its flexibility is established through the legal reasoning of divorcing women and also of Islamic religious authorities. Thus, the author argues that Islamic family law is a living law that in many ways is being driven by the circumstances and initiatives of women.

In chapter 6, Jean-Michel Landry considers Muslim divorces in the legally plural environment of Lebanon. In Lebanon, Islamic law is incorporated into the state legal system, which is based on Ottoman law, French civil law, and Islamic law. About 67 percent of Lebanon's population is Muslim, including Sunni, Shi'a, Druze, and other sects, and these different communities are subject to different divorce laws.[5] Shari'a courts are part of the state legal system and have jurisdiction over matters of personal status such as marriage and divorce; the courts are staffed by judges trained in Islamic law. The Ottoman Law of Family Rights (OLRF) is applicable to the Shi'a and Sunni communities alike (though not to the same extent in both), but the Druze community has its own family-law code. Moreover, while Sunni and Druze laws are primarily codified, Shiʿi law remains mostly uncodified. Muslims also occasionally seek out nonstate religious authorities.

In examining strategies undertaken by Muslims seeking divorce, Landry's chapter shows how everyday people navigate Lebanon's plural legal environment as well as how family courts exemplify a normative pluralism in upholding both religious and secular norms. Marital affairs are legally settled in family courts where judges enforce religion-based norms through secular juridical procedures. Landry's chapter explores how divorces are handled in Sunni, Druze, and, in particular, Shiʿi courts. His ethnographic fieldwork, which was conducted in four different family courts, established that Muslim women face excessive legal hardship in leaving problematic marriages, and much of the chapter focuses on how women navigate the complex, legally plural landscape of Lebanon. Landry is particularly interested in a type of divorce specific to Shiʿism called *ṭalāq al-ḥākim* (divorce by the judge), which Shiʿi women frequently seek out. Unlike other kinds of divorce, ṭalāq al-ḥākim is usually performed by clerics working outside the state network of family courts, but official family judges must ratify ṭalāq al-ḥākim. Landry finds that sometimes judges reject legal arrangements like these, which are made "in the shadows" of family courts. The chapter also shows how shariʿa-derived norms are enforced in a secular legal framework. Aspects of Lebanese law are discriminatory against the female citizen, and while some Islamic norms are responsible for this gender asymmetry, the chapter demonstrates that certain secular legal practices also contribute to it. Landry argues that this discrimination is rooted in the secular arrangement of spaces, procedures, and knowledge through which Islam-based precepts are implemented.

### *Islamic Divorce in the Context of Global Patterns of Mobility, Upheaval, and Changing Household Economies*

The third and final part of the volume considers how patterns of global change and upheaval are influencing divorce practices among Muslims in Mali, China, and India. The chapters deal with varying forms of social change—Islamic revival, modernization projects, rapid economic growth, and global labor migration—yet all three examine how these forms of social change affect household economies and divorce practices. Some scholars have approached economic issues in Islamic personal-status law by looking at property disputes in inheritance cases (Bowen 1998, 2003), and others have taken up this issue with particular reference to the economic aspects of divorce (Moors 1995; Sonneveld 2012, 2019; Vatuk 2019; Stiles 2019; van Huis 2019). The three chapters in this part add to this growing body of literature by considering how broad-scale social changes in Mali, China, and India are influencing local-level expectations within and outside local economies of marriage and how these changing expectations can lead to divorce. By looking at the way in which global processes play out in local practices of divorce, the chapters complement Peletz's recent argument that the institution of the Malaysian judiciaries might be viewed as a set of global assemblages in that they draw on legal regimes and organizational processes from across the globe (2020).

The Republic of Mali has been a secular state since independence in 1960. Muslims form the overwhelming majority, with about 95 percent of the population. In chapter 7, Dorothea Schulz and Souleymane Diallo note that in recent years, Islamic revival and militant Muslim movements in certain regions of Mali have generated an increasingly Islam-focused public discourse at the national and the local levels. During the colonial period, the French recognized Islamic norms as part of customary law (Schulz 2010). Today, Mali's legal system is based in large part on the French tradition, and Islamic law is not incorporated into the state. However, Schulz and Diallo argue that Islamic norms have left an "imprint" on codified law. During the colonial period, local "customary" laws and Islamic rules gradually converged, but in different ways and to different extents depending on how long particular parts of Mali had been Muslim. Today, Muslims in some regions seek out local-level Islamic legal authorities when disputing marriage and seeking divorces.

Schulz and Diallo show how Muslims in different areas of Mali account for a perceived concerning rise in the divorce rate. An expanding Islamic public discourse has catalyzed a "reframing" of divorce in terms of the proper "Islamic" regulation of personal life. In northern Mali, for example, marriage and divorce practices have been influenced by new "shariʿa regulations" imposed by militant Islamic groups that have seized control in recent years. Schulz and Diallo methodologically combine ethnographic research with an analysis of recent legal history in Mali. Their research shows that many Malians attribute the rising divorce rate to global social trends, particularly the changing economic conditions that have led more women to work outside the home. This in turn has led to a perceived decline in the influence of elders over the marriages of the young, which many observers believe has destabilized marriages. Schulz and Diallo find that many Malians also attribute the rising divorce rate to a lack of adherence to Islamic values, similar to what scholars have noted in East Africa (Stiles 2014; Keefe 2015; Caplan 2015). The chapter explores such attitudes with reference to Mali's current "Islamic awakening," which draws on global Muslim activist discourse, and responses to it that draw on global discourses of human rights and gender equity.

In chapter 8, Rune Steenberg considers Uyghur Muslim divorce practices in western China. China's Muslim population is probably less than 2 percent of the total population, and the state makes no provisions for religious divorces of any kind. All Muslims must therefore seek divorce in the state courts, but for many Uyghurs the court does little more than issue the appropriate documents and stamp divorce papers. Negotiations over divorce most often take place outside the courtroom and usually involve the litigants' families.[6]

Steenberg's chapter examines the high divorce rate among Uyghurs of Xinjiang as a consequence of rapid social change, the elements of which are economic growth, state-backed modernization campaigns, increasing integration of western

China into the state, and most recently government persecution of Muslims. All these changes have affected family and kinship structure in the region by weakening communal-based kinship patterns. Steenberg's chapter is based on extensive ethnographic research, and his analysis centers on expectations in kinship relations and, particularly, on the importance of cultivating affinal relatives as key central family members. In the city of Kashgar, Uyghurs tend to rely on affinal relatives for economic and social support and, as a result, marriage is a community affair intended to bring families together. Consequently, if a marriage does not include affinal support, the family accepts divorce as the means to ending one marriage in hopes there will be another that will be more satisfying for the parties involved. In a time of rapid social change, these kinship networks have been increasingly compromised. As Uyghur Muslims have been incarcerated in increasing numbers, Uyghur communities are suffering tremendously; divorce and other marriage-related social practices have declined as a result. The Hui (Muslim Chinese) have been treated with more tolerance by the Chinese state, but they are also subject to state law in marriage and divorce. Steenberg concludes the chapter by noting that the decline in Uyghur divorce rates since 2017 might be due to a "deterioration of normal social life" concomitant with the mass incarceration of Muslims in the region.

Chapter 9, by Katherine Lemons and Nadia Hussain, focuses on marital disputes in a shariʿa court in Patna, in the northeastern Indian state of Bihar. The chapter shows how contemporary labor-migration practices influence the political economy of marriage and divorce. India's Muslim minority makes up about 15 percent of the population. India is a secular state and the legal system is based primarily on English common law. The personal-law system accommodates religious law, and family-law cases are heard in state civil courts, where judges apply the law appropriate to the religion of the litigants. For Muslims, judges most often refer to Islamic jurisprudence and relevant legislation, much of which dates to the colonial period. However, throughout India, Muslims may also seek nonbinding, alternative legal remedies at a nongovernmental *dar ul-qaza* (*qadi* courts), where religiously trained judges, *qazis*, utilize shariʿa to mediate disputes (Vatuk 2008; Lemons 2019). In some Indian states, qazis are unpaid government appointees, while in others, such as Bihar state, they are not. In 2017, the Indian Supreme Court declared the instantaneous male unilateral divorce known as the *triple-ṭalāq* to be unconstitutional. Many hailed the end of triple-ṭalāq as a move toward women's equality in divorce. However, the Supreme Court also made the pronouncement of triple-ṭalāq a crime, which many view as a move that is more anti-Muslim than pro-woman.

Lemons and Hussain's ethnographic research shows that the dar ul-qaza function as sites for negotiating family relationships—particularly in the context of changing economics due to global migration—and the chapter adeptly connects scholarship on Islamic law in practice with current research on gender and global migration. The chapter follows the tribulations of Ruksana, a young woman who approaches the qazi courts as a space to work out changing economic relationships in her family. Twice Ruksana migrated to the Persian Gulf for employment. Although her employment abroad provided her with great satisfaction and an ability to support her children and parents, it caused a great deal of friction with her husband and in-laws, and she became involved in two marital dispute cases. In the first, her husband took her to court to sue for her return to the marital home. The numerous hearings with the qazi led to a reconciliation that met some of Ruksana's goals for her marriage in terms of shared responsibility for economic matters. However, she eventually filed for a *khula* (Arabic, khulʿ) divorce, but she was shocked when the qazi granted it as divorce was not actually her goal. Rather, she had sought to renegotiate the terms of her marriage through court proceedings. The chapter brings a new angle to other work that considers Islamic courts spaces for women to voice concerns and make claims on their husbands (Mir-Hosseini 2000; Hirsch 1998; Peletz 2002; Stiles 2009; Osanloo 2009; Lemons 2019) by considering how changing global economics impacts marital negotiations at the household level—both in and out of court.

TOGETHER, the chapters in this collection provide a much-needed look at Islamic divorce in the twenty-first century. At the personal, familial, and institutional levels, patterns of global change and the circulation of global discourses impact the practices and processes of divorcing. The chapters show how Muslims in vastly different cultural and political contexts, from Ghana to Indonesia, similarly value the ability to end marriages in religiously appropriate ways and consequently seek out Islamic means of divorcing in whatever manner is available—both within and outside the state. Through a consideration of the legal reasoning processes and the strategizing of both disputants and legal professionals, the chapters also emphasize the flexibility of the twenty-first-century Islamic legal tradition. This flexibility is nothing new, but the ways in which lay people and legal professionals draw on various legally relevant resources is. We will see that this flexibility reflects the interactional and intersubjective of handling disputes. The process of doing law is generated through the interactions of disputing parties and adjudicating authorities, of individuals and familial networks, and of local and institutional practice.

## NOTES

1. The book does not consider other types of partnerships that people form in Muslim contexts; although this is certainly an important area of study, it is beyond the scope of this volume.
2. In effect, many of the chapters take the "realistic" approach advocated by Dupret and Voorhoeve (2012).
3. For a detailed look at how "sharia-based rules" are incorporated into numerous other states, please see Otto 2010.
4. Pancasila are (1) "Belief in One Supreme God," (2) "Just Humanitarianism," (3) "Unity of Indonesia," (4) "Democracy Guided by Consultation," and (5) Social Justice.

5. Office of International Religious Freedom (2020).
6. Steenburg has noted that while husbands sometimes pronounce ṭalāq in front of their families, pronouncing ṭalāq in the courtroom would likely be deemed an illegal religious practice by the state (personal communication, July 2020).

## REFERENCES

Abū Dāwūd. 1389/1969. *Sunan Abī Dāwūd*. Edited by ʿIzzat ʿAbid al-Duʿās. Beirut: Dār al-Kutub al-ʿIlmiyya.

Abu Dawud. 2008. *Sunan Abu Dawud*, vol. 1. Translated into English by Yaser Qadhi. Riyadh: Maktaba Darus Salam.

Agmon, Iris. 2006. *Family and Court: Legal Culture and Modernity in Late Ottoman Palestine*. Syracuse: Syracuse University Press.

Allie, Shouket. 2010. "A Legal and Historical Excursus of Muslim Personal Law in the Colonial Cape, South Africa, Eighteenth to Twentieth Century." In *Muslim Family Law in Sub-Saharan Africa: Colonial Legacies and Post-Colonial Challenges*, edited by Shamil Jeppie, Ebrahim Moosa, and Richard Roberts, 63–84. Amsterdam: Amsterdam University Press.

Amien, Waheeda. 2020. "Judicial Intervention in Facilitating Legal Recognition (and Regulation) of Muslim Family Law in Muslim-Minority Countries: The Case of South Africa." *Journal of Islamic Law* 1 (1):65–114.

Bano, Samia. 2012. *Muslim Women and Shariʿah Councils, Transcending the Boundaries of Community and Law*. London: Palgrave Macmillan.

Benda-Beckmann, Kebeet von. 1981. "Forum Shopping and Shopping Forums: Dispute Processing in a Minangkabau Village in Western Sumatra." *Journal of Legal Pluralism and Unofficial Law* 13 (19):117–159.

Berger, Maurits. 2013. *Applying Sharia in the West. Facts, Fears and the Future of Islamic Rules on Family Relations in the West*. Leiden: Leiden University Press.

Bowen, John R. 1998. "'You May Not Give It Away': How Social Norms Shape Islamic Law in Contemporary Indonesian Jurisprudence." *Islamic Law and Society* 5 (3):382–408.

———. 2003. *Islam, Law, and Equality in Indonesia: An Anthropology of Public Reasoning*. Cambridge: Cambridge University Press.

———. 2016. *On British Islam: Religion, Law, and Everyday Practice in Shariʿa Councils*. Princeton: Princeton University Press.

Buskens, Léon. 2003. "Recent Debates on Family Law Reform in Morocco: Islamic Law as Politics in an Emerging Public Sphere." *Islamic Law and Society* 10 (1):70–131.

Caplan, Pat. 1995. "Law' and 'Custom': Marital Disputes on Northern Mafia Island, Tanzania." In *Understanding Disputes: The Politics of Argument*, edited by Pat Caplan, 203–222. Oxford: Berg Publishers.

———.2015. "Two Weddings in Northern Mafia: Changes in Women's Lives since the 1960s." In *Gendered Lives in the Western Indian Ocean: Islam, Marriage, and Sexuality on the Swahili Coast*, edited by Erin E. Stiles and Katrina D. Thompson, 85–115. Athens: Ohio University Press.

Carroll, Lucy. 1996. "Qur'an 2: 229: 'A Charter Granted to the Wife'? Judicial Khulʿ in Pakistan." *Islamic Law and Society* 3 (1):91–126.

Clarke, Morgan. 2018. *Islam and Law in Lebanon: Sharia within and without the State*. Cambridge: Cambridge University Press.

Creutzfeldt, Naomi, Marc Mason, and Kirsten MacConachie. 2020. "Socio-Legal Theory and Methods." In *Routledge Handbook of Socio-Legal Study and Methods*, edited by Naomi Creutzfeldt, Marc Mason, and Kirsten MacConachie, 3–8. Oxford: Routledge.

De Hart, Betty, Nadia Sonneveld, and Iris Sportel. 2017. "New Perspectives on Gender in Shariʿa-Based Family Law Studies: Moving beyond the Women's Issue." *Religion and Gender* 7 (1):42–52.

Dupret, Baudouin. 2006. *Droit et sciences sociales*. Paris: Armand Colin.

———. 2007a. "Legal Pluralism, Plurality of Laws, and Legal Practices: Theories, Critiques, and Praxiological Re-Specification." *European Journal of Legal Studies* 1 (1):1–26.

———. 2007b. "What Is Islamic Law? A Praxiological Answer and an Egyptian Case Study." *Theory, Culture and Society* 24, no. 2 (March): 79–100.

Dupret, Baudouin, Maurits Berger, and Laila al-Zwaini. 1999. "Introduction." In *Legal Pluralism in the Arab World*, edited by Baudouin Dupret, Maurits Berger, and Laila al-Zwaini, xi–xviii. The Hague: Kluwer Law International.

Dupret, Baudouin, and Maaike Voorhoeve. 2012. "Introduction." In *Family Law in Islam: Divorce, Marriage, and Women in the Muslim World*, 1–10. London: Tauris.

*The Encyclopaedia of Islam*, vol. 10. 2000. Leiden: E. J. Brill.

Fournier, Pascale. 2006. "In the (Canadian) Shadow of Islamic Law: Translating Mahr as a Bargaining Endowment." *Osgoode Hall Law Journal* 44 (4):649–677.

———. 2016. *Muslim Marriage in Western Courts: Lost in Transplantation*. London: Routledge.

Giunchi, Elisa. 2014. *Adjudicating Family Law in Muslim Courts*. London: Routledge.

Griffiths, John. 1986. "What is Legal Pluralism?" *Journal of Legal Pluralism and Unofficial Law* 18 (24): 1–55.

Haeri, Shahla. 1989. *Law of Desire: Temporary Marriage in Shi'i Iran*. Syracuse: Syracuse University Press.

Hefner, Robert W. 2011. *Shari'a Politics: Islamic Law and Society in the Modern World*. Bloomington: Indiana University Press.

Hirsch, Susan F. 1998. *Pronouncing and Persevering: Gender and Justice in an African Islamic Court*. Chicago: University of Chicago Press.

Holden, Livia. 2012. "Divorce at the Women's Initiative in India, in Pakistan and in the Diasporas." In *Interpreting Divorce Laws in Islam*, edited by Rubya Mehdi, Wener Menski, and Jorgen S. Nielsen, 131–153. Copenhagen: DJØF.

Hosen, Nadirsyah. 2007. "Human Rights Provisions in the Second Amendment to the Indonesian Constitution from Sharī'ah Perspective." *Muslim World* 97 (2):200–224.

Ibn 'Abidīn. 2003. *Radd al-Mukhtār 'alā al-Ddurr al-Mukhtār*, vol. 4. Riyadh: Dār 'Alam al-Kutub.

Ibn Hajar al-'Asqalānī. 1421/2001. *Fatḥ al-bārī bi-sharḥ al-Bukhārī*, vol. 9. Riyadh: Maktaba Mālik Fahd.

Ibn Mājah. 1952. *Sunan Ibn Mājah*, vol. 1. Cairo: Dār Iḥyā' al-Turās al-'Arabiyya.

Jaraba, Mahmoud. 2019. "The Practice of Khul' in Germany Pragmatism versus Conservativism." *Islamic Law and Society* 26 (1):83–110.

al-Jazīrī, 'Abd Raḥmān. 1423/2003. *Kitāb al-Fiqh 'Alā Madhāhib al-Arba'a*. Vol. 4. 2nd ed. Beirut: Dār al-Kutub al-'Ilmiyya.

Keefe, Susi Kreibehl. 2015. "Being a Good Muslim Man: Modern Aspirations and Polygynous Intentions in a Swahili Muslim Village." In *Gendered Lives in the Western Indian Ocean*, edited by Erin E. Stiles and Katrina Daly Thompson, 321–353. Athens: Ohio University Press.

Lau, Martin. 2010. "Sharia Law in Pakistan." In *Sharia Incorporated: A Comparative Overview of the Legal Systems of Twelve Muslim Countries in the Past and Present*, edited by Jan Michiel Otto, 373–432. Leiden: Leiden University Press.

Lemons, Katherine. 2019. *Divorcing Traditions: Islamic Marriage Law and the Making of Indian Secularism*. Ithaca: Cornell University Press.

*al-Mawsū'a al-Fiqhiyya*. 1410/1990. Vol. 19. Kuwait: Wizāra al-Awqāf wa al-Shu'ūn al-Islāmiyya.

*al-Mawsū'a al-Fiqhiyya*. 1414/1993. Vol. 29. Kuwait: Wizāra al-Awqāf wa al-Shu'ūn al-Islāmiyya.

*al-Mawsū'a al-Fiqhiyya*. 1415/1995. Vol. 32. Kuwait: Wizāra al-Awqāf wa al-Shu'ūn al-Islāmiyya.

McMahon, Elisabeth. 2015. "The Value of a Marriage: Missionaries, Ex-Slaves and the Legal Debates over Marriage in Colonial Pemba Island." In *Gendered Lives in the Western Indian Ocean*, edited by Erin E. Stiles and Katrina Daly Thompson, 60–84. Athens: Ohio University Press.

Mehdi, Rubya, Werner Menski, and Jorgen Nielsen, eds. 2012. *Interpreting Divorce Laws in Islam.* Copenhagen: DJØF.

Menkel-Meadow, Carrie. 2020. "Uses and Abuses in Socio-Legal Studies." In *Routledge Handbook of Socio-Legal Study and Methods*, edited by Naomi Creutzfeldt, Marc Mason, and Kirsten MacConachie, 35–44. Oxford: Routledge.

Mir-Hosseini, Ziba. 2000. *Marriage on Trial: A Study of Islamic Family Law.* London: I. B. Tauris.

Moore, Sally Falk. 1973 "Law and Social Change: The Semi-Autonomous Social Field as an Appropriate Subject of Study." *Law and Society Review* 7 (4):719–746.

Moors, Annelies.1995. *Women, Property, and Islam: Palestinian Experience, 1920–1990.* Cambridge: Cambridge University Press.

———. 2003. "Introduction: Public Debates on Family Law Reform. Participants, Positions, and Styles of Argumentation in the 1990s." *Islamic Law and Society* 10 (1):1–11.

———. 2013. "Unregistered Islamic Marriages: Anxieties about Sexuality and Islam in the Netherlands." In *Applying Sharia in the West. Facts, Fears and the Future of Islamic Rules on Family Relations in the West*, edited by Maurits S. Berger, 141–164. Leiden: Leiden University Press.

Nurlaelawati, Euis. 2010. *Modernization, Tradition and Identity: The Kompilasi Hukum Islam and Legal Practice in the Indonesian Religious Courts.* Amsterdam: University of Amsterdam Press.

———. 2013. "Muslim Women in Indonesian Religious Courts: Reform, Strategies, and Pronouncement of Divorce." *Islamic Law and Society* 20 (3):242–271.

Office of International Religious Freedom. 2020. "2019 Report on International Religious Freedom." U.S. Department of State.

Osanloo, Arzoo. 2006. "Islamico-Civil 'Rights Talk': Women, Subjectivity, and Law in Iranian Family Court." *American Ethnologist* 33 (2):190–209.

———. 2009. *The Politics of Women's Right in Iran.* Princeton: Princeton University Press.

Otto, Jan Michiel, ed. 2010. Towards Comparative Conclusions on the Role of Sharia in National Law. In *Sharia Incorporated: A Comparative Overview of the Legal Systems of Twelve Muslim Countries in Past and Present*, edited by Jan Michiel Otto, 613–656. Leiden: Leiden University Press Leiden: Leiden University Press.

Peirce, Leslie. 2003. *Morality Tales: Law and Gender in the Ottoman Court of Aintab.* Berkeley: University of California Press.

Peletz, Michael G. 2002. *Islamic Modern: Religious Courts and Cultural Politics in Malaysia.* Princeton: Princeton University Press.

———. 2020. *Sharia Transformations. Cultural Politics and The Rebranding of an Islamic Judiciary.* Oakland: University of California Press.

Riyani, Irma. 2020. *Islam, Women's Sexuality and Patriarchy in Indonesia: Silent Desire.* London: Routledge.

Schulz, Dorothea E. 2010. "Sharia and National Law in Mali." In *Sharia Incorporated: A Comparative Overview of the Legal Systems of Twelve Muslim Countries in the Past and Present*, edited by Jan Michiel Otto, 529–552. Leiden: Leiden University Press.

Shahar, Ido. 2008. "Legal Pluralism and the Study of Shari'a Courts." *Islamic Law and Society* 15 (1):112–141.

———. 2015. *Legal Pluralism in the Holy City: Competing Courts, Forum Shopping, and Institutional Dynamics in Jerusalem.* London: Ashgate.

Al-Sharmani, Mulki. 2017. *Gender Justice and Legal Reform in Egypt: Negotiating Muslim Family Law.* Cairo: American University in Cairo Press.

Sonbol, Amira El Azhary, ed. 1996. *Women, the Family, and Divorce Laws in Islamic History.* Syracuse: Syracuse University Press.

Sonneveld, Nadia. 2010. "Khul' Divorce in Egypt: How Family Courts Are Providing a 'Dialogue' between Husband and Wife." *Anthropology of the Middle East* 5 (2):100–120.

Sonneveld, Nadia, and Maurits Berger. 2010. "Sharia and National Law in Egypt." In *Sharia Incorporated: A Comparative Overview of the Legal Systems of Twelve Muslim Countries*, edited by Jan Michiel Otto, 51–88. Leiden: Leiden University Press.

Sonneveld, Nadia. 2012. *Khulʿ Divorce in Egypt: Public Debates, Judicial Practices, and Everyday Life*. Cairo: American University in Cairo Press.

Sonneveld, Nadia. 2019. "Divorce Reform in Egypt and Morocco: Men and Women Navigating Rights and Duties." *Islamic Law and Society* 26 (1–2):149–178.

Sonneveld, Nadia, and Erin Stiles. 2019. "Khulʿ: Local Contours of a Global Phenomenon." *Islamic Law and Society* 26 (1–2):1–11.

Stiles, Erin E. 2009. *An Islamic Court in Context: An Ethnographic Study of Judicial Reasoning*. London: Palgrave Macmillan.

———. 2014. "The Right to Marry: Daughters and Elders in the Islamic Courts of Zanzibar." *Islamic Law and Society* 21 (3):252–275.

———. 2018. "How to Manage a Marital Dispute: Legal Pluralism from the Ground Up in Zanzibar." *University of California Irvine Law Review* 8:102–123.

———. 2019. "'It Is Your Right to Buy a Divorce': Judicial Khuluu in Zanzibar." *Islamic Law and Society* 26 (1–2):12–35.

Stockreiter, Elke E. 2015. *Islamic Law, Gender and Social Change in Post-Abolition Zanzibar*. Cambridge: Cambridge University Press.

Tucker, Judith E. 1998. *In the House of the Law: Gender and Islamic Law in Ottoman Syria and Palestine*. Berkeley: University of California Press.

van Eijk, Esther. 2016. *Family Law in Syria*. London: I. B. Tauris.

———. 2019. "Khulʿ Divorce in the Netherlands: Dutch Muslim Women Seeking Religious Divorce." *Islamic Law and Society* 26 (1–2):36–57.

van Huis, Stijn Cornelis. 2019. "Khulʿ over the Longue Durée: The Decline of Traditional Fiqh-Based Divorce Mechanisms in Indonesian Legal Practice." *Islamic Law and Society* 26 (1–2):58–82.

Vatuk, Sylvia. 2008. "Divorce at the Wife's Initiative in Muslim Personal Law: What Are the Options and What Are Their Implications for Women's Welfare?" In *Redefining Family Law in India: Essays in Honour of B. Sivaramayya*, edited by Archana Parashar and Bhamidipati Sivaramayya, 200–235. New Delhi: Routledge.

———. 2019. "Extra-Judicial Khulʿ Divorce in India's Muslim Personal Law." *Islamic Law and Society* 26 (1–2):111–148.

Voorhoeve, Maaike. 2012. *Family Law in Islam: Divorce, Marriage and Women in the Muslim World*. London: I. B. Tauris.

Welchman, Lynn. 2003. "In the Interim: Civil Society, the Sharʿī Judiciary and Palestinian Personal Status Law in the Transitional Period." *Islamic Law and Society* 10 (1):34–69.

———. 2007. *Women and Muslim Family Laws in Arabic States: A Comparative Overview of Textual Development and Advocacy*. Amsterdam: Amsterdam University Press.

Würth, Anna. 1995. "A Sana'a Court: The Family and the Ability to Negotiate." *Islamic Law and Society* 2 (3):320–340.

———. 2003. "Stalled Reform: Family Law in Post-Unification Yemen." *Islamic Law and Society* 10 (1):12–33.

Zantout, Mida R. 2006. "Khulʿ: Between Past and Present." *Islamic Law and Law of the Muslim World Paper No. 08–14*. Social Science Research Network. https://ssrn.com/abstract=1094367.

Zubaida, Sami. 2005. *Law and Power in the Islamic World*. London: Tauris.

al-Zuḥaylī, Wahbah. 1985. *al-Fiqh al-Islāmiyy wa Adillatuhu*. Vol. 7. 2nd ed. Damascus: Dār al-Fikr.

# PART ONE

# State Politics and Divorce Law: Reform and Recommendations

# 1

# Divorce by *Khul*ʿ in Pakistani Courts

## Expanding Women's Rights through Reconfiguring Religious Authority

ELISA GIUNCHI

Pakistani law considers marriage a contract that can be dissolved by the death of one of the spouses, at the behest of one of them, or by mutual consent.[1] The most widely used method of ending a marriage is *ṭalāq*, a unilateral repudiation which does not require any justification on the part of the husband and requires a fairly simple procedure in order to be registered and therefore produce its legal effects. The husband, in addition to fulfilling certain formalities, must pay his wife the deferred dower (*mahr*) and provide for her maintenance for a short period, corresponding to the *ʿidda*.[2]

Obtaining a divorce without the consent of the husband in Pakistan is not as easy for women as it is for men. However, a variety of options are open to them, drawn largely from the Mālikī *madhhab* (legal school) which, when it comes to women's rights, is much less restrictive than the Ḥanafī madhhab, the dominant school in South Asia. A woman can avail herself of the delegated repudiation (*ṭalāq-i tafwīd*) as long as it is provided for in the marriage contract (*nikāḥnama*),[3] and of the "puberty option" on reaching the age of majority in the unlikely case that the marriage has not been consummated.[4] She can also apply to the judge on the ground of her husband's failure to fulfill certain essential obligations and thus obtain an annulment of the marriage (*faskh al-nikāḥ*). A more expeditious and less complicated way to obtain a divorce is by *khul*ʿ.

As explained in the introduction to this volume, the foundations for khulʿ are found in the Qur'an and the Sunna. However, the nature of these sources left the door open for the classical *fuqahā'* (jurists) to interpret God's will in different ways, with no central authority dictating who was right and who was wrong. At the time when the Islamic legal tradition was elaborated, scholars also referred to a variety of other sources to supplement what was written in the primary sources. The legal schools that emerged differed from one another on hermeneutical issues and on the relative weight given to various sources, and they responded to dissimilar cultural and social circumstances, thus arriving at inconsistent rules. Divergent opinions also coexisted within the same madhhab, with the Ḥanafī emerging as the most heterogeneous school of law. The *madhāhib* also developed different interpretations of khulʿ. According to the opinion that came to prevail, khulʿ needed the husband's consent, it could be settled with or without the intervention of state authorities, and it required financial compensation to the husband. The resulting dissolution was equated to an irrevocable ṭalāq. Most Ḥanafī jurists agreed that the husband's consent was mandatory but believed that no more than the mahr should be paid to him. According to a minority view, if the wife's request to terminate the marriage was due to some fault of the husband, no compensation was required. Mālikī jurists similarly believed that if the fault was attributed to the husband or to both spouses, nothing was due to him. Unlike most jurists of the other legal schools, they also thought that arbitrators could dissolve a marriage irrespective of the husband's consent (Munir 2015, 44–52). Historical praxis is not univocal either, as there has been great variation in the way Muslim countries have interpreted and applied khulʿ throughout the centuries. As we will see later in this chapter, on the issue of consent and compensation, Pakistani legislators and judges have departed from the majority position of fuqahā' through a variety of discursive strategies and methodological tools.

This chapter is divided into three sections. The first section reviews Pakistani legislation on wife-initiated divorce, with particular attention to khulʿ. The second discusses judicial practice pertaining to khulʿ on the basis of the court records of selected decisions—mostly drawn from Pakistan Law Decisions (PLD)—that were collected at the Federal Shariat (Arabic, shariʿa) Court (FSC) archive in Islamabad, at the Squire Law Library in Cambridge, and more recently, online.[5] The cases were heard by the High Courts and the FSC, which play a prominent role in interpreting the law and whose decisions are regularly published.[6] A problem with court records is that they provide only a brief summary of the facts and circumstances surrounding judicial khulʿ and are mostly silent on out-of-court negotiations. Nor can they shed light on the motivations of the litigants or the implications of court decisions. There is also a lack of up-to-date and systematic ethnographic research in Pakistan on private negotiations, on the socioeconomic background of the litigants, and on implications of judicial decisions on khulʿ. An interview with Majida Rizvi, a retired judge and currently chairperson of the Sind Human Rights Commission, has thus enabled me to fill some gaps in the literature and gain a glimpse of what is not recorded in the court documents.[7] The final section tackles the implications of Pakistani judicial activism in terms of religious authority.

There is a growing body of socio-legal literature on khulʿ in different countries (Vatuk 2008, 2017; Stiles 2019; Fortier 2012; Sonneveld 2012; Sonneveld and Stiles 2016, 2019; van Huis 2019; Jaraba 2020). A number of detailed studies on Pakistani family law have been published that include up-to-date discussions on female-initiated forms of divorce (Abbasi and Cheema 2018; Serajuddin 2011a and b; Mehmood 2016), and considerable attention has been given to Pakistani adjudication concerning khulʿ (Carroll 1996; Munir 2014, 2015; Serajuddin 2011a; Yefet

2011; Masud 2019 2012; Abbasi 2016, 2017; Holden 2012). While most existing studies focus on either legislation or judicial practice, this chapter attempts to combine and contextualize these two aspects and to link them to wider considerations of religious authority. My argument is that judicial practice in the field of khul', while expanding women's rights by relying on Islam and paving the way for progressive legislation, has not managed to put men and women on an equal footing and that the gains obtained through the judiciary may prove fragile.

## Legislation on Wife-Initiated Divorce

Before the granting of independence, family matters in India were mostly regulated by the personal law of each community, as transformed by British procedures and legal concepts (Anderson 1993; Kugle 2001; Giunchi 2010). So-called Anglo-Muhammadan Law was based on the main Ḥanafī works referenced in the subcontinent, the *Hidāyā* and *Fatāwā-i-'Ālamğīrī*, which provided very few options for women wanting to divorce. These treatises were translated and understood through the mediation of religious scholars (*'ulama'*) and applied by judges who, even when they were not British, were trained in English law. The combination of text-based interpretative discourses of religious scholars and British aversion to female-initiated divorce, which was foreign to them (Masud 2012, 55), made it difficult for women to escape an unhappy marriage unless they apostatized. To address women's plight and prevent apostasy, modernist thinkers such as Muhammad Iqbal, Islamist scholars such as Mawdudi, and some 'ulama' in the 1920s and 1930s advocated recourse to *talfīq* (synthesizing the principles of various Sunni schools) and *ijtihād* (independent legal thinking) in order to expand women's rights (Cheema 2019, 113). It was largely because of pressure from these sectors that some aspects of Islamic family law were codified, giving rise to a hybrid legislation that combined principles drawn from various *madhāhib* and English law. The Child Marriage Restraint Act (1929), the Dissolution of Muslim Marriage Act (1939)—known as DMMA—and the Application of Muslim Personal Law (Shariat) Act (1937) thus became the main sources of Muslim Personal Law (MPL).[8] Legal experts in India referred to these acts as well as to the precedents of the Indian High Courts and of the Judicial Committee of the Privy Council, the highest court of civil and criminal appeal in British India.

The 1937 act mentioned khul' among the issues of Islamic law that would apply to Indian Muslims, "notwithstanding any custom or usage to the contrary." However, whether replacing customs with "proper" Islam would facilitate female-initiated divorce depended on how Islamic sources were interpreted by the courts. The nature of this interpretation became clearer two years later, in 1939, when the DMMA was introduced. The DMMA drew inspiration mainly from the Mālikī legal school and thus provided, unlike the Ḥanafī majority position, a number of circumstances that allowed a wife to initiate a faskh al-nikāḥ. These included desertion, nonmaintenance, impotence, and cruelty. The DMMA also relied on the Ḥanafī madhhab by recognizing the validity of the puberty option. Women's financial rights were not affected if any of these grounds could be proved. In its final section, the DMMA provided that a woman could obtain a divorce for "any other cause [that is] valid under Islamic law" (2[ix]), a vague formulation that implicitly included khulʿ (Pearl 1979, 103).

After the introduction of the DMMA, British judges remained reluctant to grant divorce to women. They allowed khulʿ only rarely, when the husband gave his consent (Munir 2015, 52–53) or on condition that the wife fully satisfied the court that she had good reasons to divorce (Masud 2019, 77). Discord among spouses (*shiqāq*) or the wife's aversion were not considered sufficient grounds for divorce.

After Partition, no laws were enacted to further regulate MPL for over a decade. In 1955, under the pressure of the All Pakistan Women's Association (APWA) and following the example of many postcolonial governments in the Muslim world, a commission was formed to suggest how greater rights could be given to women in the family sphere. In its final report, the commission recommended a number of measures, including the introduction of regulations governing khulʿ. All the members, who with one exception had no formal religious training, advocated ijtihād as a way to adapt Islamic teachings to new circumstances without having to be constrained by the prevailing opinions of classical jurists. However, on the specific issue of khulʿ they followed the majority opinion of the *madhāhib* by stating that a woman wanting to divorce under khulʿ needed to forgo some or all of her mahr if required by the husband (Haider 2000, 328).

When Ayub Khan, an army general of modernist orientation, assumed power in a coup d'état in 1958, the commission's recommendations were partly translated into law. The 1961 Muslim Family Law Ordinance (MFLO) amended the DMMA and other acts of the colonial era by placing various constraints on traditional male prerogatives. It also expanded women's rights through a combination of talfīq and outright innovation. The minimum age of marriage was raised, the registration of marriage and divorce was made compulsory, ṭalāq was regulated and curtailed, the delegated divorce was incorporated into the marriage contract, and it was established that if a man married another wife without fulfilling certain formalities, the first wife was entitled to request a divorce.[9] Realizing that compromises were necessary since Pakistanis held divergent views on women's roles, the legislators did not accept all the commission's recommendations. Khulʿ, in particular, remained unregulated. A year later, in 1962, partly as a result of the controversies generated by the MFLO, a Council of Islamic Ideology (CII)—entirely staffed by ʿulamaʾ—was established to ensure that laws and regulations would abide by "the injunctions" of the Qur'an and sunna as per Article 227 of the constitution (the so-called repugnancy clause). The exact content of these injunctions, however, would increasingly become a matter of controversy.

In 1964, the West Pakistan Family Courts Act established family courts in each district with exclusive jurisdiction over many issues pertaining to personal status, including khul'. In the following years Ayub Khan resigned, a civil war broke out leading to the secession of East Pakistan, Saudi influence increased, and political Islam attracted growing numbers in urban areas. In this context, attempts to reform MPL to expand women's rights were shelved for decades. Under General Zia ul-Haq, who came to power in a coup in 1977, laws were enacted, mostly in the criminal sphere, in an effort to Islamize the country. While Ayub Khan had been the product of a cosmopolitan urban middle class influenced by modernist ideas, Zia ul-Haq represented a provincial Islamist lower-middle class that was entering the state apparatus. One of the laws enacted under Zia, the Zinā Ordinance, introduced *ḥudūd* penalties for rape, adultery, and fornication. Cases of zinā intersected, and at times conflicted, with issues that fell under the MFLO: as sex out of wedlock was criminalized, many cases of unregistered marriage, unregistered ṭalāq, and consensual elopement without the guardian's consent resulted in women being convicted for zinā (Giunchi 2013). Zia also directed the CII to review the MFLO. The CII determined that this ordinance was un-Islamic and recommended its repeal. A compromise was sought between divergent positions, and only two sections of the MFLO were abrogated: the age of marriage was lowered and a second marriage without the consent of the first wife would no longer constitute grounds for divorce.

Despite the expectations generated by the 1988 elections, in the "democratic decade" that followed, which saw Benazir Bhutto and Nawaz Sharif alternating in power, the ḥudūd laws were not abrogated and personal-status law was not reformed to extend women's rights. A factor that may have contributed to this was the overrepresentation within the government and major political parties of feudal landowners and 'ulama', who were interested in preserving the status quo. Nonetheless, in the 1990s there were visible signs of change within Pakistani society: during the second mandate of Benazir Bhutto, female judges were appointed to the High Courts for the first time, new NGOs emerged, and greater freedom of the press allowed advocates for women's rights to reach a wider audience.

Legislative stasis in the field of family law ended when General Pervez Musharraf assumed power through a coup in 1999. Disregarding religious and conservative opposition and in the context of a government-led policy of "enlightened moderation," Musharraf introduced laws that aimed at improving women's conditions. The legislative reforms that were ushered in at this time were made possible through the convergence of a number of factors. First, by then there was greater awareness and sympathy for the plight of women. Second, unlike Zia, Musharraf shared Ayub Khan's modernist orientation. And third, unlike Bhutto and Sharif, who had been democratically elected, the general could impose his will and ignore that of the parliament. In 2002, the Family Courts (Amendment) Ordinance regulated khul' for the first time. This ordinance, which amended the Family Courts Act of 1964, reflected positions that had emerged in previous decades in the High Courts: in the event that no compromise or reconciliation between the spouses was possible, the family court would dissolve the marriage through khul' without the wife needing to justify her request or obtain her husband's consent. To do so, she had to return the portion of mahr that had already been paid, renounce its deferred portion, and declare in the suit that she could not live with her husband "within the limits prescribed by Allah," implying that sexual relations between them had become impossible. As the act covered cases of dissolution falling under the DMMA where reconciliation had failed, women who had applied for fault-based divorce could now more easily escape an unhappy marriage. However, in doing so, they encountered an economic loss. Legislators thus chose to adopt some elements of the prevailing Ḥanafī opinions (the return of mahr) and discard others (the husband's consent). To address the problem of lengthy court trials and other hurdles that women faced (Maskiell 1984, 3), procedural requirements were amended to make it easier for women to testify in court and to expedite the trials. In addition, female judges were appointed to the family courts for the first time and the jurisdiction of the courts was extended.

The 2002 ordinance was part of a "third wave" of personal-status reform in the Muslim world (Welchman 2007, 112), which resulted in the introduction of nonconsensual khulʿ in some countries. In 2000, a law was introduced in Egypt that allowed courts to grant khulʿ irrespective of the husband's consent provided that the wife explicitly declared that she hated living with her husband, had returned the mahr, and had waived any other financial rights. A year later, Jordan followed suit by enacting a law that included a provision for judicial khulʿ. More restrictive laws were then introduced in Qatar, Algeria, and the United Arab Emirates (UAE) (Welchman 2007, 116–119). In Morocco in 2004, a new personal-status code stipulated that in cases of khulʿ, women may recover the compensation paid to obtain the divorce if they prove that they acted under duress or as the result of harm caused by their husband. However, the option of divorcing on grounds of shiqāq provided a way out of an unhappy marriage that was more advantageous to women than khulʿ since it does not require the husband's consent or the payment of compensation (Sonneveld 2019).

In 2006, the Protection of Women (Criminal Law Amendment) Act further expanded the divorce rights of Pakistani women by stipulating that a wife can obtain a divorce following a mutual oath (*liʿān*).[10] According to the Qur'an (24:6–9), if a husband accuses his wife of adultery without supplying witnesses and swears four times that his accusation is true and the wife then refutes his accusation with four oaths, their marriage is, ipso facto, dissolved. She escapes zinā and he avoids charges of *qadhf* (a false accusation of zinā). This procedure had occasionally been held as permissible by the courts under the clause of cruelty or the residual section 2(ix) of the DMMA, and it had been included in the Office of Qadhf Enforcement of Ḥadd Ordinance introduced by Zia in 1979. As part of the state attempt to regulate the private sphere, the 1979 ordinance had brought what was an extrajudicial act within the purview of the court: it had established that the oaths, if made before a court, would be followed by a decree of dissolution (section 14). The 2006 act also returned the crime of rape to the Penal Code, responding to women's rights activism in Pakistan and to international criticism of the effects of the Zinā Ordinance on women.

Modernist elites welcomed the act as a step toward greater women's right, although some activists and organizations considered it inadequate. Traditionalist and Islamist sectors—mostly the political party Jamaat-e Islami—were very critical of the law, accusing it of violating "Pakistani ideology" and Allah's sovereignty in order to please the United States. After Musharraf stepped down, subsequent democratically elected governments passed new laws that were favorable to women on a variety of issues, from domestic violence to workplace harassment to acid throwing (Weiss 2012) but did not pass personal law reforms, due to the controversies surrounding women's rights in an increasingly polarized society.

Legislative stasis, particularly in the 1970s, 1980s, and 1990s, and the limited scope and piecemeal nature of Musharraf's reforms were compensated for by the judicial activism of the higher courts, as shown in the following pages.

## Khul' and Judicial Practice

Particularly in the first decade after Partition, cases of female-initiated divorce heard by Pakistani courts were rare for a number of reasons: in most communities, women's initiation of divorce proceedings was frowned on; apart from the urban elite, women did not know their rights or the procedures to follow, nor did they have the financial means to consult a lawyer; women who lived with their husband's extended family also found it difficult to produce evidence and to appear before a court. Although Pakistani judges were less averse to ruling for divorce than their British counterparts had been, when a case under the DMMA reached a court, judges rarely determined that the circumstances necessary for a faskh had been established. Khul' was either assimilated to a fault divorce, thus requiring women to provide evidence, or expected to be accompanied by the consent of the husband. The mere incompatibility between spouses or the wife's aversion to the husband were not considered sufficient grounds for divorce (Carroll 1996, 96–102).

In 1959, the case of *Balqis Fatima v. Najam ul-Ikram Qureshi* was a turning point.[11] The High Court of Lahore established the principle that a woman who could not provide sufficient evidence to obtain a faskh under the terms of the DMMA could initiate khul' even without the consent of her husband, provided she renounced her economic rights and stated that she and her husband were incompatible. To justify this position, the judges relied on the primary sources of Islam. In particular, they referenced verse 2:229 of the Qur'an, stressing that khul' did not explicitly require the husband's consent. Although the majority position of the fuqahā' considered consent to be indispensable, the judges argued that derived religious texts could not take precedence over the primary sources. The judges added that "if we be clear as to what the meaning of a verse in the Qur'an is, it will be our duty to give effect to that interpretation irrespective of what has been stated by the jurists." Underlying this statement were the modernist ideas that the good

Muslim puts into practice Islamic values enshrined in the sacred text irrespective of fiqh and that understanding the primary sources does not require any specialized knowledge, as was to be articulated in subsequent cases.

The court also held that the phrase "if you fear" in 2:229 is addressed to the state and its officials: "The question is whether it is the husband or the state-appointed authority that determines whether the [marriage] relationship should continue, and the answer must be that it is the state-appointed authority and that the question does not depend on the benevolence of the husband." The judges relied on sunna to corroborate this position by pointing out that when the Prophet Muhammad had, in Habība's case, ordered the dissolution of the marriage, he had been acting as a qadi. The judges also appealed to reason—another hallmark of modernism—and used the language of rights: "it does not seem reasonable that while one of the contracting members [of the marriage] has full powers to terminate the contract, the other party should not be granted any rights." It is interesting that the judges relied also on Abul A'la Mawdudi, a renowned scholar who, while not in favor of equality between the sexes,[12] believed that khul', like ṭalāq, should be unconditional. The court that dissolved marriage by khul' did not need to enquire into a woman's reasons for disliking her husband or require evidence of fault on his part. Compensation was due to him but should be calculated while keeping in mind the specific circumstances of the case (cited in Munir 2009, 287–288). To support this position, Mawdudi argued that judges should give the Qur'an priority over fiqh and should apply it to the social and cultural milieu in which they live.[13]

To understand the decision of *Balqis Fatima*, one has to take into consideration the context. Ayub Khan, representing a secular and reformist elite influenced by modernism, was in power, and the idea that the recognition of new rights should be articulated in Islamic language in order to take root in the collective consciousness, as articulated by Justice A. R. Cornelius, was beginning to influence the upper judiciary (Braibanti 1999). Not surprisingly, then, the position of the High Court of Lahore was endorsed in 1967 by the Supreme Court. In *Khurshid Bibi v. Baboo Muhammad Amin* the court argued that the Qur'an and the sunna put men and women on an equal footing: in the event that the husband opposed his wife's request for divorce, the judge could, therefore, order the dissolution of the marriage if he found that the spouses could not "live in harmony and in accordance with their obligations."[14] The language of rights was accompanied by a language of love and harmony, corresponding to an upper-class notion of the ideal family, which was held by judges of the higher judiciary.[15] With regard to the role of the courts, the judge, according to the Supreme Court, was one of those who "hold authority" (*ūlī l-amr*, Q. 4:59). As such, in the exercise of his functions, he was obliged to apply the word of God and not fiqh, which is a human construction. Echoing the words of the judges in *Balqis Fatima*, the Supreme Court observed that "if the opinions of the jurists contradict the Qur'an and the sunna, they are not binding on the courts, and it is our duty, as true Muslims, to obey the word of God and the holy Prophet." It should be noted that the judges did not claim in either case that the spouses could divorce on an equal footing. Rather, the courts needed to ascertain that a "harmonious" cohabitation was no longer possible before ruling in favor of the wife, whereas the authorities were required to register out-of-court ṭalāq as long as procedural norms were respected. In similar cases adjudicated in that period, the wife was often asked to prove that her allegations were true,[16] and if she was considered to blame then the divorce was not granted.[17] The decision on "ransom" rested with the court, and khul' usually entailed a compensation that far exceeded the financial cost that a man repudiating his wife had to endure. The assumption was that a woman could not be allowed, as one reads in *Balqis Fatima*, to divorce "for every passing impulse": the paternalistic assumption was that judges must discourage divorce for frivolous reasons.

In the 1970s, the High Courts claimed in an increasing number of cases that issues not addressed by statutory law should be decided according to shari'a rather than to precedents of British origin.[18] A crucial step in the Islamization of the judicial system was the establishment in 1980, under Zia ul-Haq, of the Federal Shariat Court (FSC).[19] The FSC would hear appeals from decisions made by criminal lower courts pertaining to the offences of theft, intoxication, zinā, and qadhf regulated by the Ḥudūd Ordinances (Art. 203-DD Constitution); it would also determine, on its own initiative or acting on the petition of a citizen, a provincial government, or the federal government, whether laws and bills were "repugnant to the injunctions of Islam" (Art. 203-D Constitution). Its composition consisted of eight judges appointed by the president; not more than three should be 'ulama' who were "well versed in Islamic law" (Art. 203C[3-A]).[20] A similar Shariat Section was established at the Supreme Court to hear appeals against the decisions of the FSC.

Although overall the enforcement of the Zinā Ordinance was penalizing to women, the FSC at times used Islamic primary sources and fiqh to secure and even expand women's rights. Take, for example, unregistered marriages. The registration of marriages and ṭalāqs is prescribed by the MFLO. Without registration, the cohabitation of man and wife was to be considered, according to the Zinā Ordinance, as illegal sexual intercourse. In several cases, however, the FSC accepted unregistered marriages and ṭalāqs as valid against charges of zinā, holding that registration is not contrary to Islam but is also not required. In conformity with the views of some Ḥanafī classical jurists, including the eponym of the school, the simple declaration by a man and a woman to be united in marriage was considered sufficient to save them from the harsh punishments of zinā (Giunchi 1994, 2013).[21]

Similarly, in some cases the requirement of a minimum marriage age—set by the MFLO at sixteen for women—was considered by the FSC as un-Islamic, with the effect of acquitting young women who had eloped without their guardian's consent and had been subsequently charged with zinā: the judges again referred to the Ḥanafī madhhab when they observed that for marriage to be valid women must simply reach puberty.[22]

According to the constitution, the FSC could not actually rule on "Muslim personal law,"[23] an expression that was initially understood as covering matters that fell under the MFLO.[24] As a consequence, during the 1980s it was the High Courts that took an active role in referring to uncodified shari'a to fill in the gaps in legislation on MPL. This religiously inspired judicial activism was particularly pronounced after Article 2-A was added to the constitution in 1985, thus making the Objectives Resolution part of the constitution. The resolution, which had been adopted by the Constituent Assembly in 1949, established in vague terms that Muslims would be "enabled to order their lives in the individual and collective spheres in accordance with the teachings and requirements of Islam as set out in the holy Qur'an and sunna." According to an interpretation that the High Courts articulated in a number of cases, Article 2-A made the shari'a a normative system superior to statutory law and required that the courts apply it directly. It was held, in particular, that the High Courts and the Supreme Court could strike down as un-Islamic any law that was excluded from the jurisdiction of the FSC.

In a growing number of personal status cases, the High Courts thus referred to Islam to confirm, expand, or contradict statutory provisions, and—contrary to what many of Zia's supporters had hoped—on numerous occasions this expanded women's rights. As to khul', the High Courts held in some cases that "it is not necessary to produce evidence . . . to show the extent of [her] hatred"[25] and that judges needed merely to ensure "that the wife is genuinely determined to dissolve the marriage."[26] The Supreme Court shared the same outlook, as in several cases it considered the wife's request for divorce sufficient to prove her aversion to her husband, which in itself prevented the continuation of married life "within God's limits."[27]

The High Courts also addressed the financial implications of khul'. Mahr in Pakistan, which is established in the marriage contract, tends to be deferred and of limited value for people in the lower and middle classes. Giving up the right to receive it, then, may not constitute a disincentive for women who want to divorce (Rizvi, pers. comm., June 24, 2020). However, should the mahr be significant, the need to compensate one's husband by returning the mahr already paid and forgoing the deferred portion would be a major problem if the woman filing for divorce does not have a supportive family or private means. A substantial mahr may also induce a husband who wants to divorce to pressure his wife to demand khul' in order to keep the mahr or at least its deferred portion (Rizvi, pers. comm., June 24, 2020). In *Balqis Fatima*, the Lahore High Court had already held that if the husband is to blame for the breakdown of the marriage, then no compensation is required; the judge should also take into consideration "reciprocal benefits" received by the husband during the marriage in assessing whether anything is due to him. The High Courts subsequently held in many cases that if the wife is forced by her husband to request khul', the compensation due to him should be reduced at the discretion of the courts; if the husband is to blame for the end of the marriage, no compensation is required. The judges argued that demanding compensation would in fact be against Islamic injunctions.[28] The High Courts also reiterated that "reciprocal benefits," including those accruing from raising children and doing household chores, should be taken into consideration when calculating the amount of compensation due to the husband (Munir 2014, 15–18, 22–23). In some cases husbands have been asked to prove that mahr was paid in the first place and the judges have held that the lack of payment does not affect the validity of khul' but merely creates a civil liability with regard to the property, goods, or amount of money that may be owed by the wife to her former husband.[29]

In 1994, the Shariat Appellate Bench of the Supreme Court extended the jurisdiction of the FSC by redefining the expression "Muslim personal law": MPL was now defined as the part of personal status of each sect that is based on that sect's interpretation of the Qur'an and sunna. This meant that the MFLO was not part of MPL since it applied to all Pakistani Muslims irrespective of sect.[30] The FSC could thus be given a more active role in family-related matters covered by the 1961 ordinance, including khul'. In 2014, the FSC reaffirmed previous High Courts' decisions by declaring that khul' did not necessarily need the husband's consent since Qur'an 2:229 does not explicitly require it and the Qur'an does not support discrimination: "obviously Islam does not intend to force a wife to live a miserable life, in a hateful and unhappy union, forever."[31] The FSC, in addition to adopting a language of matrimonial harmony like the High Courts had done, decided to depart from the prevailing opinion of fuqahā' on khul' by stressing the preeminence of the Qur'an and sunna over other sources.

## Secular Judges as Mujtahids

We have seen that Pakistani High Courts and the FSC have expanded women's rights with regard to khul': they have lowered the threshold of evidence, redefined the meaning and scope of "ransom," and separated the validity of divorce by khul' from the payment of compensation. In other areas—honor killings, the restoration of conjugal rights, maintenance, the recovery of mahr, and sexual crimes—the higher judiciary has similarly ruled in favor of women (Lau 2006; Yefet 2011; Yilmaz 2014; Lombardi 2010; Giunchi 1994; Cheema 2013; Haider 2000). This has often been done by relying on the "spirit" or on specific verses of the Qur'an, in conformity with Pakistani law, which endorses the preeminence of primary sources over secondary ones. Article 2-A of the constitution commits the state to ensure that laws are in conformity with the Qur'an and sunna, not fiqh. The Enforcement of Shariat Act of 1991 affirms that "the shari'a . . . shall be the supreme law of Pakistan. By shari'a is meant 'the Injunctions of Islam as laid in the Holy Qur'an and sunna.'" Fiqh is clearly subordinate to primary sources: "While interpreting and explaining the shari'a the recognized principles of interpretation and explanation of the Holy Qur'an and sunna shall be followed and the expositions and opinions of recognized jurists of Islam belonging to prevalent Islamic schools of jurisprudence *may be* taken into consideration."[32]

The emphasis on primary sources should come as no surprise, as the call to return to the Qur'an and sunna to retrieve the dynamism of shari'a was a central element of reformist thinking since the late nineteenth century and is today a well-established principle. What is more controversial is that non-madrasa trained individuals may be entitled to practice ijtihād. As modern states encroached on the prerogatives of 'ulama' in the spheres of education and law, abridged manuals of Islamic law and collections of ḥadiths were published, and new elites emerged from state-run and missionary schools. Despite having no in-depth knowledge of religious subjects, these elites could access the primary sources of Islam and claim the right to reinterpret them to respond to novel circumstances, the more so as there was no paramount religious institution that could impose its own version of authenticity. Their claims, however, have not gone uncontested.

Many Pakistani 'ulama' do not deny that ijtihād should be practiced, and indeed some of them are in favor of it in the belief that taqlīd (adherence to the interpretations of the classical jurists) has caused the stagnation of the Muslim world. What they contest is that ijtihād is practiced by individuals with a superficial knowledge of Islam and that it may ignore *ijmā'* (consensus by scholars) and, what is worse, contradict "clear" verses and "solid" hadiths. It is this "unrestricted ijtihād" by nonreligious experts that is mostly criticized (Serajuddin 2011b, 52–57; Zaman 2018, 107–109).

Supporters of religiously inspired judicial activism by secular judges reply by pointing out that it is the right, if not the duty, of Muslims to exercise ijtihād to address novel situations with an eye to the principle of *maṣlaḥa* (the common good), as stated in *Balqis Fatima*: the good Muslim is not one who reflects on minute details of fiqh, but one who puts into practice Islamic values and principles to the benefit of society and its most vulnerable sectors. The FSC has supported the claims that secular judges are entitled to practice ijtihād: in *Saleem Ahmed*, the court expressly stated that judges with no religious background can return to the Qur'an to adapt it to new needs. As the Supreme Court held in *Khurshid Bibi*, they are among those who, according to the Qur'an, have authority (*amr*) over others. Pakistani judges do not simply go back to the Qur'an and sunna, however. An analysis of the High Courts' records, and less surprisingly, of the FSC, shows that the judges refer to a wide variety of religious sources, often within the same case, including opinions taken from fiqh. The judges thus often practice talfīq and *takhayyur* (favoring the position of one madhhab over that of others),[33] with a preference for the Mālikī legal school.[34] This is not simply a case of returning to the past: medieval legal tools are reframed and minority positions are retrieved at the expense of more established ones and integrated with global discourses on human rights. Indeed, many religious scholars criticize court decisions as a patchwork of learned references that have nothing to do with the sincere effort to understand God's will but rather aim to legitimize a foreign rights discourse and justify decisions that have already been made. Judicial activism, in sum, is seen as exemplary of the whimsical and opportunistic "Islam à la carte," as Olivier Roy calls it (2013, 15), that characterizes modern-day religiosity. However, the judges' attempts to reinterpret Islamic sources while integrating them with a global discourse on human rights could be seen in a more positive light as partaking in a tradition of flexibility and contextuality that was inherent in the Revelation and characterized classical legal doctrine and praxis. One might thus understand secular judges as returning to the original spirit of shari'a and reviving the dynamism that characterized fiqh before it was narrowed down by jurists' increasing reliance on taqlīd and, later, by the British textual approach and selective reading of Ḥanafī treatises. In this view, the judges are not betraying "authentic" Islam but rather making the divine message relevant to a radically changed world.

On women's rights, as on other issues, there is actually no clear-cut division between modernists and traditionalists, unlike what some scholars seem to assume (Haider 2000): as is the case elsewhere (Stiles 2019), Pakistani religious scholars differ among themselves as to what is "correct" Islam. In 2008, the CII, which had declared the MFLO un-Islamic in the early 1980s as it gave women rights that were not provided for by the Qur'an and sunna, recommended to the government, on the basis of Qur'an 2:228–229 and 4:35, that it amend the MFLO in order to give women divorce rights similar to those of men. If the husband did not pronounce ṭalāq within ninety days of the request for khul', the CII sustained, the marriage must be considered automatically dissolved. The husband's consent was deemed irrelevant, contrary to the prevailing opinion in fiqh. The uproar caused by this recommendation was such that it was not translated into legislation and the council was reconstituted (Masud 2019, 92). In 2015, under a new chairman, the CII reversed its position and stated that khul' needed the husband's consent.[35] In any case, its first 2008 recommendation is a reminder that reform can be affected through the dominant discourse and that the chasm between tradition and women's rights can be, at least in part, bridged.

Similarly, there is not a clear-cut opposition between the views of modernists and those of Islamists on women's rights within the domestic sphere. We have seen that Mawdudi, like the modernists, favored the primary sources over fiqh, although he believed that ijtihād should be practiced only by jurists endowed with in-depth religious knowledge. In his opinion, the Qur'an contained many injunctions that were "open to different fruitful and valid interpretations" (Mawdudi 1960, 28–29). It was on the basis of the Qur'anic text that he held that khul' should be equated to ṭalāq.

## Conclusions

Escaping an unhappy marriage is not easy for Pakistani women. Female-initiated divorce is still stigmatized, particularly in rural areas, and many women are not aware of their rights or of legal procedures, although in recent decades government bodies and nongovernmental organizations (NGOs) have provided legal aid and raised awareness of existing laws. Still, a lack of family support makes it difficult for many women to access the justice system and bear the cost of legal proceedings that can take years (Ahmed 2014, 80).

Most of the options that are open to women who want to divorce remain on paper. Hitherto there have been few cases of divorce by mubārā'a and li'ān. As to delegated ṭalāq, which, like li'ān, does not require women to show cause, it is often unavailable because the clause providing for it is often removed from the standard nikāḥnama (Ahmed 2014, 75). Finally, family courts tend to consider fault-based divorce suits filed under the DMMA as unfounded. Thus, khulʿ is often the only way out of an unhappy marriage.

Pakistani legislation and judicial practice in regard to khulʿ are more progressive than those of most other Muslim-majority countries. With some exceptions, in the contemporary Muslim world khulʿ is either unregulated or requires the husband's consent, although some legislators have decided do away with this requirement provided certain conditions are met, for example in case of an unconsummated marriage (UAE) or if the spouses disagree on the amount to be paid or forfeited by the wife (Algeria).

In some countries, judicial practice has made khulʿ less cumbersome to women. In Iran, for example, khulʿ has been allowed by courts without the consent of the husband in cases where the continuation of marriage was thought to cause hardship to the wife (Abiad 2008, 168). Undoubtedly, Pakistani High Courts have gone farther than most other courts in equating khulʿ to a nonconsensual, no-fault divorce, thus partly bridging the gap between national legislation on MPL and the principles of equality and nondiscrimination enshrined in the constitution. In regard to khulʿ, as on other issues, Pakistani judges of the High Courts and FSC have extended women's rights by advancing novel interpretations of the primary sources, emphasizing their egalitarian spirit, and relying on minority opinions of different madhāhib. This religiously inspired judicial activism has prompted a great deal of enthusiasm among scholars, with some holding that Pakistani "courts have championed women's rights by radically liberalizing Pakistani divorce law" (Yefet 2011, 557). Although Pakistani judicial practice concerning khulʿ is commendable, I would argue that this enthusiasm may be excessive.

First of all, women in Pakistan are still denied equal rights to divorce. Khulʿ, in particular, is subjected to a number of conditions: women, unlike men repudiating their wives, must go to court and satisfy the judges that their requests are reasonable; women are also usually asked to give up their right to mahr (Munir 2014, 23; Ahmed 2014, 76). It is only in rare cases that they can keep the immediate portion, let alone obtain the deferred one. Relinquishing one's mahr may in some cases discourage women from filing for divorce in the first place. Another problem is that khulʿ, more than any other form of female-initiated divorce, is associated in the collective imagination with the responsibility, if not the whim, of the wife,[36] although this social stigma has faded during the last decade. Finally, khulʿ is mostly negotiated out of court by the families of the spouses (Rizvi, pers. comm., June 24, 2020), and this factor, in a patriarchal society like that of Pakistan, is likely to have penalizing consequences for women. Private negotiations may also turn khul' into a de facto consensual divorce and thus, together with financial considerations, may prevent appeals. The progressive attitude of the higher judiciary is clearly, then, of limited significance given that most cases decided by the family courts are not appealed.

Despite these hurdles, the rate of divorce by judicial khul' is increasing.[37] However, while it is undeniable that today it is easier—both psychologically and practically—for Pakistani women to divorce than in the past, the rise in khul' cases is not alone a sign of emancipation: in addition to the fact that this is part of a general increase in divorce rates, Pakistani women tend to file for divorce under the DMMA.[38] Court records indicate that khul' is their last resort when there are no grounds for dissolution under the DMMA or these grounds cannot be proved.[39] In many cases, it is a remedy that is chosen by judges, who turn cases of fault-based divorce into khul' regardless of the wife's wishes.[40] The rise in khul' cases, then, may indicate an increase in divorce requests that is accompanied by lower courts' persistent unwillingness to accept fault-based suits under the DMMA. Furthermore, the judicial practice of Pakistani High Courts has been inconsistent and not all of these courts' divorce decisions have been favorable to women (Abbasi and Cheema 2018; Ahmed 2014, 76).[41] Some High Courts, notably in Sindh and Punjab, have ruled in ways that are more favorable to women than other courts, and the same courts have produced different decisions. Contributing to the discretionary power of the higher courts are two factors: the gaps in existing laws, which leave judges considerable leeway in deciding if khul' is justified, and the instruction to apply Ḥanafī doctrine in the absence of statutory norms, while divorce laws mostly draw on Mālikī doctrine.[42]

Despite adopting a language of rights and marital harmony, courts have also occasionally adopted the dominant patriarchal model of the family (Ahmed 2014 82) and penalized women whose attitudes do not conform to social expectations (Giunchi 1999, 80–82). We may thus conclude that what has emerged so far in Pakistani judicial practice is "a benign patriarchal interpretation of the laws" that has secured and even extended women's statutory rights but has not radically revolutionized family law

A related point is that Islamic sources can be used to support or restrict women's rights depending on how they are interpreted and on the relative weight given to one source or another. What makes the difference is the orientation of the judges who interpret and apply the law. When Justice Cornelius argued that basing human rights in Islam would contribute to entrenching them in people's consciousness, he was writing at a time when the higher echelons of state institutions—including the judiciary—were in the hands of individuals with a modernist outlook and the government's role in appointing and dismissing judges was much more pronounced. Since then, more traditionally minded and Islamist-oriented individuals have entered the state apparatus and the executive control of the judiciary has weakened. Following the nineteenth constitutional amendment of 2011, which reformed the judicial appointment procedure, the executive's power to nominate judges has been greatly curtailed. This means that the executive can no longer dismiss judges whose approach does not correspond to its own orientation. This is good news for democracy but not necessarily good news for women.

On a more optimistic note, the fact that more women have been joining the Pakistani higher judiciary may further secure and extend women's rights. Since 2009 there has been a steady increase in the number of female judges in the lower courts and, to a more limited extent, in the higher judiciary. Research shows that "lady judges," as they are usually called in Pakistan, are better at understanding the nuances of domestic strife and more attuned to women's needs, although they do not always rule in favor of women (Mehdi 2017; Rizvi, pers. comm., June 24, 2020).

It remains to be seen whether discourses that integrate human rights and Islam become pervasive and to what extent Pakistani judges with no expertise in religion will be considered by society as entitled to speak in the name of God. Further, while it should not be assumed that judges with a traditionalist and Islamist orientation will roll back women's divorce rights, the rise of militant groups may induce judges, whatever their outlook, to exercise greater caution or may pressure the legislative and the executive to abrogate or amend progressive legislation on divorce.

At least in the medium term some degree of incoherence, even in the best scenarios, may be inevitable. As Peletz suggests with regard to Malaysia (2020), judicial practice, in Pakistan as elsewhere, reflects a multiplicity of discourses, practices, incentives and constraints of different origin that interact and merge in ever-shifting articulations. Behind the apparent binary of Islamization versus secularization lie complex and hybrid dynamics that only a practice-oriented perspective can help to unearth.

### *Acknowledgments*

I wish to thank Justice Majida Rizvi for answering my questions and Nausheen Ahmed for putting me in contact with her.

## NOTES

1. In the case of *mubārā'a* nothing is owed by either party and the intervention of the family court is not required; according to section 8 of the Muslim Family Law Ordinance (MFLO) the spouses sign a mutual divorce deed and send a written notice to the Union Council, a local government body consisting of elected members and state employees. The council will treat this divorce as a ṭalāq.
2. According to section 7 of the MFLO, ṭalāq can be announced in any form, but to be effective a written notice must be sent to the Union Council, which notifies the wife and within thirty days sets up an Arbitration Council consisting of a government officer and representatives of both parties. If reconciliation attempts fail, ṭalāq has not been revoked in the meantime, and ninety days have passed since the council received the notice, divorce takes effect. If the wife is pregnant, ṭalāq will become effective at

the end of the pregnancy or after ninety days have elapsed, whichever is later. If it is not possible to deliver a ṭalāq notice to a woman, the husband can serve notice through a newspaper approved by the Union Council.

3. Under section 8 of the MFLO, if the right to divorce has been delegated to the wife and she wants to avail herself of this right, section 7 on ṭalāq will apply, as she is technically repudiating herself on behalf of the husband.
4. Ḥanafī law prescribes that on attaining puberty a woman can ask for her marriage to be rescinded provided that it has not been consummated. Under section 2(vii) of the Dissolution of Muslim Marriage Act (DMMA) as amended in 1981, if a woman is given in marriage before the age of sixteen, she can exercise the option of puberty
5. In Pakistani official documents this is the common transliteration of shari‘a and indicates the injunctions of the Qur'an and sunna. I use this spelling for Pakistani legal acts and institutions; when referring to legal terms in general, I use the Arabic spelling.
6. The higher judiciary consists of a Supreme Court and High Courts, one for each province plus one for the Islamabad Capital Territory. The subordinate judiciary consists of civil courts, criminal district courts, and specialized tribunals—such as the family courts. The disputed areas of Azad Kashmri and Gilgit-Baltistan have a separate court system.
7. Justice Majida Rizvi, interviewed on June 24, 2020 (Skype). In 1994 she became the first Pakistani woman to be appointed as a judge, and she served from 1994 to 1999. She later headed the National Commission on the Status of Women and authored several articles on women's and children's rights.
8. At the time, MPL referred to the personal law that was applicable to Indian Muslims. This is also the case in India (Vatuk 2008, 231).
9. Among other things, the husband had to obtain the consent of the existing wives before marrying a new one.
10. According to Qur'an 24:6–9, if a husband accuses his wife of adultery without supplying witnesses and swears four times that his accusation is true and the wife then refutes his accusation with four oaths, their marriage is dissolved. She escapes zinā and he escapes qadhf charges.
11. *Mst. Balqis Fatima v. Najm-ul-Iram Qureshi*, PLD 1959 Lahore 566.
12. That he had in mind a hierarchical family structure is made clear in *Purdah and the Status of Women in Islam*, first published in 1972, by his arguments against the final report of the 1955 Commission (Serajuddin 2011, 52) and by several of his speeches (Mawdudi 1981, 133–139).
13. In his book, *Purdah and the Status of Women in Islam* ([1972] 1992), he wrote that a wife can obtain separation from a husband who is cruel, impotent, or "whom she abhors" (*Ivi* 151). The clearest espousal of his thoughts on khul‘ can be found in his *Huqūq al-Zawjayn*, a series of articles published as a book in 1943 (see Cheema 2019, 130–132).
14. PLD 1967 SC 97.
15. Similar observations about judges' ideas of families have been made with regard to Egypt (Lindbekk 2014, 97).
16. *Hakim Zadi v. Nawaz Ali*, PLD 1972 Kar. 540.
17. *Siddiqui v. Sharfan*, PLD 1968 Lah. 411.
18. See, for example, *Nizam Khan v. Additional District Judge*, PLD 1976 Lah. 930.
19. The court replaced the Shariat Benches that had been introduced in 1978 in each provincial High Court. The FSC's jurisdiction and functions are spelled out in articles 203C and 203D of the constitution.

20. The constitution (18th Amendment) Act 2010 replaced this sentence with "having at least fifteen years' experience in Islamic law, research or instruction" (s. 74).
21. *Arif Hussain v. the State* (PLD 1982 FSC 42), *Muhammad Yousaf and Another v. the State* (PLD 1988 FSC 22), *Lala v. the State* (PLD 1987 SC 414), *Muhammad Ramzan v. Muhammad Saeed and Three Others* (PLD 1983 FSC 483), *Muhammad Imtiaz and Others v. the State* (PLD 1981 FSC 308), *Muhammad Ramzan v. the State* (PLDS 1984 FSC 93), *Muhammad Siddique and Another v. the State* (PLD 1983 FSC 9), *Allah Rakha v. Federation of Pakistan* (PLD 2000 FSC 1).
22. *Farrukh Ikhram v. the State* (PLD 1987 SC 5).
23. From its jurisdiction were excluded "Muslim private law," procedural norms of courts, the constitution, and, for a period of ten years, fiscal laws and norms relating to the collection and levy of taxes and fees, banking, or insurance practice and procedure.
24. *Federation of Pakistan v. Mst. Farishta*, 1981 PLD SC 120.
25. *Rashidan Bibi v. Bashir Ahmad*, 1983 PLD Lah. 549.
26. See, for example, *Shah Begum v. District Judge Sialkot*, PLD 1995 Lah. 19; *Mst Saiqa v. the Judge, Family Court Lahore*, 1994 MLD 2204, cited by Haider (2000, 333); and other cases discussed by Munir (2014, 13–15).
27. *Mst Naseem Akhtar v. Muhammad Rafiq*, PLD 2005 SC 293, cited in Munir 2014, 14.
28. *Syed Dilshad Ahmed v. Mst Sarwat Bi*, PLD 1990 Kar. 239.
29. See the cases discussed in Munir 2009, 285; Haider 2000; S. Ijaz, *A Woman's Right to Unilateral Divorce under Islamic Law: Saleem Ahmed v. Government of Pakistan*, PLD 2014 FSC 43, 80–81. In 2015 the Punjab Assembly amended the Family Court Act 1964 by establishing inter alia a ceiling for the compensation owed by the wife in case of khulʿ.
30. *Dr Mahmood-ur-Rehman Faisal v. Government of Pakistan*, PLD 1994 SC 607. For the term *MPL* and a critical appraisal of the SAB decision, see Abbasi and Cheema 2018, 13–16.
31. *Saleem Ahmed v. Government of Pakistan*, PLD 2014 FSC 43.
32. http://www.pakistani.org/pakistan/legislation/1991/actXof1991.html. Italics mine.
33. For some examples, see *Mst. Khurshid Jan v. Fazal Dad*, PLD 1964 Lah. 558; as for the eclectic approach to the sources by the FSC, see *Ansar Burney v. Federation of Pakistan and others*, PLD 1983 FSC 73.
34. For an early discussion of the sources of Islamic law and their relation, see *Mst. Khurshud Jan v. Fazal Dad*, PLD 1963 (WP) Lah. 558.
35. A few years later the CII stated that the person officiating the marriage should inform the bride-to-be of the possibility of including the provision of delegated divorce in the contract; the wording of the contract should be revised to make women's rights to delegated divorce clear; however, the CII also argued that women wanting to divorce had to return their mahr, as per the Ḥanafī madhhab: Women soon to be able to divorce husbands, https://www.thenews.com.pk/print/383020-women-soon-to-be-able-to-divorce-husbands.
36. This is the case in other countries; see Stiles on Zanzibar, for example (2019, 168).
37. To prove this point Ramzan et al. (2018) state that 13,299 cases were reported in Punjab in 2012 and in subsequent years their number kept increasing, reaching 18,901 in 2016. However, the value of these data is limited as it is not accompanied by a percentage of the total number of marriages and does not provide us with information on data gathering.
38. There are no accurate nationwide data on marriage. The number of ever-married women who were divorced or separated in 2011 was one of the lowest in South Asia: 1.5%;

however, this is not a good measure of the incidence of divorce (Dommaraju and Jones 2011, 741).

39. This is the case also in India (Vatuk 2008, 231).

40. This has been noted also Zanzibar, Palestine, and Lebanon (Stiles 2019; Moors 1995; Clarke 2014).

41. *Zarab Khan v. the State*, PLD 1981 FSC 293; *Mst. Jehan Mina v. the State*, PLD 1983 FSC 183; *Mst. Rani v. the State*, PLD 1996 Kar. 316; *Mst. Safia Bibi v. the State*, PLD 1985 FSC 120; *Mst. Siani v. State*, PLD 21984 FSC 121; *Mst. Su Khan v. the State*, 1985 P Cr.LJ 110; *Muhammad Zafar v. Zahoor and Others*, PLD 1983 FSC 480; *Zudeba Begum v. the State*, PLD 1986 FSC 268. For an analysis of these cases see Giunchi 1994.

42. The Supreme Court has held that there is a legal presumption that where the litigants are Sunni, their family law dispute falls under the Ḥanafī school unless either party proves that they follow another madhhab (Abbasi and Cheema 2018, 18).

## REFERENCES

Abbasi, Muhammad Zubair. 2016. "Women's Right to Unilateral No-Fault Based Divorce in Pakistan and India." *Jindal Global Law Review* 7:81–95.

———. 2017. "Judicial Ijtihad as a Tool for Legal Reform: Extending Women's Right to Divorce under Islamic Law in Pakistan." *Islamic Law and Society* 24 (4):384–411.

Abbasi, Muhammad Zubair, and Shahbaz Ahmad Cheema. 2018. *Family Laws in Pakistan*. Karachi: Oxford University Press.

Abiad, Nisrine. 2008. *Sharia, Muslim States and International Human Rights Treaty Obligations. A Comparative Study*. London: BIICL.

Ahmed, Nausheen. 2014. "Family Law in Pakistan: Using the Secular to Influence the Religious." In *Adjudicating Family Law in Muslim Courts*, edited by Elisa Giunchi, 70–86. Abingdon: Routledge.

Anderson, Michael R. 1993. "Islamic Law and the Colonial Encounter in British India." In *Institutions and Ideologies: A South Asia Reader*, edited by David Arnold and Peter Robbs, 165–185. London: Curzon.

Braibanti, Rudolph. 1999. *Chief Justice Cornelius of Pakistan: An Analysis with Letters and Speeches*. New York: Oxford University Press.

Carroll, Lucy. 1996. "Qur'an 2.229 'A Charter Granted to the Wife'? Judicial Khul' in Pakistan." *Islamic Law and Society* 3 (1):91–126.

Cheema, Shahbaz Ahmad. 2013. "Federal Shariat Court as a Vehicle of Progressive Trends in Islamic Scholarship in Pakistan." *Al-Adwa* 39 (28):41–52.

———. 2019. "An Unlikely Champion of Women's Rights under Muslim Personal Law: Mawdudi on Anglo-Muhammadan Law." *Journal of Islamic Thought and Civilization* 9 (2), (Fall): 110–137.

Clarke, Morgan. 2014. Shari'a Courts and Muslim Family Law in Lebanon. In *Adjudicating Family Law in Muslim Courts*, edited by Elisa Giunchi, 32–47. Abingdon: Routledge.

Dommaraju, Premchand, and Gavin Jones. 2011. "Divorce Trends in Asia." *Asian Journal of Social Science* 39 (6):725–750.

Fortier, Corinne. 2012. "The Right to Divorce for Women (*khul'*) in Islam. Comparative Practices in Mauritania and Egypt." In *Interpreting Divorce Laws in Islam*, edited by Rubya Mehdi, Werner Menski, and Jorgen S. Nielsen, 155–175. Copenhagen: DJØF.

Giunchi, Elisa. 1994. "The Enforcement of the *Zinā* Ordinance by the Federal Shariat Court in the Period 1980–1990, and Its Impact on Women." PhD diss., University of Cambridge.

———. 1999. *Radicalismo islamico e condizione femminile in Pakistan*. Turin: L'Harmattan.

——. 2010. "The Reinvention of *Sharī'ah* under the British Raj: In Search of Authenticity and Certainty." *Journal of Asian Studies* 69, no. 4 (November): 1119–1142.

——. 2013. "Islamization and Judicial Activism in Pakistan: What *Šarī'ah?*" *Oriente Moderno* 93 (1):188–204.

Haider, Nadya. 2000. "Islamic Legal Reform, the Case of Pakistan and Family Law." *Yale Journal of Law and Feminism* 12 (2):287–341.

Holden, Livia. 2012. "Divorce at the Women's Initiative in India, in Pakistan and in the Diasporas." In *Interpreting Divorce Laws in Islam*, edited by Rubya Mehdi, Werner Menski, and Jorgen S. Nielsen, 131–153. Copenhagen: DJØF.

Ijaz, Salman. No date. "A Woman's Right to Unilateral Divorce under Islamic Law: Saleem Ahmed v. Government of Pakistan, PLD 2014 FSC 43." *Lums Law Journal* 2: 77–83.

Jaraba, Mahmoud. 2020. "*Khul'* in Action: How Do Local Muslim Communities in Germany Dissolve an Islamic Religious-Only Marriage?" *Journal of Muslim Minority Affairs* 40 (1):1–21.

Kugle, Scott Alan. 2001. "Framed, Blamed and Renamed: The Recasting of Islamic Jurisprudence in Colonial South Asia." *Modern Asian Studies* 35 (2):257–313.

Lau, Martin. 2006. *The Role of Islam in the Legal System of Pakistan*. Leiden: Martinus Nijhoff.

Lindbekk, Monika. 2014. "The Enforcement of Personal Status Law by Egyptian Courts." *In Adjudicating Family Law in Muslim Courts*, edited by Elisa Giunchi, 87–105. Abingdon: Routledge.

Lombardi, Clark B. 2010. "Ever Help Promote Liberal Democracy? A View from Pakistan." *University of St. Thomas Law Journal* 7 (3):649–691.

Maskiell, Michelle. 1984. "The Impact of Islamization Policies on Pakistani Women's Lives." Working Paper 69, Michigan State University, Publication Office of Women in International Development.

Masud, Muhammad Khalid. 2012. "Interpreting Divorce laws in Pakistan." In *Interpreting Divorce Laws in Islam*, edited by Rubya Mehdi, Werner Menski, and Jorgen S. Nielsen, 43–61. Copenhagen: DJØF.

——. 2019. "Modernizing Islamic Law in Pakistan: Reform or Reconstruction?" *Journal of South Asian and Middle Eastern Studies* 42, no. 2 (Winter): 73–97.

Mawdudi, Sayyid Abul A'la. 1960. *The Islamic Law and Its Introduction in Pakistan*. Lahore: Islamic Publications.

——. (1972) 1992. *Purdah and the Status of Women in Islam*. Lahore: Islamic Publications.

——. 1981. *Selected Speeches and Writings of Maulana Maududi*. Karachi: International Islamic Publishers.

Mehdi, Rubya. 2017. "Lady Judges of Pakistan: Embodying the Changing Living Tradition of Islam." In *Women Judges in the Muslim World: A Comparative Study of Discourse and Practice*, edited by Nadia Sonneveld and Monika Lindbekk, 204–236. Leiden: Brill.

Mehmood, Ifzal. 2016. "Judicial Separation at the Wife's Initiative. A Study of Redemption (khul') in Islamic Law and Contemporary Legislation in Pakistan and Malaysia." *Journal of Islamic Legal Studies* 2 (1):1–25.

Moors, Annelise. 1995. *Women, Property and Islam. Palestinian Experiences: 1920–1990*. New York: Cambridge University Press.

Munir, Muhammad. 2009. "The Rights of Women and Role of Superior Judiciary in Pakistan with Special Reference to Family Law Case from 2004–2008." *Pakistan Journal of Islamic Research* 3:271–299.

——. 2014. "Judicial Law-Making: An Analysis of Case Law on *Khul'* in Pakistan." *Islamabad Law Review* 1 (1):7–24.

——. 2015. "The Law of *Khul'* in Islamic Law and the Legal System of Pakistan." *LUMS Law Journal* 1:33–63.

Pearl, David. 1979. *A Textbook on Muslim Law.* London: Croom Helm.

Peletz, Michael. 2020. *Sharia Transformations Cultural Politics and the Rebranding of an Islamic Judiciary.* Oakland: University of California Press.

Ramzan, Shazia, Akhtar Saiza, Ahmed Shabbir, Muhammad Umar Zafar, and Haroon Yousaf. 2018. "Divorce Status and Its Major Reasons in Pakistan." *Sociology and Anthropology* 6 (4):386–391.

Roy, Olivier. 2013. "Secularism and Islam: The Theological Predicament." *International Spectator* 48 (1):5–19.

Serajuddin, Alamgir Muhammad. 2011a. *Muslim Family Law, Secular Courts and Muslim Women of India, Pakistan and Bangladesh.* Oxford: Oxford University Press.

———. 2011b. *Shariʿa Law and Society. Tradition and Change in South Asia.* Karachi: Oxford University Press.

Sonneveld, Nadia. 2012. *Khulʿ Divorce in Egypt: Public Debates, Judicial Practices, and Everyday Life.* Cairo: American University of Cairo Press.

———. 2018. "The Case of Women's Unilateral Divorce Rights in Egypt Revolution or Counter-revolution?" In *Women and Change in North Africa: What Counts as Revolutionary?* edited by Doris H. Gray and Nadia Sonneveld, 331–352. Cambridge: Cambridge University Press.

———. 2019. "Divorce Reform in Egypt and Morocco: Men and Women Navigating Rights and Duties." *Islamic Law and Society* 26 (1–2):149–178.

Sonneveld, Nadia, and Erin E. Stiles. 2016. "Divorce and Custody: Contemporary Practices: *Khulʿ*." In *The Encyclopedia of Women in Islamic Cultures*, General Editor Suad Joseph. \First Published online 2016.

———. 2019. "*Khul*ʿ: Local Contours of a Global Phenomenon." *Islamic Law and Society* 26 (1–2):1–11.

Stiles, Erin E. 2009. *An Islamic Court in Context: An Ethnographic Study of Judicial Reasoning.* New York: Palgrave Macmillan.

———. 2019. "It Is Your Right to Buy a Divorce: Judicial Khuluu in Zanzibar." *Islamic Law and Society* 26 (1–2):12–35.

van Huis, Stijn 2019. "*Khul*ʿ over the Longue Durée: The Decline of Traditional *Fiqh*-Based Divorce Mechanisms in Indonesian Legal Practice. *Islamic Law and Society* 26 (1–2):58–82.

Vatuk, Sylvia. 2008. "Divorce at the Wife's Initiative in Muslim Personal Law: What Are the Options and What Are Their Implications for Women's Welfare?" In *Redefining Family Law in India: Essays in Honour of B. Sivaramayya*, edited by Archana Parashar and Amita Dhanda, 200–235. London: Routledge.

———. 2017. *Marriage and Its Discontents. Women, Islam and the Law in India.* New Delhi: Women Unlimited.

Weiss, Anita M. 2012. *Moving Forward with the Legal Empowerment of Women in Pakistan*, Washington, DC: United States Institute of Peace.

Welchman, Lynn. 2007. *Women and Muslim Family Laws in Arab States: A Comparative Overview of Textual Development and Advocacy.* Amsterdam: Amsterdam University Press.

Yefet, Karin Carmit. 2011. "The Constitution and Female-Initiated Divorce in Pakistan: Western Liberalism in Islamic Garb." *Harvard Journal of Law and Gender* 34 (2):553–615.

Yilmaz, Ihsan. 2014. "Pakistan's Federal Shariat Court's Collective *Ijtihād* on Gender Equality, Women's Rights and the Right to Family Life." *Islam and Christian-Muslim Relations* 25 (2):181–192.Zaman, Muhammad Qasim, 2018. *Islam in Pakistan. A History.* Princeton. Princeton University Press.

# 2

# Male-Initiated Divorce before the Egyptian Judiciary

NATHALIE BERNARD-MAUGIRON

In January 2017, Egyptian president Abdel-Fatah al-Sisi declared that in order to give divorcing husbands a chance to reconsider their decision, only repudiations (*ṭalāq*) pronounced in the presence of the government official (*ma'dhūn*)[1] should be officially recognized (Al-Hayah TV Network 2017, 22:30). The president added that he had recently learned from the head of the state Central Agency for Public Mobilization and Statistics (CAPMAS) that about 40 percent of Egypt's 900,000 annual marriages end in divorce after five years (CAPMAS 2016; Diaa 2016) and was alarmed by Egypt's escalating divorce rate, which threatened social stability.[2]

The National Council for Women welcomed Sisi's proposal. Relying on religious and social arguments, it declared that, "Islamic Sharia calls for the unity and stability of families. Having a ma'dhūn official administer the divorce would give couples a chance to reconsider a decision they might have made out of anger. This would reduce the number of divorces, preserving family unity and cohesion and protecting children against the pain they might suffer as a result of their parents' split" (Rashwān 2017; El Shalakani 2017).

The council praised the president's determination to preserve Egyptian family ties and keep up with a renewed religious discourse to promote a new vision of Islam in line with the modern age. Sisi also received the support of the Grand Mufti, the state-appointed highest religious authority in the country, who, however, put the blame on the 2000 *khul'* law for the increase in the divorce rate (Dār al-Iftā' 2017; Qāsim 2017) by making it easier for a wife to get a no-fault divorce.[3]

However, the president's statement met with a strong protest from Al-Azhar's Council of Senior Scholars.[4] The council was convened by Shaykh al-Azhar, and two weeks after President Sisi's announcement, it declared on February 5, 2017, that verbal divorce had been an undisputed practice since the days of Prophet Muhammad and that it did not need to be documented to be considered valid as long as the husband was fully conscious and of sound mind. As a compromise, they proposed to enforce harsher penalties against husbands who failed to record such divorces within a reasonable time frame.

In traditional *fiqh*, the dissolution of the marriage by the husband is not submitted to any condition nor to judicial review. A simple willful, unilateral pronouncement is enough to instantaneously break spousal bonds. This form of marriage dissolution remains the most common means of divorce in Egypt, but the Egyptian state has tried to limit its use by instituting procedural and substantive hindrances (Abu-Oudeh 2004a; Anderson 1951; Fawzy 2004; Hefner 2005; Lindbekk 2016; Linant de Bellefonds 1962; Singerman 2005; Zulficar 2008).

Following the formation of the modern Egyptian state in the nineteenth century, personal status law has gone through a process of codification and traditional fiqh was transformed into written statutory law (Abu-Odeh 2004b; Bernard-Maugiron 2016; Bernard-Maugiron and Dupret 2002; El Alami 1994; Linant de Bellefonds 1955; Sonneveld and Lindbekk 2015). The Egyptian state attempted to curb the right of the husband to divorce his wife unilaterally. At the same time, women have been allowed to apply for divorce on several grounds and even to get a unilateral divorce through the khul' procedure.

Verbal repudiation is still allowed in Egypt, but since 1985 it has had to be registered by the husband before the ma'dhūn within thirty days of the date of pronunciation and the ma'dhūn must inform the wife that she has been repudiated.[5] Criminal sanctions are applied in case of nonobservance of these procedures. Even if it was not registered, unilateral divorce takes effect from the date of its occurrence, though in terms of inheritance and other financial rights, it becomes effective only from the date the wife was notified. In 2000, the legislature decided that if the husband or the wife denies that repudiation has taken place, it could only be proven by the official registration document. This provision, however, was declared unconstitutional by the Supreme Constitutional Court in 2006.

Since 1929, a male-initiated divorce has been considered null and void if uttered in a state of inebriation or if it was subject to coercion; it cannot be conditional and its wording cannot be ambiguous.[6] In addition, triple repudiation pronounced in one sitting counts only as one revocable repudiation and not as three irrevocable ones.[7] In 2000, the parliament declared that if the wife or the husband denies that marital relations have resumed, their resumption can be proven by the husband only in the official registration document, though the wife can use any means of proof. Finally, since 1985, in addition to her waiting-period maintenance (*nafaqa al-'idda*) and deferred dower (*mu'akhkhar al-ṣadaq*), the divorced wife can receive a financial compensation (*mut'a*) if she did not consent to the divorce and did not cause it. The Supreme Constitutional Court decided in 1993 that such a compensation does not violate the right of the husband to repudiate his wife as granted by the shari'a.

The Egyptian parliament did not go so far as abolishing unilateral divorce, as Tunisia did, or demanding that it be pronounced before a judge on legitimate grounds, as in Algeria, Morocco or Syria, but it did establish several barriers to limit its use by husbands. This chapter analyzes the stance taken by the judiciary toward these different reforms of male-initiated divorce in Egypt. It relies on the decisions of the two supreme courts of the country: (1) the Supreme Constitutional Court's arguments on the conformity of such reforms with the constitution in general[8] and with Article 2 in particular;[9] and (2) the Court of Cassation,[10] which is in charge of establishing binding judicial principles in that field.[11] The implementation of these legal reforms by ordinary Egyptian judges[12] will also be analyzed to stress how family judges did not oppose the implementation of this new legislation even when the laws moved away from the predominant opinion of the Ḥanafī *madhhab* (legal school), which is the official Sunni school in Egypt.[13] The introductory notes to the laws regulating male-initiated divorce will also be analyzed to identify the arguments used by the state to limit men's ability to repudiate their wives.

## Egyptian Judges and the Validity of Male-Initiated Divorce

In 1929, the Egyptian legislature required a husband's real intention to repudiate his wife and declared that a triple repudiation made at one time would be equivalent to a single repudiation. Since 1985, the repudiation has had to be registered and the wife has had to be notified. Since 2000, the ma'dhūn have been required to try to reconcile the spouses before registering the divorce.

### *Repudiation in a State of Inebriation or under Duress*

In traditional Ḥanafī fiqh, words articulated by the husband and referring unambiguously to repudiation give divorce legal effect regardless of his real intention. The pronunciation made in a state of culpable intoxication or under pressure is valid and will lead to the dissolution of the conjugal bond (Schacht 1913–1936). In that matter, "the accepted Ḥanafī rules are more right and retrogressive than those of any other school for . . . they not only leave the power of the husband unilaterally to repudiate his wife completely unfettered, as do all the Sunni schools, but go further than any other in regarding as valid, binding and even final various expressions of divorce never really intended to have that effect" (Anderson 1951, 271). This position was codified by the Qadri Pasha code at the end of the nineteenth century.[14] That code stipulated expressly that "a repudiation pronounced even under duress [*mukrah*] or by joke [*hāzil*] will produce its legal effects."[15] The code likewise considered as valid "any repudiation pronounced by a husband in case of willful drunkenness [*ṭā'i'an mukhtār*] caused by a forbidden drink."[16]

Law No. 25 of 1929 stated that repudiations conditionally pronounced[17] or uttered in a state of inebriation (*sakran*) or under duress (*mukrah*) would be deprived of any legal effects.[18] The explanatory memorandum that accompanied the law justified such a departure from the validity of a repudiation pronounced in a state of inebriation in the Qadri Pasha code by invoking better-suited solutions adopted by other schools of fiqh, in particular "an authoritative [*rājih*] opinion of Aḥmad Ibn Ḥanbal and the opinion of the other three rites and by many subsequent disciples [*al-tābi'īn*]" as well as the fact that "no opinion of the companions [*ṣaḥāba*] of the prophet is known for admitting its validity." The memorandum adds that "the Shāfi'ī and Mālikī rites as well as the opinions of Aḥmad, Dāwūd, and many other companions of the Prophet" refuse to consider a repudiation made under duress.

Such a strategy to bypass the often-rigid rules of the Ḥanafī school followed a legal method called *takhayyur* (innovative selection). Reformers also combined legal rules from different schools to produce new solutions, in a process known as *talfīq*. This allowed the reforms to be presented as in accord with the shari'a and thus to avoid significant attacks from conservative religious circles.

The Court of Cassation implemented Article 1 of Law No. 25 of 1929 and declared that repudiations made under duress were to be invalid. In its rulings, the court stressed that this provision had codified the solution of "the majority of fuqahā'," in spite of the fact that "the fiqh of the Islamic shari'a only requires that the husband be adult and conscious."[19] The court added that "it is established in the Ḥanafī fiqh, which has to be implemented according to Article 280 of the Rules of procedure of the shari'a courts, that the divorce of the furious [*ghaḍbān*] [husband] is not valid if the anger [*ghaḍab*] reached such a level that he became unable to be aware of his words or acts or becomes in a kind of madness [*hadhayān*] where the confusion [*iḍṭirāb*] reigns over his words and acts because he lost his sound will and reason."[20]

The Court of Cassation therefore endorsed and even extended the Egyptian legislature's stand according to which fiqh invalidates a divorce made by an angry husband. Furthermore, the court justified this interpretation as following the Ḥanafī school. The court also argued that a repudiation made under coercion is not valid if it was uttered under a serious threat (*khaṭar jāsim*) to the husband or his property, since this could be considered as duress neutralizing his consent.[21] The court added that the trial judge has discretionary power to evaluate the means, the intensity, and the effects of such constraints.[22] The state of intoxication or duress can be established by testimony.

### *Egyptian Judges and Triple Repudiations*

In classical fiqh and Egyptian law, a repudiation is revocable during the wife's waiting period, meaning during her first three menstruations after repudiation. During this period, the spouses are still considered to be married and the spousal bond is simply suspended. They continue to live together and the husband can decide to take his wife again with or without her agreement, explicitly or implicitly, by resuming marital relations and married life. If this is the case, he does not need to conclude a new marriage contract or pay a new dower (*ṣadaq* or *mahr*). The wife is not asked for her opinion, nor is her consent required. If the husband dies during her 'idda, she inherits from him as his wife.[23] At the end of the 'idda period and in the absence of a resumption of the marital relations, the marriage is dissolved and repudiation becomes irrevocable. The spouses are divorced and neither has inheritance claims on the other. If the husband has pronounced the ṭalāq over his wife only once or twice (*ṭalāq bā'in baynūna sughrā*), he is entitled to remarry her by drawing up a new contract with a new dower, but only if she consents to it. If she was repudiated thrice (*ṭalāq bā'in baynūna kubrā*), not only does the separation become irrevocable before the end of the 'idda, but the husband may not return to his wife unless she contracts a marriage with another husband and then is repudiated after the consummation of that marriage.[24]

As noted, since 1929 the Egyptian legislature has considered[25] a triple repudiation made at one time (e.g. "you are repudiated, you are repudiated, you are repudiated!") to be equivalent to a single revocable repudiation.[26] Therefore, to be considered irrevocable, a triple repudiation must be uttered in three separate pronouncements. To avoid any risk of confusion, the Ministry of Justice requires the ma'dhūn, when registering an irrevocable repudiation, to specify the dates of the two previous (revocable) ones.

Such a stance is contrary to the accepted views of all four Sunni schools. The Qadri Pasha code, thus, stated that "repudiations can be pronounced successively in three separate times, when the marriage is consummated, or in one and the same formula, whether the marriage is consummated or not."[27] Article 239 of the code also stated that a repudiation is irrevocable "if the formula is expressly accompanied by the number three or a sign of the fingers" and "if he declares that he intended to repudiate her by three." The introductory memorandum to Law No. 25 of 1929 justified this departure from the traditional rule by referring to the opinions of a number of isolated fuqahā' as well as to various scholars of Cordova (*mashāyikh qurṭuba*), and "according to the later jurist Ibn al-Qayyim, this was the opinion of most Companions of the Prophet [*al-ṣaḥāba*] as well as some disciples [*ṣāḥib*] of Mālik, some Hanafites as well as some disciples [*aṣḥāb*] of Aḥmad."

On the basis of the 1929 law, the Court of Cassation ruled that repeated acts or words made in one session count only as one divorce and that such a divorce is revocable.[28] It has also argued that three repetitions of a divorce at one time count as one revocable divorce and not as three irrevocable ones. For the court, requiring three separate pronouncements allows the husband to examine himself after the first and second divorces and to exercise patience (*ṣabr*) and forbearance (*iḥtimāl*). The wife will also have the opportunity to reflect. The court underscores that in the end, if the experience is not fruitful and a third divorce is pronounced, the spouses will be assured that there is no benefit to staying in the relationship and that a definitive break is preferable.[29]

### *Conciliation and Arbitration Attempts before the* Ma'dhūn

Since 2000, before proceeding to registration, the ma'dhūn has been required to warn the spouses of the dangers of divorce and ask them to choose one arbiter each, if possible from among their relatives, to attempt to reconcile them (Art. 21). If the spouses insist on immediate divorce or declare that their marriage has already been broken down or if the husband declares that he has already repudiated his wife, the divorce will be registered.

The novelty introduced by that law lies in the requirement that reconciliation will be attempted by the notary and the fact that the notary must draw the spouses' attention to the dangers of divorce. The law, however, does not specify the extent to which the notary must intervene and whether the notary should attempt to reconcile the spouses or merely draw their attention to the seriousness of the consequences of divorce. The 2000 law also does not specify the time limit within which the arbitration attempt must be made, although its introductory memorandum mentions a minimum length of one month.

Although this procedure has strengthened the role of the ma'dhūn, who is no longer limited to recording the repudiation but now plays a more active role in the interaction with the spouses, interviews show that in practice, the ma'dhūns tend to have a very narrow interpretation of this provision and make little effort to try to reconcile the couple or warn them of the danger of breaking up a marriage. Their lack of training and the fact that they receive remuneration for each registered repudiation are probably not unrelated to this attitude.

The conciliation attempts by two arbiters do not seem to be very successful either. Field research and interviews show that most ma'dhūns simply propose that the witnesses who accompany the spouses try to reconcile them. Very often these are "professional witnesses," who stand in front of the notary's office and do not even know the spouses personally. When spouses refuse to reconcile or when the repudiating spouse declares that the repudiation has already taken place, notaries then proceed to register the divorce.

In 2000 the Egyptian parliament decided to introduce conciliation attempts for all kinds of divorce procedures, including repudiation, in an attempt to limit marriage dissolution "in order to preserve the family unit."[30] During the debates on the 2000 law before the parliament, the minister of justice justified this procedure as having its source in the Mālikī school. According to the explanatory memorandum of the 2000 law, this reform was intended to preserve married life and avoid divorce, which according to the hadith, is "among permitted [ḥalāl] things the most hated by Allah."

### *Egyptian Judges and Nonregistered Male-Initiated Divorce*

In 1985, the Egyptian parliament required all repudiations to be registered within thirty days. In 2000, the state went even further by stating that if the husband or the wife denied that repudiation had taken place, divorce could be proven only by certification (*ishhād*) and registration (*tawthīq*). That provision, however, was declared unconstitutional by the Supreme Constitutional Court in 2006.

### *Registration of the Repudiation in Law No. 100 of 1985 and Law No. 1 of 2000*

According to fiqh, a divorce does not need to be registered and the wife does not need to be informed of her repudiation. Registration should only be a means of proof, not of validity of the divorce. However, Law No. 100 of 1985 required verbal repudiations to be registered by the ma'dhūn within thirty days following the declaration.[31] Witnesses need to be present when the husband divorces his wife. They can be two men or one man and two women. The husband does not need to give the reasons for his decision and registration can take place in the absence and without the knowledge of his wife.[32]

According to this law, a copy of the repudiation certification (*ishhād al-ṭalāq*) must be sent to the wife in person by a bailiff (*'alā yad muḥḍir*) within seven days from the authentication of the repudiation.[33] Penal sanctions are provided in case of nonobservance of these procedures. Article 23 of Law No. 100 of 1985 stipulated a prison term of six months maximum and/or a fine not exceeding 200 Egyptian pounds (LE) to be imposed on the husband who refuses to respect such a procedure. As to the ma'dhūn, he risks a prison term of one month maximum and a fine not exceeding LE 50 if he infringes such provisions; he can also be dismissed or suspended of his duties for a maximum of one year.[34] The validity of the repudiation made in the absence of notification, however, is not affected.

The 1985 law stated that the consequences of the divorce take effect from the date of its occurrence. However, if the husband tried to conceal the repudiation from his wife, her inheritance and financial rights would not be affected until the moment she learned of it. As long as the husband did not inform his wife that she had been divorced, he would have to pay her maintenance. The wife was entitled to prove by any means, including witnesses, that she was not aware of the divorce and that her husband had intentionally tried to conceal it from her. However, she could not claim to be uninformed if she refused to receive or open the notification sent by the notary to her address.

This provision was adopted in order to prevent wives from continuing normal marital relationships with their husband without knowing that they had been repudiated. It was meant to "protect women, particularly among the popular classes, from their husband's frivolous abuse of the oath of ṭalāq" and was a guarantee "of women's rights, protecting her against continued intimacy with a man who has divorced her without her knowledge" (Fawzy 2004, 78). The explanatory memorandum of Law No. 100 of 1985 stressed that some husbands divorce their wives in their absence without telling them, which causes a prejudice since they become "suspended" (*ta'līq*) without any justification. According to the memorandum, some husbands even registered the divorce but kept the divorce paper with them and resumed marital life until a conflict broke out between them, whereupon they produced the paper and tried to deprive their wife of her rights. The introductory note underscores that some jurists from the Ḥanafī school had decided to postpone the beginning of the 'idda until the husband acknowledges repudiation in order to fight against hidden divorces.

The ma'dhūn could not refuse to register a repudiation even if it took place more than thirty days earlier, but its effects would only start from the date of registration unless the husband could prove it started earlier. The Court of Cassation ruled that according to the shari'a, the waiting period should start from the date of the repudiation even if the husband did not notify his wife.[35] According to the court and to the shari'a, therefore, the spouses were divorced after the pronouncement by the husband, though according to Law No. 100 of 1985, the financial and inheritance effects would only start from the day the wife was informed of the divorce (Fawzy 2004, 68). In a case where the repudiation was pronounced verbally but not registered and the husband denied it had taken place, wives could go to courts to have it recorded. It could be proven by any means, including testimony.

In 2000, Article 21, paragraph 1, of Law No. 1 stated that in case of denial (*'ind al-inkār*), only witnessed (*ishhād*) and registered (*tawthīq*) divorces could be proven. All legal effects of the repudiation were to start from the day of its pronouncement if the wife was present or from the date she received official notification if she was not present. According to the explanatory memorandum, the parliament decided to extend to male-initiated divorce the solution adopted for nonregistered marriages in 1931, according to which, in case of denial (*'ind al-inkār*), only registered marriages can be brought before the courts: both are religiously valid according to the shari'a but only registered divorces will have legal effects in the case where one spouse denies its occurrence (Mansour 2001, 275).[36]

The law made it extremely difficult for a wife to prove that she had been divorced verbally. If a husband repudiates his wife in public and then denies that he did and the wife goes to court to claim that she was divorced, the court will refuse to consider her divorced because the repudiation was not registered. On the basis of the shari'a, therefore, the wife will consider herself as divorced but according to Egyptian law she will still be married to her husband.

### *The Supreme Constitutional Court Rules Article 21 of Law No. 1 of 2000 Unconstitutional*

Article 21 was challenged before the Supreme Constitutional Court in 2004 by the Court of Personal Status of Shibin al-Kum. A wife had required the trial court to establish that she had been divorced irrevocably by her husband for the third time in May 2003. Her husband had recognized before witnesses that he had divorced her but refused to register his statement. After the wife left him to stay with her family, he sent her a notification of obedience (*indhār al-ṭā'a*) requiring her to come back and live with him. The trial court decided to stop the examination of the case and refer it to the Constitutional Court, stating that Article 21 violated the principle established in the shari'a according to which a divorce can be proven by all means of proof, including testimony, oath, or statement. The trial court argued that allowing proof only by registration entails a contradiction between prohibited marital relations according to the shari'a and the persistence of marital relations according to the law, which violates Articles 2 and 12 of the constitution.

The Supreme Constitutional Court decided to follow the trial court. It recalled the basic principle it had established for the first time in 1993 and systematically repeated in all its decisions regarding the conformity of laws with Article 2 of the constitution.[37] A distinction should be made between absolute and relative principles of the Islamic shari'a. Only the principles "whose origin and significance are absolute [*al-aḥkām al-shar'iyya al-qaṭ'iyya fi thubūtihā wa dalālatihā*]"—in other words, that represent uncontested Islamic norms because of their source or their meaning—must necessarily be applied. They are fixed, cannot be subject to interpretative reasoning (*ijtihād*), and cannot evolve with time. They represent the fundamental principles and fixed foundation (*thawābit*) of Islamic law. However, relative rules (*aḥkām ẓanniyya*), either because of their origin, their significance, or both, evolve in time and space, are dynamic, give rise to different interpretations, and are adaptable to the nature and the changing needs of society. It is up to the "person in authority" (*wali al-amr*), namely, the legislature, to carry out the task of interpreting and establishing the norms related to such rules, guided by their individual reasoning and in the interest of the shari'a.

The Supreme Constitutional Court asserted that the right to interpretive reasoning of relative principles is circumscribed; it should always respect the universal principles (*al-uṣūl al-kulliya*) of the shari'a and its stable prescriptions and protect its five fundamental objectives (*maqāṣid al-kulliya*): religion, life, reason, dignity, and property. The "person in authority" should always choose the easiest legal option and should not adopt rules that overburden people or their affairs with difficulty (*'usran*). Otherwise, the person in authority will violate the verse, "God does not impose on any soul a burden superior to its capacity" (Q. 2:286).

As far as repudiation is concerned, the court declared that it is an act of God's mercy for his servants and one of the means of breaking the marital relationship with a special expression, whether explicit or tacit. The court recalled the introductory memorandum to Law No. 100 of 1985 according to which a divorce shall be proven before the courts by all means of proof. It added that although Article 21 remained within the limits of the right of interpretation of the wali al-amr, it put a divorced wife in a stressful religious situation since she knew that she had been divorced but could not prove it because her husband refused to register his statement. The court argued that this was a violation of the rules of interpretive reasoning and of the fundamental objectives of the Islamic shari'a.

For the Constitutional Court, this was also a violation of the right of divorced women to personal freedom and even an infringement on their right to life, as guaranteed by Article 41 of the constitution. The right to marry and divorce is part of the right to personal freedom and cannot be exercised in isolation from the community's customs. In Article 9, the constitution declares that the state shall protect the Egyptian family and in Article 12 it declares that the society shall promote Egyptian traditions. Individual freedom is also guaranteed by the constitution in Article 41. The court concluded that the parliament shall not limit or violate these constitutional rights under the pretext of regulating them (*tandhīm*).

The Constitutional Court therefore declared Article 21 unconstitutional for having violated Articles 2 and 9 (protection of the family), Article 12 (protection of morality), and Article 41 (personal freedom) of the 1971 constitution. Article 21 thus was considered unconstitutional for having violated women's rights by depriving them of the right to have their divorce legalized and putting them in a distressing religious situation. This is paradoxical, since Article 21 had been adopted to protect women's rights against the abusive use of repudiation by their husband. To avoid having Article 21 ruled unconstitutional, the parliament could have adopted the solution provided by Article 22 of Law 1 of 2000 regarding the resumption of marital relations: allow wives to prove their divorce by all means of proof while restricting husbands' right to prove repudiation to registered statements only.

### *Courts and Registration of the Resumption of Marital Relations*

According to fiqh, the resumption of marital relations can take place following words or acts; registration of such a resumption is only required for evidentiary purposes and does not constitute a condition of validity. Until 2000 the resumption was not registered and the law did not even require that the wife be informed.[38] The husband could prove he had returned to his wife, in conformity with the Ḥanafī rules of evidence, by the testimony of two witnesses.

The Court of Cassation ruled that in case of a conflict between the wife and her husband on whether the resumption had taken place within the ʿidda period, the wife must be trusted when under oath since she is the only one to know the occurrence of her menstrual cycles.[39] The court added that the shortest length of ʿidda in the predominant opinion in the Ḥanafī school is sixty days.[40] In a case brought before the Court of Cassation, a husband who had divorced his wife claimed to have recalled her before the end of her ʿidda period while his wife replied that her ʿidda had already expired at that time and that the divorce had therefore become irrevocable. The Court of Cassation declared that since the husband had divorced his wife on June 16, 1994, and decided to recall her on September 4, 1994, his wife's statement under oath, according to which her ʿidda had expired on August 16, 1994, "was plausible [*taḥtamil dhālika*]."[41]

In a similar case, the court, after having recalled the same principles, declared implausible the statement by a wife under oath that her ʿidda had expired since the divorce took place on November 30, 1991, and her husband had decided to resume marital relations less than two weeks after that and had even lodged a request before the courts on December 17, 1991, stating that they were still married. The court decided that the resumption of the marital relations had taken place during the ʿidda of the wife since the shortest length of the ʿidda is sixty days.[42]

In another case, the Court of Cassation declared that Ḥanafī fiqh establishes that a revocable divorce does not change anything in the marital relations until the end of the ʿidda. The only effect is to decrease the number of repudiations the husband can use against his wife. The court confirmed that the husband can resume marital relations by words or acts as long as his wife is in her ʿidda period and that the resumption does not need the approval of the wife nor even her knowledge to be valid.[43]

The court also ruled that the wife's return to the marital home during her 'idda period without opposition from her husband is not sufficient to prove that the marital relations have resumed since a revocable divorce does not impact the marital relations as long as the wife is in her 'idda period. She has the right, therefore, to remain in the marital home.[44] In another case, the Court of Cassation declared that the resumption of marital relations could be proven by witness testimony since the relations can be resumed by words or acts.[45]

Since 2000, however, according to Law No. 1 of 2000 (Article 22), if the wife denies that her husband returned to her, the only possibility for her husband to prove that he did resume marital relations within the 'idda period is to prove that he informed her by an official letter before the expiration of sixty days—if his wife was not menopausal—or otherwise, within ninety days following the day of registering the repudiation. If the wife is pregnant, it is proof of the resumption of spousal relations and her recognition of the fact that she had not finished her 'idda period when she was informed that her husband wanted her back. This notification must be done through bailiff rather than by mail or through witnesses. If the two spouses agree that the marital relations have resumed, however, then the marriage will be considered as having resumed even if the husband did not formally notify his wife.

The introductory memorandum to Law No. 1 of 2000 justified this reform by the fact that devious husbands were taking back their wives without informing them and therefore wives only discovered that their marriage had resumed when they were trying to arrange a new marriage or, even worse, after they had married again and the first husband insisted they were still married. Since 2000, if the wife denies that the relations have resumed, the husband can only prove the resumption by producing a written notification as evidence. Article 22, however, gives the wife the right to prove by any means that spousal relations have resumed. The law, therefore, made it easier for wives, but more difficult for husbands, to prove the resumption of marital relations. This provision extended to the resumption of marital relations the solution already adopted regarding the divorce itself: its effects will only start from the date the wife is notified. If the 'idda has expired, the husband can only bring his wife back under his authority with a new contract and a new dower.[46]

## Egyptian Courts and Financial Compensation of the Repudiated Wife

The Supreme Constitutional Court decided in 1993 that the financial compensation for repudiated wives introduced by the Egyptian parliament in 1985 did not violate the constitution or the shari'a.

### *Mut'a in Law No. 100 of 1985*

Since 1985, a divorced wife has been entitled to financial compensation if the marriage was consummated and the divorce occurred against her will and without any cause on her part.[47] The amount of the compensation must not be less than two years of maintenance and is evaluated according to the husband's financial means, the circumstances of the divorce, and the length of the marriage. The judge decides whether the wife is entitled to such compensation and sets the amount.

Before 1985, the only financial consequences of the husband's right to unilateral divorce were the wife's entitlement to the deferred portion of the dower and to maintenance (*nafaqa*) during the waiting period. The Court of Cassation, however, allowed trial courts, on a case-by-case basis, to order husbands to give their wives a financial compensation: the court declared that such a compensation did not violate the principles of the shari'a or public order and could be given when the wife was not the one who initiated the divorce. This was left to the determination of the trial court according to the circumstances of each case.[48]

The explanatory note of Law No. 100 of 1985 stressed that it is well established in the shari'a that repudiation is a right of the husband and that the law that is currently in force does not make mut'a obligatory for a woman who was divorced after the consummation of the marriage. However, the note explains, human kindness (*murū'a*) has waned in these times, in particular between spouses, and divorced wives are in need of greater material support than merely maintenance during the waiting period. Mut'a provides additional material support, which might discourage husbands from carrying out a hasty divorce. The note stressed that this principle was based on several sources: Qur'an 2:236, "But give them [a gift of] compensation—the wealthy according to his capability and the poor according to his capability"; the Shāfi'ī school; an opinion of Aḥmad Ibn Ḥanbal as selected by Ibn Taymiyya; an opinion of the Zāhirī; and an opinion of Mālik.

In practice, trial courts examine the circumstances of the divorce to ensure that the conditions for entitlement to mut'a are present. In 2006, for instance, a women filed a claim before the Family Court of Badrashin against her husband, to whom she had been legally married for eighteen years, asking him to pay her mut'a because he had divorced her in absentia after she had filed for her *nafaqa zawjiyya* (marital maintenance). The court referred to Article 18 of Law No. 25 of 1929 as amended by Law No. 100 of 1985 and, quoting entire paragraphs from the explanatory memorandum of that law, recalled that the legal basis for mu'ta came from the Shāfi'ī school. The court then ensured that all the conditions for the wife to deserve mut'a were fulfilled: a valid and consummated marriage and a final divorce effected without the wife's agreement and not due to any cause on her part. The court considered the fact that the husband had divorced the wife without her presence as a presumption of her lack of agreement and put the burden of proof of her consent on the husband.[49] The fact that he divorced his wife after she had brought a case before the court to get her due maintenance was not considered a valid reason to claim that she was responsible for the divorce and for depriving her of her mut'a. In its decision, the Family Court referred to several rulings of the Court of Cassation[50] and to contemporary law books.[51]

### *The Supreme Constitutional Court Confirms the Constitutionality of Mut'a: May 15, 1993*

A repudiated wife claimed before the courts the right to receive compensation of an amount equivalent to ten years of maintenance. Her ex-husband refused to comply with her request and, arguing that this provision was not in conformity with Article 2 of the constitution, referred the case to the Supreme Constitutional Court, which decided on the case in 1993.

After recalling the distinction it had established between absolute and relative principles of the Islamic shari'a, the Supreme Constitutional Court denied the petitioner's claim and ruled that there was no violation of Article 2 of the constitution. The court held that if the origin of this compensation was to be sought in the Qur'an, the meaning itself of the verse had given rise to different interpretations among the jurists.[52] There was no consensus on the amount of the mut'a or whether it was mandatory for the husband to offer compensation. The court therefore considered that it was a relative rule in regard to its meaning and not an absolute principle. The wali al-amr could set the conditions for granting such a compensation, making sure, however, that they did not contradict an absolute principle of the shari'a.

The provision required two conditions for a wife to be able to benefit from the mut'a: that the marriage must be legally valid and that the divorce must not have been initiated by the wife (or that she was not responsible for the breakdown of the marriage). The court found that this article was in accordance with the principles of Islamic law because the mut'a aims to compensate the wife for the material and moral injury she suffered: "Mut'a legislation aims at comforting the repudiated woman, psychologically healing her from the sufferings of divorce. Comforting her is part of the human kindness demanded by the Islamic shari'a and which has obviously been neglected in practice, particularly between two spouses whose emotional ties have broken down."[53] It is different when the wife initiates the divorce or consents to it. In that case she does not have to be compensated for harm that she has not suffered. The conditions fixed by the parliament for granting mut'a, the court concluded, are therefore in accordance with the principles of shari'a.

As for the amount, the court found that there was no absolute principle either. Therefore, the parliament was free to regulate it by taking into account the interest of society. By fixing an amount representing at least two years of maintenance, to be assessed by the judge according to the financial situation of the husband, the circumstances of the divorce, and the duration of the marriage, the law had pursued realistic and moderate objectives. This provision had sought not to restrict the right to divorce but rather to ensure that the amount be as realistic as possible without being excessive. The court concluded that the decision to set a lower limit but not an upper one was within the discretion of the legislature and outside the constitutional review framework.

## Religious and State Law in Egypt

Male-initiated unilateral divorce outside the court is still legal in Egypt, but the state has subjected such divorce to several restrictions and the judiciary has implemented these reforms without contesting their legitimacy. Both the state and the judiciary claim they apply repudiation as stated in the shari'a, but in fact they apply the interpretation of the shari'a by the Egyptian legislature. Male-initiated divorce in contemporary Egyptian law is thus quite different from traditional Islamic fiqh as it was applied in Egypt before the codification of personal status law in the 1920s.

The state referred to the shari'a in its reforms but did adopt an interpretation that fit with the transformations in the Egyptian society. Thus, in its introductory note to Law No. 25 of 1929, the legislature stated: "The policy regarding Islamic law is to facilitate the practice of the law by interpreting it in a broad way and consulting the scholars ['ulama'] whenever it is necessary to find a cure for a social illness that has become difficult to cure, so that men feel that the law brings a solution to all difficulty and deliverance to any adversity." The law must therefore evolve according to the needs of society. This is also confirmed by the Constitutional Court, which considers that the relative principles of the shari'a should adapt to changing times. The reform of personal-status law in Egypt, however, has been limited in its scope and constrained by the political context, the survival of patriarchy, and the role played by conservative and religious opposition movements. It is not easy to amend these laws because of the resistance of society and conservative religious groups.

Egyptian supreme and trial courts have implemented these laws without objection even though they reformed considerable aspects of traditional male-initiated divorce. In their decisions, the courts refer to these laws and to decisions of the Court of Cassation. Trial courts do sometimes refer to fiqh or the shari'a, but only to legitimize the legislative reforms by emphasizing that they conform to shari'a or Ḥanafī fiqh. In such cases, they refer vaguely to "fiqh," to "the shari'a," or to law books written by colleagues or law professors, not to traditional fiqh books.[54] Having been trained in the law faculties of Egyptian universities on contemporary Egyptian law, as codified on the model of Western law since the late nineteenth century, most judges do not have a strong enough background in classical Islamic jurisprudence to delve into classical fiqh books for guidance. Furthermore, when the Supreme Constitutional Court opposed the 2000 reform of nonregistered male-initiated divorce, it based its reasoning on the defense of women's rights, not on tradition or a respect of men's prerogatives.

## Conclusion

The 2017 debates about a possible new reform of male-initiated divorce must be situated in the context of a conflict between the top political and top Islamic authorities in Egypt over the control of the religious sphere and attempts by the presidency to curtail the autonomy of the religious establishment.[55] President Sisi's proposal took place during a ceremony attended by Shaykh al-Azhar and was directed to him—"What do you think, honorable Imam?" (Al-Hayah TV Network 2017). This shows how law, religion, and politics are intrinsically linked when it comes to family law. The president was calling for the amendment of the family law, but he acknowledged implicitly that a religious institution, al-Azhar, needed to back that suggestion.

Nathan J. Brown and Mariam Ghanem argue that by relying on social considerations (the stability of the society) in his statement, "the president seemed implicitly to be suggesting that the shaykh and his institution were undermining Egyptian family life with their old-fashioned approach to divorce" (2017). He also positioned himself as the defender of women's rights. Al-Azhar replied by relying on religious but also on social grounds, holding the state responsible for countering divorce and underlining the fact that "the correct treatment for this phenomenon is through the care of young people and their protection from all kinds of drugs, and in educating them through different media, art, culture and general knowledge."[56] No matter how high the authority of the president, it should never override that of the Prophet, Al-Azhar maintained. Apart from prescribing solutions revolving around improving education, countering drug abuse, and providing good guidance through the media, Al-Azhar's Council of Senior Scholars also called on husbands to document a divorce as soon as it is pronounced in order to preserve the rights of the wife and the children. The council also added that "rising divorce rates will not be countered by ending verbal divorce, especially as the cases included in the divorce statistics are already documented" (Shams El Din 2017). If the cases included in the statistics are indeed documented, there may be many other cases of verbal divorces that are not documented.

This confrontation with al-Azhar on such a sensitive issue gave the president an appearance of modernity in contrast to the perceived conservatism of the religious body. Although the debate evolved around women's rights, women were not part of the debate. As Sahar Mandour underlines, "The only role of women in these debates is as objects of sympathy or fear, and always within the context of the nuclear family and the ramifications of verbal divorce on the state. No research was conducted on the effects of divorce on women's lives, which would have necessitated consulting with civil society organizations and would have imposed a different hierarchy of demands than those stated by the authorities" (2017). It is obvious that women's rights were not the main concern of the religious and political bodies when addressing restrictions on male-initiated unilateral divorce.

## NOTES

1. The ma'dhūn is a state employee who administers marriages and male-initiated divorces for Muslims.
2. According to this report, the divorce rate increased by 50 percent from 1996 to 2008 in both urban and rural areas.

3. Divorce by khulʿ is a unilateral means of breaking up a marriage that allows women to dissolve their union in exchange for material compensation. For a study of this kind of marriage dissolution, see Sonneveld 2012, 2019.
4. The Council of Senior Scholars, formed in 2011, is al-Azhar's highest religious authority. It is made of twenty-two clerics who are in charge of issuing fatwas. Since 2012, they have elected the grand Shaykh of al-Azhar.
5. Art. 5a of Law No. 25 of 1929, added by Law No. 100 of 1985.
6. Art. 1 and Art. 2 of Law No. 25 of 1929.
7. Art. 3 of Law No. 25 of 1929.
8. The Supreme Constitutional Court reviews the conformity of laws and regulations to the constitution.
9. Art. 2 of the 1971 (as amended in 1980) and 2014 Egyptian Constitutions: "Islam is the religion of the state, Arabic its official language. The principles of the Islamic shariʿa are the main source of legislation."
10. The Court of Cassation is the highest court in the judiciary. It decides whether the rules of law have been correctly applied by the lower courts. Its main purpose is to harmonize case law and ensure that texts are interpreted in the same way throughout the country.
11. In 2004, Law No. 10 establishing family courts was adopted. The law stated that rulings in family law issues would no longer challengeable before the Court of Cassation. Since 2004, only the public prosecution is allowed to challenge a ruling before that court, on certain conditions. All the decisions of the Court of Cassation analyzed in this chapter, therefore, were adopted before 2004.
12. Family courts were established to bring relief to an overburdened judicial system and speed up the legal process. All family-related disputes (alimony, custody, divorce, etc.) are now heard by one court, potentially reducing delays, instead of being examined by different courts in different places.
13. According to Art. 280 of Decree-Law No. 78 of 1931 concerning the organization of shariʿa courts, if no law was applicable to the case, the judge had to follow the most authoritative opinion in the Ḥanafī school. This means that noncodified shariʿa applied only to matters where the law was silent. If a legal provision existed, the judge had to apply it even if they personally disagreed with its content. That provision was abrogated by Art. 4 of Law No. 1 of 2000 concerning some rules and procedures of litigation in matters of personal status and replaced by Art. 3 of the law promulgating that law.
14. Qadri Pasha, Egypt's minister of justice, codified the rules of the Ḥanafī school relative to personal status affairs in 1875. The code was never promulgated and did not acquire binding legal status but it remains a fundamental reference for judges adjudicating in the field of personal status.
15. Qadri Pasha Code, Art. 217.
16. Qadri Pasha Code, Art. 218.
17. Law No. 25 of 1929, Art. 2. A conditional repudiation is submitted to a condition or circumstance or postponed to a future time.
18. Law No. 25 of 1929, Art. 1.
19. See for instance Court of Cassation, No, 31/50, December 8, 1981.
20. Court of Cassation, No. 28/48, February 13, 1980.
21. Court of Cassation, No. 468/65, November 24, 2001.
22. Court of Cassation, No. 468/65, November 24, 2001.

23. Art. 11 of Inheritance Law 77 of 1947.
24. Art. 5 of Law No. 25 of 1929 and Qadri Pasha Code, Arts. 226–250.
25. Law No. 25 of 1929, Art. 3.
26. Law No. 25 of 1929, Art. 3.
27. Qadri Pasha Code, Art. 224.
28. See, for instance, Court of Cassation, No. 34/28, June 23, 1960.
29. Court of Cassation, No. 34/28, June 23, 1960. See also Court of Cassation No. 667/67, December 22, 2001. Those were also the words of the Introductory Memorandum to Law No. 25 of 1929.
30. Introductory memorandum to Law No. 1 of 2000.
31. Law No. 25 of 1929, Art. 5a, as added by Law No. 100 of 1985.
32. The Court of Cassation confirmed that a repudiation is valid even if the wife is not present when it is pronounced. The court argued the shari'a establishes it as the right of the husband, which he can use independently and without the wife's approval (Court of Cassation, No. 30/44 28 April 1976).
33. Art. 2 of the Decree of the Minister of Justice No. 3269 of 1985.
34. Law No. 100 of 1985, Art. 23a, para. 3.
35. Court of Cassation, No. 182/63, 24 June 1997.
36. For the debates before al-Azhar Islamic Research Academy on the adoption of Art. 20, see (Mansour 2001, 275).
37. Supreme Constitutional Court, May 15, 1993, No. 7/8e.
38. Qadri Pasha Code, Art. 231.
39. Court of Cassation, No. 18/38, May 31, 1971.
40. Court of Cassation, No. 182/65, June 9, 2001, and Court of Cassation, No. 530/66, May 28, 2001.
41. Court of Cassation, No. 182/65, June 9, 2001.
42. Court of Cassation, No. 326/63, March 20, 1998.
43. Court of Cassation, No. 30/46, March 1, 1978.
44. Court of Cassation, No. 17/43, November 5, 1975.
45. Court of Cassation, No. 34/28, June 23, 1965.
46. Court of Cassation, No. 18/38, May 31, 1972.
47. Art. 17 and 18 of Law 25/1929 and Art. 18a (1), added to Law 25/1929 by Law 1/1985.
48. Court of Cassation, No. 67/9, February 29, 1940.
49. See for instance Family Court of Badrashin, No. 121/2007, January 30, 2008.
50. To prove, for instance, that the trial court has a discretionary power to assess the facts of the case.
51. One was a book by Judge Mohammed Azmi al-Bakri, *Mawsu'āt fī al-fiqh wa al-qada fī al-awhāl al-shakhsiyya* (Encyclopedia of Fiqh and jurisprudence in personal status), 6th edition, 1997, regarding the conditions that the mut'a shall fulfill; another book by Judge Ashraf Mustafa Kamel, *Qawānīn al-Aḥwāl al-Shakhṣiyya* (Personal-status laws), Judges Club, 3rd edition (no date), was used to justify the fact that the divorce in absentia entails a presumption of lack of agreement of the wife.
52. Qur'an 2:241.
53. Supreme Constitutional Court, May 15, 1993, No. 7/8.
54. For similar findings, see Lindbekk 2016, 114.

55. For the dispute between the president and al-Azhar see Brown and Bardos Cassia 2018.

56. Al-Azhar 2017.

## REFERENCES


Abu-Oudeh, Lama. 2004a. "Egyptian Feminism: Trapped in the Identity Debate." *Yale Journal of Law and Feminism* 16 (2):145–191.

———. 2004b. "Modernizing Muslim Family Law: The Case of Egypt." *Vanderbilt Journal of Transnational Law* 37:1043–1146.

al-Azhar Council of High Scholars. 2017. Statement. February 5. Http://www.azhar.eg/ArticleDetails/ArtMID/6131/ArticleID/11377.

Al-Hayah TV Network. 2017. "Ceremony Marking Police Day." January 24 at 22:30. Https://www.youtube.com/watch?v=MN3O8nTK5oc.

Anderson, J. N. D. 1951. "Recent Developments in Sharia Law (V): The Dissolution of Marriage." *Muslim World* 41 (4):271–288.

Bernard-Maugiron, Nathalie. 2016. "Egyptian Family Law Reform: Between Law in the Books and Law in Action." In *Changing God's Law: The Dynamics of Middle Eastern Family Law*, edited by Nadjma Nassari, 181–203. Farnham: Ashgate Publishing.

Bernard-Maugiron, Nathalie, and Baudouin Dupret. 2002. "From Jihan to Suzanne: Twenty Years of Personal Status in Egypt." *Recht van de Islam* 19:1–19.

Brown, Nathan J., and Bardos Cassia. 2018. "Power Politics or Principle?" *Carnegie Middle East Center.* December 12. Https://carnegie-mec.org/diwan/77928.

Brown, Nathan J., and Mariam Ghanem. 2017. "Divorce, Egyptian Style." *Carnegie Middle East Center.* February 15. Https://carnegie-mec.org/diwan/68001.

CAPMAS (Central Agency for Public Mobilization and Statistics). 2016. Press Release. July 4, Http://www.capmas.gov.eg/Pages/ShowHmeNewsPDF.aspx?page_id=/Admin/News/PressRelease/201674105616_889.pdf&Type=News.

Dār al-Iftā'. 2017. Press Release. February 2. Http://www.dar-alifta.gov.eg/ar/Viewstatement.aspx?sec=media&ID=4772.

Diaa, Rahma. 2016. "Divorces up by 10.8 percent in 2015—Official Statistics Agency." *Aswat Masriya*, July 5, http://en.aswatmasriya.com/news/details/17277. According to this report, divorce rate increased by 50 percent from 1996 to 2008 in both urban and rural areas.

El Alami, Dawood S. 1994. "Law No. 100 of 1985 Amending Certain Provisions of Egypt's Personal Status Law." *Islamic Law and Society* 1 (1):116–130.

El Shalakani, Sarah. 2017. "Sisi's Call to Annul Verbal Divorce Sparks Controversy." El-Monitor, February 20, https://www.al-monitor.com/originals/2017/02/egypt-sisi-call-law-annul-verbal-divorce.html#ixzz7L5IXEjKp https://www.al-monitor.com/originals/2017/02/egypt-sisi-call-law-annul-verbal-divorce.html.

Fawzy, Essam. 2004. "Muslim Personal Status Law in Egypt: The Current Situation and Possibilities of Reform through Internal Initiatives." In *Women's Rights and Islamic Family Law: Perspective on Reform*, edited by Lynn Welchman, 17–94. London: Zed Books.

Hefner, Robert. 2005. "Rewriting Divorce in Egypt: Reclaiming Islam, Legal Activism and Coalition Politics." In *Remaking Muslim Politics: Pluralism, Contestation, Democratization*, edited by Robert Hefner. Princeton, NJ: Princeton University Press.

Linant de Bellefonds, Y. 1955. "Immutabilité du droit musulman et réformes législatives en Egypte." *Revue internationale de droit comparé* 1 (7):5–30.

———. 1962. "La répudiation dans l'islam d'aujourd'hui." *Revue internationale de droit comparé* 14 (3):521–548.

Lindbekk, Monika. 2016. "Inscribing Islamic Shari'a in Egyptian Divorce." *Oslo Law Review* 3 (2):103–135.

Mandour, Sahar. 2017. "Verbal Divorce: A Man-to-Man Fight in the 'Year of Women,'" *Madā Maṣr*, March 14. Https://madamasr.com/en/2017/03/14/opinion/u/verbal-divorce-a-man-to-man-fight-in-the-year-of-women/.

Mansour, Hosni Hassan. 2001. *al-Muḥīṭ fī Sharḥ Masā'il al-aḥwāl al-Shakhṣiyya*. Cairo: Maṭba'a Sāmī.

McKernan, Bethan. 2017. "Egypt's Top Religious Authority Rejects Reform to Law Allowing Men to Verbally Divorce Their Wives as Unconstitutional." *Independent*, February 20. Https://www.independent.co.uk/news/world/middle-east/egypt-religious-council-law-reform-verbal-divorce-men-wives-gender-equality-abdel-fattah-al-sisi-a7565306.html.

Qāsim, Muhammad. 2017. "Muftī al-jumhūriyya: qanūn al-khul' ahad asbāb ziyāda nisbat al-talāḳ fī misr." February 20, https://www.masrawy.com/News/News_Egypt/details/2017/2/2/1022934.

Rashwān, Hodā. 2017. "al-Qawmi li-l-Mar'a: Da'wā al-Ra'īs li-Tanzīm al-Talāq Intiṣār Jadīd li-l-Mar'a," *al-Waṭan*, January 25. Https://www.elwatannews.com/news/details/1815791.

Schacht, Joseph. 1913–1936. "Ṭalāḳ." In *Encyclopaedia of Islam*, edited by M. Th. Houtsma, T. W. Arnold, R. Basset, and R. Hartmann. Http://dx.doi.org/10.1163/2214-871X_ei1_SIM_5639.

Shams El Din, Mai. 2017. "Tensions Arise between Al-Azhar and Presidency over Verbal Divorce Debate." Mada Masr, February 7, Https://www.madamasr.com/en/2017/02/07/feature/politics/tensions-arise-between-al-azhar-and-presidency-over-verbal-divorce-debate/.

Singerman, Diane. 2005. "Rewriting Divorce in Egypt: Reclaiming Islam, Legal Activism and Coalition Politics." In *Remaking Muslim Politics: Pluralism, Contestation Democratization*, edited by Robert Hefner, 161–188. Princeton: Princeton University Press.

Sonneveld, Nadia. 2012. *Khul' Divorce in Egypt: Public Debates, Judicial Practices, and Everyday Life Cairo*. New York: American University in Cairo Press.

———. 2019. "Divorce Reform in Egypt and Morocco: Men and Women Navigating Rights and Duties." *Islamic Law and Society* 26 (1–2):149–178.

Sonneveld, Nadia, and Monika Lindbekk. 2015. "A Revolution in Muslim Family Law? Egypt's Pre and Post-Revolutionary Period (2011–2013) Compared." *New Middle Eastern Studies* 5:1–19. Http://www.brismes.ac.uk/nmes/archives/1409.

Zulficar, Mona. 2008. "The Islamic Marriage Contract in Egypt." In *The Islamic Marriage Contract: Case Studies in Islamic Family Law*, edited by A. Quraishi and F. E. Vogel, 231–274. Harvard Series in Islamic Law no. 6. Cambridge, MA: Harvard University Press.

# 3

# Problems of and Possibilities for Islamic Divorce in South Africa

FATIMA ESSOP

Muslims have been part of the political and socioeconomic fabric of South Africa for over 350 years (Allie 2010). They have always practiced Muslim personal laws of marriage, divorce, and inheritance in the private sphere, facilitated by Muslim clergy and Muslim judicial bodies and with limited or no state recognition (Moosa 2011; Allie 2010; Moosa and Dangor 2019; Amien 2019). Muslim marriages that are concluded only through a *nikāḥ* (Muslim marriage ceremony) have not been recognized or regulated under any form of legislation, unlike South African civil marriages, which are registered and recognized by the state.[1] The absence of state regulation has been detrimental to parties married by Muslim rites only, and especially for Muslim women, who have often found themselves without rights and protection following the dissolution of their marriage (Gabru 2004; Amien 2010; Moosa 2011; Hoel 2012).

The advent of South Africa's constitutional democracy in 1994 brought the expectation that Muslim marriages would finally be recognized, given that section 15(1) of the Constitution of the Republic of South Africa, 1996 (hereafter referred to as "the Constitution) expressly provides that "everyone has the right to freedom of conscience, religion, thought, belief and opinion" and section 15(3)(a) further stipulates that "this section does not prevent legislation recognizing marriages concluded under any tradition, or a system of religious, personal or family law; or systems of personal and family law under any tradition, or adhered to by persons professing a particular religion." However, such recognition has not transpired as to date no legislation has been enacted to recognize and regulate Muslim marriages or the different forms of Muslim divorce (Amien and Leatt 2014).[2] At present, three pieces of legislation govern valid marriages, namely, the Marriage Act,[3] which regulates heterosexual monogamous marriages; the Civil Union Act,[4] which regulates same-sex or heterosexual partnerships; and the Recognition of Customary Marriages Act,[5] which regulates monogamous and polygamous African customary marriages. There is no legislation that recognizes and regulates religious marriages. As an Islamic marriage concluded by nikāḥ is not recognized as a valid legal marriage in South Africa, the concomitant divorce processes are also not regulated by the state.[6] The South African judiciary has stepped in to offer piecemeal relief to Muslim women in regard to divorce, but the remedies are largely unknown or not understood within the Muslim community, and they have little impact on the lived reality of Muslim women (Rautenbach 2019; Essop 2018).[7] At present, a Muslim woman who wishes to dissolve her religious marriage must persuade her husband to *ṭalāq* (unilaterally divorce) her or apply for a *faskh* (annulment) to a Muslim judicial body. This chapter illustrates the challenges encountered by women in their interactions with Muslim judicial bodies when applying for a divorce.

The findings in this chapter are based on ethnographic research undertaken at the Muslim Judicial Council (MJC), a Muslim judicial body situated in the Western Cape, one of the nine provinces in South Africa. The MJC is one of three Muslim judicial bodies in the Western Cape that runs its own Shari'a Court, which facilitates faskh applications. The other two Muslim judicial bodies that run Shari'a Courts are the Muslim Assembly and Shura Al-Islam. Given the scant research on the functioning of Shari'a Courts within Muslim judicial bodies in South Africa,[8] this chapter seeks to shed light on the divorce services offered by one such body, namely, the MJC, through observing their divorce proceedings, the remedies granted by their Shari'a Court, and the challenges experienced by women when applying for a divorce. My findings illustrate that there are numerous procedural and substantive shortcomings in the MJC's administration of divorce proceedings. Because of these shortcomings, Muslim women suffer numerous injustices when trying to exit their Islamic marriages. I therefore argue that the state should enact legislation that would regulate and standardize Islamic divorce proceedings. If such legislation is not enacted, I argue that the MJC and similar Muslim judicial bodies have the responsibility to ensure that divorce processes in their Shari'a Courts are standardized and conducted in a just manner.

The chapter first describes the sample community and the methodology employed in the ethnographic research. Then it provides an overview of the divorce services offered by the MJC, including a discussion of the problems encountered in the pre-divorce proceedings and Shari'a Court proceedings itself. Finally, the chapter discusses the limitations of the remedies offered by the Shari'a Court and concludes with recommendations for the improvement of Muslim divorce proceedings.

## The Community

The first Muslims were brought to Cape Town[9] from five main regions of the world, namely, the Indonesian archipelago, Bengal in the South Indian Coast, Ceylon (Sri Lanka), Madagascar, and the East African Coast (Davids 2011). They arrived in the seventeenth century as enslaved people and political prisoners. Islam spread rapidly at the Cape in the eighteenth and nineteenth centuries and was firmly established in the twentieth century with the introduction of numerous *masājid* (mosques), *madāris* (Muslim religious schools), and nongovernmental social welfare organizations (Dangor 2003). As of 2013, Muslims compromised 2 percent of the total South African population, with the most Muslims concentrated in the Western Cape, followed by KwaZulu Natal and Gauteng (Schoeman, 2017). This chapter focuses on the Cape Muslim community, which is situated in the Western Cape and is the oldest Muslim community in South Africa (Moosa 2011).

The Muslim community in the Western Cape is, however, not necessarily reflective of Muslim communities in other parts of South Africa, as Muslims in South Africa do not constitute a single homogeneous community. Muslims in the Western Cape are generally considered to be more liberal and to have a more moderate view of gender relationships than in other parts of South Africa (Moosa 2011). The experience of Muslim women navigating Muslim divorces in other provinces, which espouse more conservative views on gender equality, might therefore be very different from the experience of Muslim women in the Western Cape. Muslims in South Africa generally adhere to two of the four Sunni-based schools of law, the Ḥanafī and the Shāfiʿī, and the MJC predominantly applies the Shāfiʿī (Moosa 2011; Abduroaf, 2019).[10] Where circumstances justify, judges at the MJC may resort to the other schools of thought when arriving at a *ḥukm* (legal ruling) in a particular case.

Muslim judicial bodies in South Africa are responsible for administering the religious and spiritual affairs of the community, including matters of personal law (Moosa 2011). Throughout South Africa there are numerous Muslim judicial bodies, which are essentially constituted as nongovernmental organizations. These bodies oversee Muslim marriage, divorce, and inheritance matters but have no official legal recognition in South Africa. Accordingly, they have no state-sanctioned enforcement powers and rely solely on religious and moral injunctions when issuing their rulings. They operate and coexist alongside the official legal system. Muslims adhere to the normative authority of these nonstate bodies because they feel socially and morally obliged to do so. The MJC, the judicial body that is the subject of this study, was established in 1945. It is a nonprofit organization that provides "religious guidance, education, *Fatawa*, *Da'wah*, *Halaal* certification and Social Development (especially marriage counselling)" to the community. The MJC describes itself as "the most representative and influential Muslim religious organization in the Western Cape, [which is] recognized locally, nationally and internationally for the religious, cultural and organizational roles it plays in South Africa" (MJC 2019). Many Muslims consider it the leading Muslim judicial body in the Western Cape, and therefore it plays an influential role in the Muslim community. It is for this reason that I chose the MJC and its Shariʿa Court for my research.

## Methodology

I adopted a socio-legal methodology in my research with the aim of understanding the impact of decision making by semi-autonomous bodies, like the MJC, who operate normative systems that are alternative to the official legal system. I draw on Sally Falk Moore's concept of the semi-autonomous social field: "The semi-autonomous social field has rule-making capacities and the means to induce or coerce compliance; but it is simultaneously set in a larger matrix which can and does, affect and invade it" (Moore 1973, 720). I undertook ethnographic research at the MJC, which entailed participant observation and qualitative interviews. I observed forty-five faskh hearings in the MJC's Shari'a Court and three ṭalāq facilitations in the MJC's offices over a period of three months from August to November 2019. I also conducted interviews with the imams (Muslim clergy) who preside as judges in the Shari'a Court at the MJC and with one male and one female counselor from the Social Development Department (SDD) at the MJC. Finally, I conducted qualitative interviews with three women who applied for a faskh at the MJC.[11] These women were either not granted a faskh or their faskh was granted after a protracted period.

I also conducted in-depth qualitative interviews at the other two Muslim judicial bodies in the Western Cape that run their own Shari'a Courts: the Muslim Assembly and Shura Al-Islam. Owing to time constraints, I was unable to observe faskh hearings at the Shari'a Courts of these two Muslim judicial bodies but I interviewed a counselor at the Muslim Assembly and an administrator at Shura Al-Islam. Based on these interviews I was able to compare the procedures and approaches adopted by the Shari'a Court at these bodies with those of the MJC.

## Muslim Divorce Services Offered by the MJC

The MJC offers various services to the community, including providing marriage counseling, facilitating ṭalāq pronouncements, and hearing faskh applications. The Shari'a Court is the body that hears faskh applications. Despite the fact that the MJC Shari'a Court fulfills the function of a conventional state court when adjudicating matters pertaining to divorce, it receives no state funding.[12] Muslim judicial bodies like the MJC have the mammoth task of administering and adjudicating Islamic divorces with limited resources at their disposal and no assistance from the state.

### *Counseling*

On any given day the reception lobby of the MJC is filled with men and women waiting to be assisted. They are waiting for either their faskh hearing, their ṭalāq facilitation, or a marriage counseling session. Marriage counseling is offered by the SDD at a nominal fee of R50 for a forty-five-minute session, and for the period March 2018 to February 2019, over 2,451 counseling sessions were conducted.[13] The SDD has four permanent counselors and four volunteer counselors; the latter are counselors or social workers by profession who offered their services on a voluntary basis at the MJC for a few days a week. The four permanent counselors consist of two men and two women; the men are imams with qualifications in Islamic law. One of the men had limited experience as a counselor, while the other had over thirty years of counseling experience. The women counselors had over twenty-five years' combined experience in marriage and trauma counseling.

One counselor, Ayesha, whom I interviewed at the MJC offices, cited extramarital affairs as one of the main reasons for the breakdown in marriage relationships and mentioned that the inappropriate use of cell phones and social media has been a contributing factor to the increase in extramarital affairs. Substance abuse by husbands was another recurring ground, which inevitably resulted in a myriad of problems, such as abusive behavior by the husband or his unemployment. Abuse, whether physical, verbal, or emotional, was another common ground for women seeking to exit their marriages, as was a husband's refusal to maintain (*nafaqa*) his wife and children. As a policy, counselors first encourage couples to reconcile, based on the MJC's understanding that while divorce is *ḥalāl* (permissible), it is nevertheless *makrūh* (morally reprehensible). Research has shown that the MJC's practice of encouraging reconciliation at all costs can be detrimental to women (Hoel 2012). Only if reconciliation proves impossible is the matter to be referred to ṭalāq facilitation or Shariʿa Court for a faskh hearing.

### Ṭalāq *Facilitation*

It is commonly understood within the South African Muslim community that a husband may unilaterally pronounce a ṭalāq against his wife without having to comply with any formalities. Although the MJC strongly discourages the triple ṭalāq, it still occurs within the community, usually when the husband is in a state of anger or out of ignorance of the consequences of such a divorce pronouncement. According to Faizel, one of the counselors I interviewed at the MJC, "It [the triple ṭalāq] still occurs frequently," and he cited a recent case where the husband pronounced a triple ṭalāq against his wife "because she goes into the bathroom without shoes." Ayesha, the female counselor, confirmed that pronouncement of a triple ṭalāq still occurred within the community. Faizel furthermore indicated that pronouncing a ṭalāq via email or WhatsApp was on the increase and resulted in much uncertainty and trauma on the part of the wife. In order to ameliorate the difficulties women experience as a result of the unilateral ṭalāq, the MJC encourages both parties, especially husbands, to undergo counseling. If the husband still wishes to pursue a ṭalāq, then the SDD counselors or the imam in the Ṭalāq Court will facilitate the ṭalāq process. Calling this court the Ṭalāq Court is somewhat of a misnomer as the couples simply appear before the imam in his office and he then facilitates their ṭalāq. This entails the imam advising the husband through the process of pronouncing the verbal ṭalāq, reminding him of his responsibilities to support his wife during her ʻidda (waiting period), explaining to the wife what is permissible during her ʻidda, and issuing a ṭalāq certificate.[14]

The parties are also advised that the ṭalāq is revocable and only becomes irrevocable if the parties do not reconcile during the wife's ʻidda. It was interesting to note that the imam facilitating the ṭalāq in the Ṭalāq Court advised the parties that according to the Shāfiʿī school of law, the husband must clearly express his intention to reconcile with his wife for a reconciliation to take effect. He explained that unlike in the Ḥanafī school, it did not suffice for the parties to simply resume sexual relations. The imam adopted a highly conservative Shāfiʿī interpretation of reconciliation, emphasizing that reconciliation was the husband's prerogative and that the wife's consent was not necessary to resume the marriage.

### Faskh *Hearings*

In addition to counseling and facilitating ṭalāq, the MJC also hears faskh applications in its Shariʿa Court. Countless women from different socioeconomic backgrounds approach the MJC for a faskh, usually after they have undergone counseling at the MJC offices or elsewhere. Women seek a faskh when the husband has deserted them or refused to grant a ṭalāq. The Shariʿa Court hears faskh applications every Thursday. The court is held in a boardroom at the MJC offices with two imams presiding. The more senior of the imams acts as the presiding judge (*qadi*), who makes the final decision on whether to grant the faskh, while the second imam fulfills multiple roles as an assessor, scribe, and clerk of the court (I refer to him as the "the clerk"). I interviewed the clerk, who was present at all the faskh hearings. The presiding judges would rotate every week, with a different imam acting as judge each Thursday.

Although there are three Muslim judicial bodies in the Western Cape with Shariʿa Courts that hear faskh applications (MJC, the Muslim Assembly, and Shura Al-Islam), the number of faskh applications heard by the MJC far outnumber those processed by the other two bodies. All three bodies respect the jurisdiction of the others and do not take on a case being processed by another. Although this prevents "forum shopping," it also means that women who are unhappy working within a particular judicial body are locked in, with no recourse to move to another forum. This proved to be an obstacle for women who were not happy with the service they received at the MJC.

## Challenges to Pre-Divorce Procedures

Once parties file for divorce at the MJC, they must undergo three compulsory counseling sessions before the case is referred to the Ṭalāq Court or Shariʿa Court. However, husbands frequently refuse to attend the counseling sessions, resulting in protracted proceedings and a delay in the dissolution of a marriage. Recalcitrant husbands are often not pursued by the MJC due to poor administration or lack of capacity on the part of the administrators. One of the female participants, referred to here as Azraa, related her difficulties in this regard.

In July 2018, Azraa left her husband, Irfaan, and the marital home as the result of emotional abuse. In September 2018 she approached the MJC for a faskh. She was advised that it would be easier if Irfaan gave her a ṭalāq; however, both first had to undergo individual counseling. Irfaan attended the first counseling session and initially agreed to grant Azraa a ṭalāq, but he subsequently refused to do so and failed to return to the MJC offices or respond to any further requests to resolve the matter. Over the next year, Azraa made repeated calls and personal visits to the MJC offices to enquire about a ṭalāq or, alternatively, a date for a faskh hearing, but she received no clear response. She expressed immense frustration with the lack of follow-up on the part of the MJC and the inefficient way in which her matter was handled, stating, "I was very frustrated because for me, sorry to put it bluntly, it was a whole *koeksister* process.[15] Candy-coated in coconut. I don't know how more to explain it because I kept on saying to the Mawlana[16] it is not an Islamic issue anymore. This is an admin issue with the MJC because nobody follows up."

Unfortunately, Azraa's experience is the norm and results from the MJC's lack of enforcement powers and inability to ensure that a husband appears before it. There are no punitive consequences for a recalcitrant husband who refuses to appear before the MJC or who refuses to release his wife from a marriage that has irretrievably broken down. The MJC could have dealt with the matter in a more efficient, professional manner by keeping the wife informed of all developments and, after a reasonable period, referring the matter to the Shari'a Court for a faskh hearing. Moreover, Azraa had to wait for more than a year before her faskh application was heard in the Shari'a Court, and even then she faced challenges, which I discuss later in this chapter.

## The Limited Forms of Divorce Available to Women: *Khul*ʿ as an Option

The two main forms of divorce available to women through the MJC are the ṭalāq facilitation process and faskh hearings. Khulʿ is very seldom utilized at the MJC. In other countries, as other chapters in this volume explain, khulʿ is a non-fault-based divorce that allows the wife to divorce her husband in exchange for forfeiting her *mahr* (dower or marriage gift) or giving him other financial compensation (*mut'a*).

There are conflicting views on whether the husband must grant his consent to khulʿ, with the majority of classical jurists stipulating that the consent of the husband is necessary (Al-Sharmani 2017; Sonneveld and Stiles 2019). Nonetheless, khulʿ, as a form of divorce, would be a viable alternative for Muslim women in South Africa because it gives them a quick and efficient way out of a marriage as opposed to the stringent criteria required when applying for a faskh.

However, women are generally ignorant about khulʿ and it is not promoted by the MJC. During my fieldwork, I observed khulʿ only being granted once, and that was most likely a result of my presence. Between two faskh hearings I questioned the judge on why women were not encouraged to use khulʿ to exit the marriage if they were unable to prove grounds for a faskh. The judge responded, "Khulʿ is not really part of our custom in the Cape." However, in the very next case he suggested a khulʿ to the parties, even though there were sufficient grounds for a faskh as the husband had not maintained his wife for several years. The judge stated that the husband had to consent to the khulʿ and in return the wife would pay him a certain amount. As the parties were unfamiliar with khulʿ as a form of divorce, the judge first explained the process to them and then suggested to the wife that she pay her husband R50 for the khulʿ, to which she tellingly responded, "I have paid for everything so far in this marriage, I might as well pay to get out of it." The husband was uncertain about how the khulʿ operated and delegated his right to the judge, who pronounced the ṭalāq against the wife in exchange for the R50 paid to the husband.

This particular khulʿ was unusual, as by all accounts khulʿ is rarely utilized as a form of divorce at the MJC or in the broader community. However, I argue that the MJC and other Muslim judicial bodies should seriously consider advocating for the use of khulʿ within the Muslim community because it alleviates the burden of proof on women trying to exit a marriage and could possibly balance out the husband's right to a unilateral ṭalāq.

## The Shortcomings of the Shariʿa Court Hearings

The Shariʿa Court fulfills an essential function in the community. It assists women in ending their marriages when the husband is at fault but refuses to release the wife by pronouncing a ṭalāq. Although the MJC tries its best to run an efficient court system, I observed various shortcomings.

### *The Male-Dominated Court*

Two male imams preside over the Shariʿa Court every Thursday, with the more senior of the imams acting as the presiding judge, who makes the final decision on faskh applications. The second imam fulfills multiple roles. The presiding judges rotate every week, with a different imam acting as judge each Thursday while the same clerk is present every week, as his responsibilities are to ensure the smooth running of the court by, inter alia, ensuring that the files are in order on the morning of the hearing.

Some women were not intimidated by the all-male court setting but others appeared to feel overwhelmed and anxious. One participant explained, "You have to share your problems with them; I mean other women maybe have worse problems where they were abused, maybe sexually or physically by their husbands. How do you tell all of this to a man?" It is not surprising that female lay participants would find the court setting intimidating. Husbands who attended the hearings shook hands with the judges as a form of greeting, immediately excluding the wife, who, for reasons of piety, could not greet the judges in a similar fashion. The judges seemed oblivious to the partisan impression that this innocuous act potentially created.

The clerk of the court defended the lack of gender representation as follows: "No, I mean gender is not an issue in determining the verdict. . . . The qadi is not worried whether you [are] a male or a female. . . . That's not the issue here. The qadi has to be—the text of *fiqh* will always be his yardstick of getting to his conclusion . . . that's why I said gender is irrelevant when it comes to this case. It's just what the fiqh says, it's what [the] text says, and we will grant the verdict based on that."

However, the Qur'an and hadith texts are open to interpretation, as can be gleaned, for instance, from the conflicting views on whether khulʿ requires the consent of the husband. I propose that a panel of judges with diverse views and perspectives would assist in providing more balanced interpretations that would be in the best interest of justice and of both spouses. The experience of women complainants would be significantly improved by a greater female presence in the court, a suggestion that was confirmed by the three participants I interviewed.

In contrast with the MJC's Shariʿa Court, both the Muslim Assembly and Shura Al-Islam had either female counselors or a female attorney present in their Shariʿa Courts.[17] These women sit on a panel with the male judges to hear the faskh applications. The participation of women in these Shariʿa Courts helped the wives feel more comfortable and less alienated in the faskh hearing than they would feel in an all-male court. There are sufficiently qualified female Islamic law scholars within the Cape Muslim community who could act as judges and assessors in the various Shariʿa Courts, and there is no reason why the MJC couldn't include women as judges in its Shariʿa Court.

### *Judicial Preparation and Lack of Training*

On the morning of the faskh hearings, the judge receives from the clerk a batch of files that were sent down for that day. It is the first time the judge sees the file, and he therefore has very limited time to peruse it before the clerk calls the parties into the court. On more than one occasion the presiding judge mentioned to the clerk that it would have been better if he had received the file earlier so he could have familiarized himself with its content before the faskh hearing. The files contain the history of the matter at hand and include the counselor's recommendations and relevant documents, for example, protection orders that a wife may have taken out against an abusive husband.[18]

Presiding judges in the faskh hearings do not have sufficient time to read the applicant's file and prepare for each hearing. This usually results in a very superficial hearing of the matter, with many of the judges proceeding rapidly through the case. After one particularly brief faskh hearing, the presiding judge commented, "It feels like we [are] running a sausage machine," and then asked the clerk if he could send the files through earlier. In some instances, the faskh hearing was over in five minutes, especially if the husband was not present and the wife had sufficient evidence to show that he had not maintained her. One participant, Rabia, stated the following about the imam presiding over her faskh hearing: "You could see that he was agitated because he is not there for a discussion. He is there ready to write this piece of paper out. He is pressured for time, yes, you can be pressured for time, but it's not for me to be able to pick that up from you because you serve in a social service environment. I mustn't feel that I must get done quickly because my matter is a very important matter of a family that affects a household and children. It's not a five-minute thing, so if they feel they are understaffed, then they must get more staff."

Judges are not interested in long drawn-out proceedings, as one participant, Faiza, tellingly indicated: "You are being cut off even before you started. He [the qadi] cannot expect me to explain my life in a few minutes. I feel that they are just strapped for time. They want to get this over and done with. Next case, next case, you know." One of the husbands who opposed his wife's application, Adiel, expressed a similar sentiment. On being interrupted by the judge before he could even finish recounting his version of events, Adiel retorted, "Shaykh, if you in a hurry then I am going to be very disappointed."[19]

### *The Nonappearance of Husbands at* Faskh *Hearings*

In twenty-six of the forty-five faskh hearings I observed (57 percent), the husbands were absent, either because they were not aware of the hearing or because they were simply not interested in attending. The MJC informs both parties of the hearing date through written registered letters or an SMS.[20] Absentee husbands often indicated that they never received notice of the faskh hearing or only received the text message the day before and could not attend on such short notice. Female participants also complained about the insufficient notice they received from the MJC concerning their hearing dates. Because the Shari'a Court is not an official state court, a sheriff cannot be employed to serve notices of the hearings to the parties. The clerk intimated that the MJC might in future employ someone to deliver the hearing notice to the husband personally but that this had huge cost implications that needed to be considered at the highest level of the organization.

Of the twenty-six cases I observed in which husbands were not present, the wives were granted a faskh in eighteen. In some instances the judge would make every attempt to contact the husband by telephone to establish his version of the events, while in others a judge would simply accept the wife's version and would grant the faskh in the husband's absence. The clerk explained that judges did not always call husbands to enquire about their version of events because they had had sufficient opportunity to refute the wife's allegations in their counseling sessions. If a husband did not use the opportunity, then he essentially waived his right to defend himself at the faskh hearing. It is a cause for concern that so many faskhs are granted in the absence of the husband, but the MJC's hands are more or less tied: either they grant the faskh in cases where husbands are absent or they delay the faskh indefinitely until the husband appears before them at the hearing. There is no provision for a husband to file a written notice indicating that he has no intention of opposing the wife's application.

Where the husband was present for the faskh application, the hearing would usually take longer either because the husband would oppose the faskh application or the judges would want to hear the husband's response to the wife's allegations. If the husband confirmed the wife's claim that he was not maintaining her, the judges would very quickly conclude the matter by granting the faskh, even if the husband provided reasons for the lack of maintenance. In one case a husband claimed he had fallen seriously ill and was thus unable to work and maintain his wife. The judges listened sympathetically to his defense but explained to him that they had no choice but to grant the faskh because his wife had proved that he had not maintained her, even though he had a reason for not fulfilling his responsibilities. This particular case emphasized the importance attributed to defaulting nafaqa as grounds for obtaining a faskh at the MJC.

### *Judicial Bias against Certain Grounds for Divorce*

When applying for a faskh, the wife must prove valid legal grounds before the court can grant it. The MJC does not have a written list of grounds in the form of a legal code that wives can rely on when applying for a faskh. Traditionally, grounds for a faskh were almost nonexistent in the Ḥanafī school, while the Shāfiʿī school allowed more leeway to a wife to obtain a faskh on grounds such as the husband's desertion, impotence, detention or imprisonment, insanity, or failure to maintain his wife (Black, Esmaeli, and Hosen 2013). The Mālikī school has the most favorable position toward women, whereby physical, verbal, or emotional abuse or harm constitute grounds for a wife to obtain a faskh.

The MJC generally applies the Shāfiʿī school of thought but may resort to other schools when arriving at a ruling on a particular case. This depends on the facts before the court and the flexibility of approach of the judge presiding over the matter. The judges I interviewed confirmed that they preferred to apply Shāfiʿī grounds for a faskh; where a wife could prove those grounds, she would have no difficulty in obtaining it. Of the forty-five faskh hearings I observed, 77 percent of the women raised the fact that their husbands were failing to maintain them and their children financially and 20 percent cited the fact that their husbands had abandoned or deserted them. When the wife was able to prove desertion or lack of maintenance, the faskh would be granted. However, if the wife only alleged verbal or emotional abuse in the absence of any of the other Shāfiʿī grounds for a faskh, she would have a far harder time obtaining a judicial divorce. One judge confirmed that allegations of emotional abuse and infidelity on their own would not suffice for a faskh. This is problematic for a woman who is married to an adulterous husband or to a husband who, despite fulfilling his financial responsibilities, is emotionally abusive. In such cases a woman will find it very difficult to obtain a faskh at the MJC. This is illustrated by the case of Azraa, who sought a faskh based on emotional abuse.

Azraa is a professional woman in her mid-thirties who was married by Muslim rites only to a divorcé, Ilyaas, a man fifteen years her senior. She was financially independent when she married him in 2015 and was able to support herself. In September 2018 she approached the MJC for a faskh on the grounds of emotional abuse. Her husband refused to grant her a ṭalāq despite being encouraged to do so by the MJC counselors, and furthermore he refused to respond to any of the MJC's correspondence or calls. The MJC administrator and counselors eventually stopped contacting Ilyaas. After badgering the MJC administrators for more than a year, Azraa was finally, and with very little notice, granted a faskh hearing date in October 2019. Her husband did not appear at the hearing. At the hearing, which I observed, the judges inquired about her grounds for wanting a faskh. She responded that her husband was emotionally abusive and a narcissist. She explained: "My grounds were never maintenance. . . . My issue was I'm not happy in this abusive marriage, get me out."

In spite of her evidence before the court, the judges persistently asked Azraa if lack of nafaqa was not actually the main reason she sought a faskh. Completely frustrated, she responded irately that, "I am not interested in my husband's money or nafaqa. I just want out of the marriage because he is a narcissist!" The judges appeared taken aback by her response. They discussed the matter with each other in Arabic while Azraa waited for their decision. They granted Azraa the faskh at the end of the hearing, more than a year after she had moved out of her marital home and approached the MJC for dissolution of her marriage.

### *Judicial Preparation*

The imams who preside over the court are not trained as lawyers or judges and are therefore not equipped to lead or cross-examine witnesses in order to identify where the truth lies. This has a direct impact on the manner in which the faskh hearings are conducted because when a husband is present and disputes the claims of his wife, the judges are ill-equipped to deal with conflicting evidence. They are unable to cross-examine either party to determine the truth. They do not call further witnesses to confirm either party's version or have the parties attest to documentation on record to support their case. The parties are not allowed any legal representation and are completely reliant on the judges to act fairly, objectively, and in both their best interests, which does not always happen. This was illustrated in the case of Faiza.

This was the second time Faiza had appeared before the court for a faskh hearing. In 2016 she had also applied to the MJC for a faskh, but her application was denied. At the 2016 faskh hearing, her husband, Fahmy, had opposed the application and denied all the allegations she made. She explained: "Like with the first time, three years back that I went, I hardly got to speak. Fahmy was just dominating the whole conversation. . . . I actually had photos of where he tipped over [broke up] the whole place, my knees being busted, marks over my chest of how he abused me. They didn't even want to look at it." Despite having a protection order against her husband and evidence of abuse, the court accepted the husband's version of events and refused to grant Faiza a faskh. Faiza explained her devastation at the refusal: "Then they declined my faskh. I cannot put into words what it did to me. I cannot explain to you how I felt that very moment when they declined me. . . . I couldn't fathom what more reason I needed to have for them to take my faskh into consideration and obviously it gave him the upper hand. . . . So when we got home it was a case of 'van jy lè net stil, van ons is nou getroud,'[21] and I felt stuck and I felt trapped and I felt betrayed. I felt betrayed because these are the people that's supposed to be looking out for us women."

Faiza eventually moved out of the marital home with her children, despite not being granted a faskh. In 2019, she returned to the MJC to reapply for a faskh. She felt that she stood a better chance the second time because in addition to the grounds of abuse, she and her husband had been living separately for more than a year. However, her 2019 faskh application was also denied due to her husband's opposition. She explained that she did not approach another Muslim judicial body or imam because her husband would only accept a faskh that was granted by the MJC. In the absence of a divorce decree from the MJC, he would insist that they were still married.

Faiza alleged that her husband had physically, emotionally, and verbally abused her throughout their twenty-two-year marriage. She indicated that all the proof was in her file, including the protection order she had obtained against her husband. At her faskh hearing in September 2019, the husband denied her allegations and told the court that he did not want the marriage to end.[22] The presiding judges did not refer to the supporting documentation on file, did not call additional witnesses, and did not cross-examine either party to establish the veracity of their statements. They declined the faskh and referred the parties to arbitration.[23]

The judges who preside in the Shariʿa Court received no training on eliciting evidence from parties appearing before them, nor are they equipped with skills to cross-examine witnesses. I argue that in the absence of these skills, it becomes very hard to conduct a fair hearing, especially when the judges are confronted with husbands who oppose the faskh application and deny all the allegations made by the wives. The judges inevitably gave the husbands the benefit of the doubt because they lacked the skills to expose false evidence. One of the participants, Rabia, had the following to say: "I feel that the shaykhs, they don't really want to point out the husband or the man's wrong. They, for me, I feel they are more on the man's side than on the woman's side."

## The Limits of Shariʿa Court Remedies

After hearing the faskh application, the court either grants the faskh or refers the parties for further counseling or to arbitration. When a faskh is granted, the judge explains to the parties that the faskh is an irrevocable divorce and that if the parties wish to reconcile, they must contract a new marriage. The judges also explain the intricacies of the 'idda to the wife and advise her on what is permitted during this period. Most of the judges adopt a very conservative approach with respect to the 'idda and usually advise the wife that she can only leave home for necessities such as going to work or buying groceries. The judges even discourage her from visiting her parents or siblings.

On many occasions, after the faskh is granted, women ask the judges about the status of immovable property acquired during their marriage or about the maintenance and care of minor children born of their marriage. Judges explain that they are not equipped to provide any other remedies aside from granting the faskh. They advise women that husbands must maintain their wives during the 'idda period, but this is of little comfort to most women as husbands who default on paying maintenance during the marriage are unlikely to pay maintenance during the 'idda period. Thus, the courts provide no practical enforceable remedies as to the division of property, spousal maintenance postdivorce, maintenance for minor children, or parenting plans for minor children.[24] In South African civil divorce cases, these issues are all included in a consent paper, which is usually drawn up by the spouses' attorneys and then becomes a court order.

The Shari'a Court judges furthermore do not have a list of service providers, such as state or private family-dispute mediation services, to whom they can refer women seeking further assistance with maintenance claims and parenting plans. Women are simply granted an order dissolving their marriage. As recounted by Rabia, "Yes, so I asked the Mawlana because he was ready to write this faskh out . . . but so I asked him, if he's going to write that out now, then what support system is there from the MJC for when I go home from here, and I need to get rid of Malik out of the house because he's not going to leave the house." Rabia mentioned that even if the MJC granted her the faskh, there was no way her husband would leave the matrimonial home. She would have to institute eviction proceedings in the South African courts, and she did not have the finances to do so. She therefore opted to go for further counseling, even though she had sufficient grounds for faskh.

When a faskh is not granted, the judges can refer the parties back to counseling. Alternatively, they can refer the matter to arbitration. Each party is allocated an arbitrator, typically an imam at the MJC. The arbitrator speaks to the spouse by phone in order to establish if there is any possibility of the parties reconciling. Each arbitrator then makes a recommendation to the Shari'a Court, and the judges then make the final decision on whether to grant a faskh based on the recommendations of the arbitrators. Although the process appears straightforward, it is often complicated.

Faiza's matter was referred to arbitration, and despite the fact that she repeatedly explained to the arbitrator that she wanted to exit the marriage because her relationship with her husband had broken down irretrievably, her matter was never referred back to the Shari'a Court for a final decision on her faskh. Her husband once again managed to convince his arbitrator that the marriage could still work, which resulted in reluctance on the part of both arbitrators to recommend that a faskh be granted. The MJC offices never contacted Faiza nor returned any of her calls when she tried to enquire after the status of her divorce. At the time of writing this chapter, the MJC had still not contacted her or granted her a faskh, leaving Faiza despondent and disillusioned with its system of justice.

## Conclusion

The failure of the South African state to recognize Muslim marriages has created problems for Muslim women seeking divorce. Islamic judicial bodies such as the MJC have, out of necessity, tried to solve the problems by facilitating the dissolution of marriages. Despite their concerted efforts, my ethnographic research has shown that there are numerous challenges and limitations to the divorce procedures currently employed at the MJC. These include problems that arise from the pre-divorce procedure, shortcomings in the Shari'a Court hearings, and the limited remedies available to women seeking a divorce.

The most efficient way to address these issues would be for the South African state to enact legislation that would clearly regulate Muslim divorce proceedings, whether through Muslim judicial bodies or within conventional state courts. I argue that the state has a constitutional obligation to formally recognize Muslim marriages and to protect the rights of Muslim women who are currently suffering inequity in divorce procedures because of the nonrecognition of Islamic marriage and divorce. The state has failed in its constitutional obligation for over twenty years.[25] With the enactment of state legislation, Islamic divorce could be standardized and consistently regulated.

In the absence of state intervention, I propose that Muslim judicial bodies such as the MJC adopt a series of steps in order to substantively improve the experience of parties navigating Islamic divorces. These include the advocating and acceptance of khul' as an alternative form of divorce, creating a more efficient pre-divorce notification system, having a more gender-representative Shari'a Court, producing clear written guidelines for court procedures, expanding the grounds for a faskh to include the Mālikī grounds of *ḍarar* (harm), and, finally, adequately training judges in the Shari'a Court to equip them to conduct hearings that are just and fair to both parties. Adopting these recommendations would go a long way in alleviating the injustices suffered by Muslim women when seeking divorce from Muslim judicial bodies.

### *Acknowledgments*

I wish to thank the University of Cape Town (UCT) Research Office and the Engaged Scholarship Programme, who provided funding for a writing retreat in which this work was developed. I would furthermore like to thank the Family and Research Unit (FASRU) at the Centre for Social Science Research, UCT, for providing support and ethical clearance for the empirical research undertaken for this chapter. I also wish to acknowledge and thank the Muslim Judicial Council for allowing me to observe the divorce processes in their Shari'a Court and for agreeing to the various interviews and to thank the Muslim Assembly and Shura Al-Islam for allowing me to conduct interviews with their relevant officials. Finally, I wish to thank Dr. F. Osman for commenting on the earlier drafts of this chapter.

## NOTES

1. Historically, couples who wished to conclude a marriage recognized under South African law had to conclude a civil marriage in terms of the Marriage Act of 1961, which made provision for heterosexual couples to conclude a monogamous civil marriage. Muslim marriages concluded in terms of Islamic law only were considered potentially polygamous and were therefore regarded as unlawful and invalid by the courts. However, since 1994 the South African courts have recognized Muslim marriages in various instances. In *Daniels v. Campbell NO and Others* 2004 (5) SA 331 (CC), spouses in a Muslim marriage were recognized as spouses for the purpose of inheriting intestate from each other and for maintenance claims against the estate of the deceased spouse. In *Hassam v. Jacobs NO and Others* 2009 (5) SA 572 (CC), the court recognized that all wives in a polygamous Muslim marriage were entitled to inherit from their husband intestate.
2. The Department of Justice and Constitutional Development released a Muslim Marriages Bill (MMB) in 2010, but to date the MMB has never been passed as an Act of Parliament. See Amien and Leatt (2014) for a discussion of the complexities surrounding the enactment of the MMB.
3. Act 25 of 1961.
4. Act 17 of 2006.
5. Act 120 of 1998.
6. There are Muslim women who marry according to both Islamic rites and civil law, but they remain in the minority.
7. In the case of *Rylands v. Edros* 1997 (2) SA 690 (C), the court held that an Islamic marriage was a contract, and hence recognized commonly implied consequences occurring at the termination of an Islamic contract through divorce. The court upheld the wife's right to nafaqa (maintenance) during the 'idda (postdivorce waiting period), the right to claim arrears maintenance, and the right to claim *mut'a* (a conciliatory gift) from her husband. While this was a groundbreaking case for Islamic divorce, most women are not aware that they can enforce these remedies in a South African court. And for those who are aware of the fact, the cost of a lengthy court case serves as a disincentive to pursue these remedies in conventional court.
8. See Hoel (2012), who discusses the experience of Muslim women in divorce initiatives at the MJC.
9. Cape Town is the capital city of the Western Cape. It is also the legislative capital of South Africa and is where the country's Parliament is found.
10. This was confirmed in a fatwa (legal ruling) issued by the MJC and dated July 19, 2017, as well as through my observations of faskh hearings in the MJC Shari'a Court and interviews with imams (Muslim clergy) who presided in these courts.
11. The names of all participants in this study have been changed to ensure anonymity.
12. In South Africa any matter that affects the legal status of an individual, such as divorce, has to be heard by the High Courts.
13. 50 Rands (R) is the equivalent of approximately 3.40 USD at the time of writing this chapter.

14. The ṭalāq certificate serves as evidence of their marital status in Islamic law and may be required by various state or corporate entities as proof of marital status.
15. A koeksister is a spicy sugared coconut doughnut specific to Cape Town. A "koeksister process" in this context denotes an unprofessional or haphazard process.
16. *Mawlana* is a term used to describe an imam or a member of the Islamic clergy.
17. This information was gleaned from my interviews at the Muslim Assembly and Shura Al-Islam.
18. Parties in a domestic relationship can obtain a protection order in terms of the Domestic Violence Act 116 of 1998.
19. Members of the community use the terms *imam* and *shaykh* interchangeably when referring to Muslim clerics.
20. In the past they would also broadcast a notice on the local Muslim community radio informing the husband that he had to appear in Shari'a Court on a particular date. This practice has been stopped because of privacy concerns.
21. Translated from Afrikaans to English as "You will just lie still because we are still married."
22. I observed this hearing, and it was apparent to me that the judges were incapable of dealing with conflicting evidence.
23. Arbitration is discussed in the following section.
24. A parenting plan sets out the contact time each parent will have with the minor children.
25. In the recent case of *President of the RSA and Another v. Women's Legal Centre Trust and Others Minister of Justice and Constitutional Development v. Faro and Others; and Minister of Justice and Constitutional Development v. Esau and Others* (Case no 612/19 [2020]) ZASCA 177 (18 December 2020), the SCA found that the nonrecognition of Muslim marriages is a violation of the constitutional rights of women and children in particular, including their rights to equality, dignity and access to court. The judgment obliges the president and parliament to pass new legislation within twenty-four months in order to ensure the recognition of Muslim marriages as valid marriages for all purposes in South Africa and to regulate the consequences arising from such recognition. The judgment is currently on appeal before the Constitutional Court, which is the highest court in the Republic of South Africa.

## REFERENCES


Abduroaf, Muneer. 2019. "The Consequence of an Islamic Divorce." *Without Prejudice* 19 (9):31–32.

Allie, Shouket. 2010. "A Legal and Historical Excursus of Muslim Personal Law in the Colonial Cape, South Africa, from the Eighteenth to the Twentieth Century." In *Muslim Personal Law in South Africa—Evolution and Future Status*, edited by Najma Moosa and Suleman Dangor, 26–43. Cape Town: Juta.

Al-Sharmani, Mulki. 2017. *Gender Justice and Legal Reform in Egypt—Negotiating Muslim Family Law*. Cairo: American University in Cairo Press.

Amien, Waheeda. 2010. "A South African Case Study for the Recognition and Regulation of Muslim Family Law in a Minority Muslim Secular Context." *International Journal of Law, Policy and the Family* 24 (3):361–396.

———2019. "The Gendered Benefits and Costs of Legal Pluralism for Muslim Family Law in South Africa." In *Muslim Personal Law in South Africa—Evolution and Future Status*, edited by Najma Moosa and Suleman Dangor, 94–112. Cape Town: Juta.

Amien, Waheeda, and Dhammamegha A. Leatt. 2014. "Legislating Religious Freedom: An Example of Muslim Marriages in South Africa." *Maryland Journal of International Law* 29 (1):505–547.

Black, Ann, Hossein Esmaeli, and Nadirsyah Hosen. 2013. *Modern Perspectives on Islamic Law.* Northampton: Elgaronline.

Dangor, Suleiman. 2003. "The Establishment and Consolidation of Islam in South Africa: From the Dutch Colonization of the Cape to the Present." *Historia* 48 (1):203–220.

Davids, Achmat. 2011. *The Afrikaans of the Cape Muslims.* Pretoria: Protea Book House.

Essop, F. 2018. "Maintenance on Divorce." *Muslim Views*, December, 19.

Gabru, N. 2004. "Dilemma of Muslim Women Regarding Divorce in South Africa." *Potchefstroom Electronic Law Journal* 7 (2):1–15.

Hoel, Nina. 2012. "Engaging Religious Leaders: South African Muslim Women's Experiences Matters Pertaining to Divorce Initiatives." *Social Dynamic* 38 (2):184–200.

MJC (Muslim Judicial Council). 2018. "Significance of the MJC." Https://mjc.org.za/about-mjc/significance/.

Moore, Sally Falk. 1973. "Law and Social Change: The Semi-Autonomous Social Field as an Appropriate Subject of Study." *Law and Society Review* 7 (4):719–746.

Moosa, Najma. 2011. *Unveiling the Mind: The Legal Position of Women in Islam—A South African Context.* Cape Town: Juta.

Moosa, Najma, and Suleman Dangor. 2019. "An Introduction to Muslim Personal Law in South Africa: Past to Present." In *Muslim Personal Law in South Africa—Evolution and Future Status*, edited by Najma Moosa and Suleman Dangor, 1–25. Cape Town: Juta.

Rautenbach, C. 2019. "The Contribution of the Courts in the Integration of Muslim Law into the Mixed Fabric of South African Law." In *Muslim Personal Law in South Africa—Evolution and Future Status*, edited by Najma Moosa and Suleman Dangor, 145–170. Cape Town: Juta.

Schoeman, Willem J. 2017. "South African Religious Demography: The 2013 General Household Survey." *HTS Theological Studies* 73 (2):1–7.

Sonneveld, Nadia, and Erin Stiles. 2019. "*Khul'*: Local Contours of a Global Phenomenon." *Islamic Law and Society* 26 (1–2):1–11.

# PART TWO

# Gendered Strategies and Judicial Responses in Marital Disputing

# 4

# Women in the Search of Sexual Pleasure

## Divorce on Grounds of Sexual Dissatisfaction in Indonesian Religious Courts

AYANG UTRIZA YAKIN

On the morning of March 30, 2016, I attended an extraordinary court session during which a revealing dialogue ensued between the plaintiff and the chief judge. An attractive young woman, dressed fashionably and wearing a veil, entered the religious court in South Jakarta after her name was announced via the public address system loudspeaker. The senior chief judge headed the session with the assistance of two additional judges and a female clerk. After the plaintiff sat down, the door was closed, although noises from outside still infiltrated the courtroom. I sat in the right-hand corner of the courtroom, observing, taking notes, and recording the day's judicial proceedings.

The chief judge began to question the woman according to court procedures. After about ten minutes, he asked if she had any children. This question revealed the surprising reason she was filing for divorce. At first, she hesitated and seemed ashamed to answer the question. However, she ultimately told the judges that her husband could not engage in sexual relations. The dialogue continued, and she was insistent about continuing her divorce case. Accordingly, the chief judge read a petition summarizing her claim: "The reason for the divorce is that the husband cannot meet her conjugal needs [*nafkah batin*]. It is not enough. That is the core problem." The judges did not explore what she meant by "it is not enough."[1]

As the dialogue between the judge and the plaintiff reveals, the young woman filed for divorce because of problematic sexual relations. I asked the judge for permission to leave the courtroom so I could catch up with the plaintiff to request an interview. She agreed, and from the interview I came to understand what she meant by "it is not enough." As she explained: "Day by day, the sexual relations' duration has become shorter and shorter until it is less than ten seconds. I am not satisfied sexually, and this has been going on for years. . . . In fact, when we have sexual relations, I feel nothing: because he has already ejaculated even before I feel something. This is suffering."

The plaintiff failed to attend the two subsequent hearings and the court decided to drop the case that June.[2] Thanks to the kindness of the clerk and the permission of the court, I obtained the complete case file. The woman's divorce petition, dated January 29, 2016, stated: "The plaintiff has suffered from a lack of sexual relations since the beginning of the marriage due to the [sexual] performance problems of the defendant, which makes her feel traumatized about having sex with him."[3]

Irma Riyani has found that cultural discourses and religious teachings about sexuality in Indonesia shape women's understanding and knowledge in gendered ways. She argues that Indonesian women have often felt unable to express and explore their sexual desires within marriage. Riyani provides rich ethnographic data on married women's sexuality, and her interviews indicate that in recent years Indonesian women have become more vocal about their sexual needs and feelings (2020). Today many Indonesian women believe that, as a matter of their sexual rights, they are entitled to enjoy sex in marriage. Arzoo Osanloo (2009) found that religious courts in Iran are "dialogical sites" where women can discuss their rights, including sexual problems with their spouse. Those women can negotiate through the divorce process to speak for their rights. The same might be said of Indonesian courts. An unsatisfactory sex life leads to irritations, quarrels, and in some cases, petitions for divorce, as in the case just described. Although the amount of academic literature dealing with Islamic divorce in Indonesia has increased in the last twenty years (Nakamura 1993, 2006; Heaton, Cammack, and Young 2001; Cammack, Donovan, and Heaton 2007; Cammack, Young, and Heaton 2010; Cammack and Heaton 2011; Nurlaelawati 2010, 2013; Bowen 2003; Nasir 2013; van Huis 2015, 2019), little attention has been paid to divorce on the grounds of sexual dissatisfaction.[4] This chapter aims to fill that gap.

According to Indonesian law, sexual dissatisfaction is not a legitimate ground for divorce. Three pieces of legislation regulate divorce: the Marriage Law (Undang-Undang Perkawinan [UUP]) No. 1/1974; Government Regulation (Peraturan Pemerintah [PP]) No. 9/1975 (as an explanation of Law No. 1/1974); and the Compilation of Islamic Law (Kompilasi Hukum Islam [KHI]) No. 1/1991.[5] A divorce petition may be filed on the following grounds: adultery, drug addiction, alcoholism, if a spouse is a gambler, a spouse's absence of two years in succession or imprisonment for five years or more, cruelty, incapacity to carry out spousal duties and obligations due to illness, continuous and irreconcilable discord, violation of conditional divorce, and apostasy.[6] Although an unsatisfactory sexual relationship is not specifically listed as grounds for divorce, judges will frequently grant a divorce in such a case.

The chapter considers why spouses file for divorce on the grounds of sexual dissatisfaction and how the religious courts deal with these cases when the legislation is uncertain in this regard. I answer these questions based on Baudouin Dupret's praxiological approach to socio-legal studies (2006, 2007, 2010, 2011). *Socio-legal* is a generic term that encompasses all approaches to the law and that "emphasizes the importance of understanding the context of the law and the exploration of social context" (Creutzfeldt, Mason, and MacConachie 2020, 3–4). A praxiological approach to law seeks to understand judicial practice and reasoning in context and is particularly interested in the judgment itself as situated action in a specific context that is carried out through a particular mode of deployment (Dupret 2006, 173–189). This chapter aims to describe in an empirically documented way how judges in Indonesian religious courts adjudicate the issue of divorce due to sexual dissatisfaction. The merit of the praxiological approach is that it completely avoids any presuppositions about the law. The law is not determined in advance by theoreticians or social scientists; instead, people's common uses determine the law (Dupret 2011, 34).

The chapter first describes several cases involving divorce petitions on grounds of sexual dissatisfaction. Then I examine the legal reasoning of the judges who have accepted sexual dissatisfaction as proof of "a broken marriage" (*syikak* or *syiqaq* in Indonesian; Arabic, *shiqāq*) for the legitimate reason of "continuous and irreconcilable discord" under article 19 (F) of the PP 1975 and article 116 (F) of the KHI. Finally, I argue that the judges adjudicate cases by linking the disputants and witnesses' information to existing written laws and developing legal arguments to support their decision. Because sexual dissatisfaction is not grounds for divorce in Indonesian law, judges prepare formal rulings that suit the needs of the case yet comply with the existing law. I found that to support their rulings, judges extend the meaning of "a conjugal bond," expand the grounds of "continuous and irreconcilable discord" in Indonesian legislation, and refer to *fiqh* (Islamic law) books.[7]

## Religious Courts and Divorce

During Indonesia's sultanate period, from the thirteenth to eighteenth centuries, the qadi (Islamic judge) court existed in various independent Islamic kingdoms. In the sultanate of Aceh, the grand qadi carried the title of Kali Malikon Adé (Arabic, Qāḍī Mālik al-ʿĀdil) and judges working under him bore the title Kali Rabon Jalé (Arabic, Qāḍī Rabbun Jalīl) (Hurgronje 1906, 2:96–97). In the sultanate of Banten, the grand qadi bore the official title Kiyahi Peqih Najmuddin and his adjuncts working in remote areas carried the titles *pangulu*, *karta*, *jaksa*, and *paliwara* (Yakin 2015, 470–471; 2016a, 25–27). In this precolonial period, the qadi (sometimes also called *hakim*) was the highest authority in legal matters and had the authority to judge all kinds of conflicts, from family disputes to criminal issues (Yakin 2015, 405–422; 2016b). However, the arrival of Europeans changed Indonesia's legal landscape.

During the colonial period, the Dutch introduced a plural legal system and a hierarchically organized system of courts.[8] This included the qadi court (*priestraad*) for religious cases, including family issues, among the Muslim population and the civil court (*landraad*) for secular, civil, and criminal cases. Nevertheless, the qadi court's decisions had to be validated by a civil court, and qadi courts were marginalized and not supported by the state. After Indonesia gained its independence in 1945, legal pluralism was maintained, with different names, systems, and procedures for religious courts. The Ministry of Religious Affairs (MORA) was a fervent defender of religious courts, and it tried to unify the judicial system to replace all colonial legislation on Muslim family law (Laws No. 22/1946 and 32/1954) and judicial procedures (Law No. 8/1/735, 1958). In 1989, Muslims finally had their own unified and centralized religious court systems for the first time, when Religious Court Law (Undang-Undang Peradilan Agama: UU PA) No. 7/1989 was promulgated (modified later by Laws No. 3/2006 and 50 /2009). This marked the end of marginalization and different systems for various religious courts (Hisyam 2002, 218–230; Lev 1972, 2000).

Following this, judges were called *hakim* rather than qadi. To be appointed a hakim of a religious court, Art. 13(1) of the UU PA No. 50/2009 stipulates that a person should meet the following conditions: "Indonesian, Muslim, honest, fair, behaving impeccably, being authoritative and loyal to Pancasila and the Constitution, holder BA in shari'a or law, aged between 25–40 years old, [passed] judge's training, being capable of spiritually and physically to carry out duties and obligations, and having no criminal record." The judge's selection is under the authority of the Supreme Court of the Republic of Indonesia (Mahkamah Agung Republik Indonesia: MARI),[9] which also imposes additional conditions on candidates for hakim (being Muslim and capable of reading and understanding Arabic fiqh books).[10] All candidates must complete two years of training, after which they are appointed as judges. Almost all Indonesian religious court judges have graduated from the Faculty of Shari'a and Law at one of Indonesia's fifty-three state Islamic universities or institutes.

According to the UU PA, the religious court comprises two levels of jurisdiction: the Religious Court of First Instance in each county and the Religious Court of Appeal in each provincial capital. Both courts are administered by the MARI and the judges are civil servants. In 2016, there were 359 courts of first instance and 29 courts of appeal across Indonesia; the courts have jurisdiction only over family-law cases for Muslims, including divorce. According to Indonesian law, all divorces must be pronounced in a religious court and divorce outside the court is not recognized as legal. Petitions for divorce must be filed in the religious court in the county where the litigants live. To register a case, litigants must present all relevant documents (identity card, birth certificate, marriage certificate, household composition card, etc.) and a reason for divorce. Generally, they must also pay an administrative fee, but there is an exemption for the poor.

The head of the religious court of the first instance (which first takes the case) appoints a panel to adjudicate divorce cases, consisting of three judges (one of whom acts as a chief judge) and a clerk. The litigants are called to start the process one week later. At the first hearing, the case is presented and the court tries to reconcile the litigants through mandatory mediation.[11] The maximum period of reconciliation is forty days and the process almost always fails. If reconciliation fails, the panel of judges begins the judicial process. In the subsequent hearings the court hears the litigants' issues and asks for evidence and two witnesses to support their claim. One hearing usually takes fifteen to thirty minutes and the entire judicial process takes about three months. Two weeks after the judges' decision the litigants receive the divorce certificate, provided there is no appeal.[12]

## Divorce, Women, and Sexual Pleasure

By 2016, the number of marriages between Muslim couples in Indonesia had reached almost 2 million per year,[13] but the recorded number of divorces per year amounted to at least 365,633.[14] This indicates that approximately 18 percent of Muslim marriages in Indonesia end in divorce. Indeed, 100,000 divorce petitions are filed at the religious courts each year. One of the more interesting reasons for divorce is sexual dissatisfaction, and in most cases it is the wife who is sexually dissatisfied.

This chapter examines cases from Indonesian religious courts gathered during fieldwork in 2016 and collected from the database of MARI in 2017; one case is from my fieldwork and thirty-one are from the online repository of the Directorate General of Religious Courts Body (Badan Peradilan Agama [BADILAG]) of MARI from the years 2007 to 2017. Twenty of these cases were filed by women (*cerai gugat*) and the remaining twelve were filed by men (*cerai talak*). Two were rejected by the court (one due to the fault of the relevant jurisdiction of the court[15] and the other due to an unproven divorce petition[16]) and one was dropped by the court due to the absence of litigants (the applicant did not come to hearings).[17] The remaining twenty-nine cases form the basis of this chapter. Of these cases, the majority involved younger men and women who were relatively well educated. Fifty-two out of the fifty-eight litigants (90 percent) were aged twenty to forty. Forty (68 percent) had completed secondary school (65 percent of the men and 35 percent of the women). Most were employed: twenty-eight (48 percent) were unskilled workers, eighteen (31 percent) were skilled workers (civil servants, police officers, and teachers), and twelve (20 percent) were homemakers.

In seventeen cases the divorce petition cited sexual dissatisfaction as the sole reason for the divorce. In fourteen of these the claim of sexual dissatisfaction was taken into consideration by the judges, while in three cases it was not. As we shall see later in the chapter, in thirteen of these cases other factors were incorporated into the divorce petition to support the issue of sexual dissatisfaction and to strengthen the case. Sixteen cases were heard by judges of both sexes, twelve by male judges only, and one case by female judges only. Twelve cases had two male judges and one female judge and four cases had two female judges and one male judge.

I will analyze twelve cases: six *cerai gugat* (divorce filed by women) and six *cerai talak* (divorce filed by men).[18] In the following section, I present the primary reasons why people petitioned for divorce based on sexual dissatisfaction. It should be noted that all citations of the cases are taken from the court clerks' notes on the judicial process. The language used in the court is Indonesian and all translations are my own.

### *Complaints about the Duration of Sexual Intercourse*

Three cases involve complaints from women who expected their husbands to engage in longer-lasting sexual relations. The first was from the religious court in Central Java.[19] The wife (who was in her mid-twenties) argued that her husband (a man in his early thirties) ejaculated before penetration, which caused the wife stress. In the first hearing, in December 2010, the clerk summarized the wife's testimony thusly: "The plaintiff and the defendant have never had sexual relations. . . . Indeed, the defendant has suffered an ejaculatory dysfunction during each sexual intercourse, [and] the defendant ejaculated even before penetrating the sex organ of the plaintiff." At the second hearing, the defendant challenged the claim and produced the attestation letter with the results of his medical check tests. According to him, the cause of the dispute was that the plaintiff was ashamed to stay in a rented house and also because of their difference in opinion regarding religion. During the third and fourth hearings the plaintiff and defendant each insisted on their versions of the conflict. At the fifth hearing the plaintiff produced two witnesses, her mother and a neighbor. The mother stated that the couple had not lived together for two months. The neighbor had once seen the wife, the plaintiff, crying after a quarrel with her husband. The wife had also shown the neighbor a text message from the husband that read: "If you do not enjoy a genital relationship, you can use a cucumber or eggplant." At the end of the process, the court granted a divorce to the plaintiff.

The second case, also brought by a woman, was from the religious court in West Kalimantan.[20] In her petition the plaintiff (who was in her late twenties) gave many reasons for the divorce. At the first hearing in March 2011, she said that she did not love her husband (a man in his late thirties) because it was an arranged marriage and she was sexually dissatisfied with him due to his premature ejaculation. At the second hearing the husband refused to agree that the problem was related to his wife's sexual dissatisfaction. In the subsequent four hearings there were reply-rejoinders on the issue of sexuality.[21] The clerk's notes summarize the plaintiff's position as follows: "Related to the premature ejaculation, it was the plaintiff who experienced the sexual relationship. The defendant has always ejaculated prematurely. For five months, the plaintiff was patient and never complained. When the plaintiff asked the defendant to seek medical treatment, the defendant casually said: 'We'd have been ashamed if people knew about it. That is a dishonor for us. I don't want to go back to the defendant to continue conjugal life.'" When the defendant argued that this was untrue, the plaintiff responded: "Do not make your weakness a 'weapon' to defend yourself. As a man and a husband, you must make every effort to ensure the happiness of married life. Indeed, for the goodness [virtue and chastity] of life on this earth and the hereafter, this marriage must end to avoid things that we do not want. I, as a normal woman, have a libido and a lust for sex. Can you, Honorable Judges, assume and bear responsibility if I commit the great sin [*zinā*] if you force me to continue this marriage?" At the next hearing the plaintiff brought three witnesses: her mother, her mother-in-law, and her aunt. The clerk's summary of their testimony states that "the defendant is not romantic [and] the plaintiff did not take sexual pleasure during the sexual relationship with the defendant." After two months of the judicial process, the court granted her a divorce.

The third case was from the religious court in North Sumatra and was also filed by a woman.[22] According to the plaintiff (who was in her early twenties), the husband (a man in his early forties) engaged in sexual intercourse for only three minutes. At the first hearing in October 2013, the clerk summarized the plaintiff's testimony as follows: "The defendant and the plaintiff engaged in sexual intercourse twice a week, but the defendant always had premature ejaculation within three minutes." At the second hearing, also in October 2013, the clerk's notes state that the defendant argued that his wife was not dissatisfied: "In fact, when the defendant had sexual relations with the plaintiff before the marriage, the defendant asked whether it had given her pleasure and she affirmed that it had. After the marriage, the defendant also asked the plaintiff whether she enjoyed the sexual relations; the plaintiff said that she was satisfied sexually." He added: "It is untrue that the defendant can only sustain for three minutes, as he can have sex for about ten minutes and, having followed the traditional treatment, there is a significant change in the duration of sexual relations, because the defendant can have sex that lasts about twelve minutes." Two following hearings were reply-rejoinders from both parties, and at the fifth hearing, the plaintiff produced her parents as witnesses. They testified that the defendant was lazy, a gambler, an alcoholic, and unable to have sex normally because he had a problem with premature ejaculation. Ultimately, after two months, the judges granted the divorce to the wife.

### *Issues Regarding the Size of the Male Sex Organ*

This section examines two cases in which women claimed their husbands' genitals were too small. The first case is from the court in East Java and was filed by a wife in her early thirties.[23] The case file indicates that the marriage's core problem was that the plaintiff was dissatisfied sexually with her husband (a man in his early forties). At the hearing the defendant argued that they actively had sex but the plaintiff had never enjoyed it because, according to her, his sex organ was small. He informed the judges that "when my wife came to my parents' house, she told my mother that every time she made love with me she was never satisfied and said that my penis is small. Moreover, she told her son, 'Your father's cock is like a chili pepper, too small.' I am asking, 'What kind of mother, is she?'" Two witnesses testified to the couple's problems. They said that the husband engaged in domestic violence and extramarital sex and had threatened his wife with a machete. Finally, after nine months of the judicial process (which was longer than average), the court granted a divorce to the plaintiff.

The second case was from the court in South Kalimantan and was also filed by the wife.[24] After one year of marriage, the woman (who was in her twenties) petitioned for a divorce. Her case shows that she was sexually dissatisfied with her husband (a man in in his early thirties) from the very beginning of their marriage. At the third hearing the plaintiff insisted on her claim before the judges that she had never enjoyed the sexual relationship because her husband's penis was short and so he could not satisfy her. At the fourth trial the husband rejected his wife's claim and explained to the judges that his sex organ's size was normal. The plaintiff brought her cousin and sister as witnesses. The cousin told the judges that the plaintiff no longer liked the defendant and that their marital life was not very good, and the plaintiff's sister stated that the couple did not know each other before marriage, as it was a kind of arranged marriage. The two witnesses also testified regarding the wife's sexual dissatisfaction. After two months the court granted the divorce.

### *Frequency of Sexual Relations*

Three cases reveal that women's disappointments about infrequent sex with their husbands can lead to divorce. It is interesting that men opened many of these cases. The first case, which was from the religious court in Central Java, was filed by a husband in his mid-fifties due to "a quarrel and dispute over the wife's lack of sexual pleasure."[25] His wife, who was in her early fifties, expected to have sex at least once a week but the husband was unable to fulfil her sexual needs. At the first hearing, in November 2007, the clerks record the defendant's statement as follows: "Since April 2004, the defendant has been dissatisfied sexually with the plaintiff. The defendant wants to have sex at least once a week, but the plaintiff cannot do so because of a lack of desire due to fatigue and problems." The wife was so upset by this condition, which had gone on for three years, that she even told the court that she considered her husband to be *najis* (impure).[26] At the subsequent hearings, two witnesses, both male neighbors, testified that the couple had been separated for more than eighteen months because of the dispute. The case file reports that the witnesses said "the plaintiff is no longer able to have sex as requested by the defendant." After only a month of the judicial process, the judges granted a divorce to the wife. The husband did not attend the judgment.[27]

The second case is from the court in North Sumatera. This divorce case was filed by a husband in his forties because "the wife is not sexually satisfied."[28] The wife (who was in her twenties) expected to have sex at least twice a week, which her husband was unable to do. At the first hearing, in January 2011, the defendant informed the judges that her husband could only have sex twice a month and that she required sex twice per week to fulfil her desires. The plaintiff agreed that he could not meet his wife's sexual needs. Two witnesses appeared at the next hearing, both of whom were brothers-in-law of the plaintiff. Both witnesses confirmed that the source of the complaint was the "wife's sexual dissatisfaction." After only three weeks, at the end of January 2011, the court granted a divorce.

The third case, from the religious court in Banten, was filed by a husband (who was in his early fifties) for several reasons: financial problems, domestic violence, and sexual dissatisfaction.[29] In the hearings, the wife (a woman in her thirties) claimed that she wanted to have sex with her husband on a daily basis but he was incapable of this. At the first session, in March 2011, the case files recorded the statement that "the defendant said to the plaintiff that she wants to marry a younger handsome man and asked for a divorce." The wife denied all the plaintiff's charges except for one: the lack of sexual enjoyment. She said to the court: "He always refuses if I ask him to have sex. As a woman, it is normal to ask your husband to have sex once a day. It is also normal if the wife asks her husband to fulfil her sexual desires." She continued: "My husband does not want to have sex with me, even if I ask to make love to such an extent that it happened one day that I opened the zipper of my husband's pants and pulled down his pants, but he refused to have sex." At the second session the plaintiff replied to the defendant's statement: "I have always met my wife's sexual needs, at least once a week, but she wants to have sex every night. It is impossible for me to satisfy her sexual desires because I am tired after work and I had an accident that broke my right foot, so I need rest, so . . . I cannot satisfy my wife's sexual desires." At the third and fourth hearings, the wife insisted that her husband was incapable of fulfilling her sexual desires and that this had been the case for three years. She requested custody of the children and compensation for not having had sex for two years (15 million rupiah [Rp.], equivalent to about $1,500). Two witnesses testified about the financial problem and domestic violence, but they did not know about the couple's sexual problems. Ultimately, after five hearings, the court granted a divorce.

### *Experience with the Former Husband*

In some cases, women compared sex with their current husbands unfavorably to sex with their former husbands. At the first hearing in a case from the court in Bangka-Belitung, the man who opened the case claimed that his wife (a woman in her late twenties) was not sexually satisfied and compared him to her ex-husband: "Specifically, she said that she was not satisfied sexually in each sexual relationship with me."[30] The husband brought two witnesses to support his claim: his younger brother and a friend. They testified that his wife did not want to take care of her husband's children from his former marriage and that she was always angry and yelled at the children. After one month of the judicial process, the court granted the divorce.

### *Sexual Performance Due to Age Difference*

Two cases involved women who thought that a younger husband would be more able to satisfy them sexually. The first case is from the court in East Java and was filed by the husband (who was in his mid-fifties).[31] The defendant (a woman in her late twenties) complained that her husband was incapable of fulfilling her sexual needs because he was too old. At the first hearing, the plaintiff said that his wife was unsatisfied because he was too old. The plaintiff brought two witnesses to the next hearing to confirm his account. After two hearings in only one month, the court granted a divorce.

The second case is from the religious court in Banten and was filed by a husband in his eighties.[32] He wanted to divorce his wife (a woman in her late thirties), who had left the marital home three years earlier. At the first hearing, the case file records the plaintiff's view as follows: "The defendant cannot accept his condition that he is sick and the defendant is always unsatisfied in each sexual relationship." He brought two witnesses, who testified: "The defendant never took pleasure in sexual intercourse because the plaintiff is already old, while the defendant is still young." Based on the plaintiff's incapacity to fulfil the sexual needs of the wife due to the forty-three-year age difference, the court granted the divorce.

In the twelve cases examined here, the primary reason for the divorce petitions was the wife's sexual dissatisfaction. The judges granted divorce in all the cases; the following section analyzes their legal reasoning.

## Judges' "Invention" of a Legal Basis for Divorce Based on Sexual Dissatisfaction

The religious courts accept the grounds of sexual dissatisfaction as a reason to end a marriage even though it is not listed as grounds for divorce under Indonesian law. Euis Nurlaelawati found that other grounds that are not specifically listed are also often accepted by the courts, such as polygamy, a husband's bad behavior, or a poor relationship with the wife's parents-in-law. Judges accept these other grounds as evidence of a "protracted dispute" (2013, 258–261). The cases of sexual dissatisfaction are similar. I argue that the religious courts resolve the legal ambiguity of these cases by referring to fiqh texts and existing articles of Indonesian family law that specify "continuous and irreconcilable discord" as grounds for divorce (Art. 19-F of PP 9/1975 and Art. 116-F of the KHI 1/1991). According to Cammack, Donovan, and Heaton, the religious courts equated "the continuous and irreconcilable discord" with the principles and procedures for *syiqaq* (discord) in fiqh (2007, 115). Although the grounds of syiqaq makes divorce easier for Indonesian women, some judges feared that its acceptance would give wives too much power (Bowen 2003, 206).

I have found that in the Indonesian religious courts, using sexual dissatisfaction as grounds for divorce rests on two legal principles, namely, that marriage is based on "a physical and psychological union" and that a "broken marriage" has "continuous and reconcilable discord." In the twelve cases presented in this chapter—as in the larger data set of twenty-nine cases—the religious courts referred to three legislative acts. The first two, Art. 1 of UUP No. 1/1974 and Art. 3 of KHI No. 1/1991, concern the meaning of marriage: "Marriage is a physical and psychological union between a man and a woman as husband and wife to found a happy and eternal marital life based on the belief in one God" and "the purpose of marriage is to create a marital life in peace, love, and compassion." The third is Art. 19 (F) of PP No. 9 /1975 and Art. 116 (F) of the KHI No. 1/1991: "The husband and the wife have continuous and irreconcilable discord, making it impossible to achieve a harmonious family life." Based on this legislation, judges interpret the meanings of "conjugal bond," "peace, love, and compassion," and "discord" to resolve the gap in the law as written. Subsequently, judges supplement their decisions by referring to the Qur'an 30:21 and the hadith "lā ḍarar wa lā ḍirār [one must not harm himself and bring harm to others]." Finally, the judges referred to the fiqh books to explain the uncertainty in the law. Thus, the judicial practices of Indonesian religious courts exemplify how judges draw on plural legal sources in cases of legal absence or uncertainty (Dupret, Berger, and al-Zwaini 1999, xi). In the following section I explain how the court referred to the legislation and these three sources to resolve the apparent lack of clarity in the law.

### *Extending the Meaning of a Conjugal Bond*

To justify using sexual dissatisfaction as grounds for divorce, the courts first interpreted Art. 1 of UUP No. 1/1974, to mean that the *ikatan batin* (conjugal bond) is the essential factor in marital life. In the decisions described earlier, the judges specifically linked the conjugal bond to sexual relations. In the case from East Java, for example, the court reasoned that "one of the elements of marriage is the conjugal bond—the explanation of the article saying that the conjugal bond has an important role, and if this element no longer exists, then the marriage bond is essentially broken and its connections severed."[33] To explain the meaning of "ikatan batin," the court referred to Art. 1 of the UUP in the PP No. 9/1975 to assert that a conjugal psychological or spiritual element plays an important role. The term *conjugal* is further connected to sexual activities between husband and wife, without which the marriage bond will be weakened. In the case from Southeast Sulawesi, the court reasoned,[34] "It is understandable that it is impossible for a wife who still wants to continue her marriage to leave her household for a long time, if she gets [sexual] satisfaction from her husband. Therefore this [sexual dissatisfaction] is kind of hidden discord."[35] In other words, the conjugal bond includes sexual relations. When this element no longer exists, the marital bond has been broken. In the eyes of the judges, if the wife cannot find pleasure in the marital sexual activities, the objective of marriage has not been achieved.

The court also referenced Art. 3 of the KHI 1991 in stating that the purpose of marriage is "to create a marital life in peace, love, and compassion." Art. 3 is derived from Qur'an 30:21, to which the judges frequently referred to support their legal reasoning.[36] For example, the religious court in East Java reasoned:

> Considering that the purpose of marriage is as God said in the Qur'an 30:21 *"And among His Signs is this, that He created for you mates from among yourselves, that you may dwell in tranquility with them, and He has put love and mercy between your [hearts]: verily in that are signs for those who reflect,"*[37] in article 1

> of the UUP 1974 and article 3 of the KHI 1991, the dignity and quality of marriage have been lost in the conjugal life of the couple mentioned. Tranquility, love, and compassion no longer exist in their married life. If they continue this conjugal life, harm and disaster can further occur between them and the solution for this conflict of marriage is divorce.[38]

Similarly, the religious court in West Kalimantan reasoned that:

> to realize a tranquility, love, and compassion in the household as the purpose of marriage in the Qur'an 30:21, the article 1 of UUP No. 1/1974 and the article 3 KHI No. 1/1991, requires a condition of mutual respect and love for each other between the plaintiff and the defendant. With the proof of disputes and quarrels between the plaintiff and the defendant, as well as the plaintiff's attitude stating that she does not want to reconcile with the defendant and the defendant continuing to insist on the divorce lawsuit she [the applicant] filed, it proves that the interpersonal relationship between the plaintiff and the defendant is increasingly distant because the plaintiff has not loved the defendant. Therefore, the Panel of Judges is of the opinion that the plaintiff and defendant's households are included in the category of broken marriage, so that the marriage is impossible to be maintained and rescued.[39]

Qur'an 30:21 is crucial in almost all Indonesian religious court decisions involving divorce. Although the Qur'an does not state specifically that a marriage can be ended on grounds of sexual dissatisfaction, it offers a general condition for marriage—*sakinah* (peace, tranquility)—without which the marriage has effectively ended. In the cases examined here, the judges referenced Qur'an 30:21 to establish that because of the conflict between the wife and husband, the objective of the marriage, sakinah, was gone.[40]

### *Judicial Expansion of Irreconcilable Discord*

In addition to extending the meaning of the conjugal bond, the courts also reasoned that the divorce petitions filed on the basis of sexual dissatisfaction could be supported through Indonesian legislation. Article 19 (F) of PP No. 9/1975 and Article 116 (F) of the KHI 1991 state, "The husband and the wife have continuous and irreconcilable discord [*syiqaq*], making it impossible to achieve a harmonious family life." Although Article 19 does not address sexual dissatisfaction, the courts take it into account as the legal reason for "continuous and irreconcilable discord": thus, the court considered the consequence (discord) and not the cause (sexual dissatisfaction). The courts ground their legal reasoning in MARI No. 38.K/Ag/1990, which stated, "If the court is convinced that the marriage is broken in line with the article 19-F PP No. 9 /1975, one should not seek the cause of the dispute and quarrel that has arisen between the applicant and the defendant, but rather the actual condition of their marital life, where the marriage is already broken and torn apart."[41]

The courts thus interpret "sexual dissatisfaction" as a form of "discord." They are under no obligation to search for a reason for the discord but only to establish that the marriage had broken down, and the proof is the syiqaq of the husband and wife. Stijn van Huis (2019, 76) argues that divorces that are grounded in this way have become "no-fault divorces." Whether the marriage is already broken or not, a religious court has five criteria to assess during the hearing: (1) whether the judges fail to reconcile the spouses (in the first two hearings through a mediator); (2) whether the spouses live separately; (3) whether the spouses still speak to each other; (4) whether the spouses fulfil their duties as wife and husband; and (5) whether one spouse has had an extramarital sexual relationship. If any of these criteria are established, then the judge can proceed to a divorce hearing. As can be seen in the judicial process described earlier, the courts have taken all these steps (mostly steps 1 to 4). Even in cases where conflict arose from the first day of marriage, judges may grant a divorce following syiqaq procedures since the five criteria do not consider the duration or frequency of discord.

In Indonesia, where the Supreme Court once ruled that a divorce petition itself is an indicator of a broken marriage, it is not surprising that judges rule that an unsatisfactory sexual relationship is indicative of a broken marriage when it leads to a petition for divorce.[42] Another Supreme Court ruling, No. 534.K/AG/1996, also influences the judges' legal reasoning. According to this ruling, "The court believes that it is not necessary to look at the cause of the dispute, but whether the household of the plaintiff and the defendant is worth maintaining or not, or whether there is a benefit or not if the plaintiff's and the defendant's household is maintained."[43]

Based on this, Indonesian judges expand the meaning of syiqaq to include sexual dissatisfaction. In a case from the religious court in North Sumatera, the judges reasoned the endless quarrels caused by unsatisfactory sexual relationship made it impossible for the couple to live together: "Considering that with the conditions mentioned above, if the marriage is retained, it will be able to cause misery for the plaintiff or both, the judges argued that despite the marriage being the Sunnah of the Prophet Muhammad which must be followed, but if it turns out that in the household a fight arises and this cannot be eliminated except by divorce, then divorce as an effort to eliminate this misery must take precedence over taking advantage."[44] In all the cases examined in this chapter, the religious court granted the divorce petition for sexual dissatisfaction on grounds of "continuous and irreconcilable discord," referring to the existing legislation described here.

### *Reference to Fiqh: The Marital Bond Should Not Create Harm*

The religious courts also refer to fiqh books to resolve uncertainty in Indonesian law and strengthen their reasoning.[45] In the cases examined here, the judges referred to the principle that "dar'u al-mafāsid muqaddamun 'alā jalb al-maṣāliḥ [preventing mischief is better than bringing benefits],"[46] which is articulated in two works of fiqh, *al-Ashbāh wa al-Naẓā'ir* of al-Suyūṭī[47] and *Hāshiya al-'Aṭṭār 'alā Sharḥ al-Maḥallī 'alā Jam'i al-Jawāmi'* of al-Aṭṭār.[48] In some cases, the courts also referred to a third fiqh book, *Ghāya al-Marām* of Shaikh al-Majdī.[49] They cited the principle, in the third book, that "when the wife is very displeased with her husband, the judge can divorce her from the husband with one divorce." In some cases, the judges referred to the contemporary book *Fiqh al-Sunna*.[50] For example, the judges in the religious courts of South Kalimantan, of East Java, of Central Java, and of East Lombok, wrote that,[51] "in line with the provisions in the laws as mentioned earlier,[[52]] the court must provide the *dalil syar'i* [Islamic legal argumentation] that is written in the book of *Fiqh al-Sunna*, vol. 2, p. 290"; this section reads as follows: "Suppose the divorce petition has already been proven by the wife's evidence or by a husband's confession. In that case, their marital relationship can no longer be maintained because the harm makes it unbearable to continue marital life as husband and wife, and the court cannot reconcile them, the judge pronounces the divorce accordingly."

The judges cited this paragraph for making their decision "more Islamic" and in conformity with shari'a, and they wrote it clearly as a dalil syar'i. However, *Fiqh al-Sunna* does not address divorce on grounds of sexual dissatisfaction but rather establishes that the marriage is broken. In the paragraph cited previously Sābiq discusses divorce for harm (*al-taṭlīq li-l-ḍarar*) by citing the opinion of the Mālikī school, verses from the Qur'an, and a hadith of the Prophet, ostensibly to justify Art. 6 of Egyptian Family Law No. 25/1929 on divorce, from the fiqh perspective (Sābiq, 2004, 654). Indirectly, the Indonesian religious courts "borrowed" this Egyptian law on divorce for harm through *Fiqh al-Sunna*. In the same vein, the religious courts referred indirectly to the Mālikī opinion on divorce for harm to explain syiqaq in the ambiguous Indonesian legislation. By citing the Mālikī opinion and Egyptian law indirectly, the Indonesian courts expanded the meaning of the "continuous and irreconcilable discord" that "broke" a marriage by categorizing "sexual dissatisfaction" as a form of syiqaq, which is a legitimate reason for divorce in Indonesian law.

## Comparison with Other Muslim Countries

Divorce on the grounds of sexual dissatisfaction has not been adequately studied. The closest similarities observed in other Muslim countries are divorce based on impotence or sterility, where we find similar judicial reasoning and legal arguments. Historians have found records of divorce on grounds of impotence in Syria and Palestine in the seventeenth and eighteenth centuries. There divorce for impotence was possible, but the wife had to wait one year and testify before the qadi that she was still a virgin (Tucker, 1994, 272).

Divorce on grounds of impotence is also common in other Muslim countries today. Erin Stiles has found that a satisfying sexual relationship is also considered a necessary element of marriage in Zanzibar, where women sometimes file for divorce before the *kadhi* (Islamic judge) on grounds of lack of sexual activity. Zanzibari courts consider that a fulfilling sexual relationship is a legal requirement of marriage. Petitions on such grounds typically result in divorce (2015). However, Stiles found that Zanzibari women's reason for divorce was usually impotence, which is grounds for divorce according to fiqh (al-Jazīrī 1987, 4:180–198), while the Indonesian cases cited in this chapter were not dealing with impotence (which is a legitimate reason for divorce in Indonesia),[53] but with sexual dissatisfaction. In other words, although the Zanzibari kadhi's reasoning was the same as that of the Indonesian religious court judges, the causes were different (impotence versus lack of sexual satisfaction).

Carolyn Fluehr-Lobban studied divorce on the grounds of impotence in Sudan (1987, 163–166). She found that a wife can file for divorce because of her husband's impotence but the process is complicated, and the burden to prove the husband's impotence is on the wife. A wife must provide medical proof that she is still a virgin and she must live with her husband for one to two years to allow him to attempt to perform sexual activities. In Iran, a husband's impotence is grounds for divorce but with more lenient procedures than in Sudan. For example, Arzoo Osanloo (2009, 130–133) described a case of a woman filing for divorce through faskh due to her husband's impotence. The woman claimed that she shared a bed with her husband but also produced a doctor's virginity certificate. The woman claimed her husband had not touched her for the five months they shared a bed because, according to her, he was impotent, and the court granted her a divorce. In Malaysia, the husband's impotence is also a legitimate reason for divorce, and women can easily file for faskh on grounds of impotence. Michael Peletz observed that impotence was among the chief reasons for faskh in Malaysia in the 1950s and 1960s (2020, 198–199).

Sterility may also be grounds for an Islamic divorce. In Kuwait, a woman asked the mufti (Islamic juristconsult) Shaykh Hasan Murād Mannā‘ if she could file for divorce due to her husband's sterility. Shaykh Mannā‘ responded in his fatwa (Islamic legal opinion) that she could not file for divorce if the husband could perform sexually, although he advised her to end her marriage through khul‘. Here we see that marriage is not just about procreation but also about sexual fulfilment, which is, according to the mufti, an essential part of marriage (Rispler-Chaim 1995, 92–99). This is similar to the seventeenth- and eighteenth-century fatwas of Syrian and Palestinian muftis (al-'Amidī, Ibn 'Abidīn, and al-Ramly), which emphasized the importance of sexual activities in marriage in order to channel sexual desire and satisfy both partners, without any reference to procreation (Tucker 1994).

The classical fiqh acknowledges the importance of female sexual satisfaction, and women are entitled to file for divorce through faskh or khul‘ if they are not satisfied. According to one opinion of the Shāfi‘ī school, a wife has a right (*khiyār*) to end her marriage through faskh if she finds that her husband's genitals are small (al-Māwardī 1994, 9:340.). In the same vein, if a wife finds that her husband's lack of prowess leaves her unsatisfied, she is entitled to divorce through khul‘ (al-Māwardī 1994, 10:5). Moreover, if a husband's premature ejaculation leaves his wife unsatisfied, the wife has right to annul her marriage in court (al-Haythami 2016, 257). Apparently Islamic judges in Indonesian religious courts did not delve into vast Shāfiʿī fiqh literature due to the time constraint.

## Conclusion

This chapter considers the various types of unsatisfactory sexual relationships presented as the reason for initiating divorce proceedings in Indonesia and how judges reason in such disputes. Although sexual dissatisfaction is not a ground for divorce according to Indonesian legislation, judges often grant these divorce requests. As indicated by these examples, Indonesian religious courts understand that there is no clear, specific legislation regarding divorce on the grounds of sexual dissatisfaction. Hence, they base their reasoning on existing legislation. The courts must hear these cases as by law, they cannot refuse claims brought before them. Law No. 48/2009 on Judicial Authority, Art. 10, states that "the court is prohibited from refusing to examine, hear, and decide upon a case filed under the pretext that law is absent or uncertain, but rather shall be obliged to examine and adjudicate it."

Ultimately, the judges in the religious courts extended the meaning of a conjugal bond and expanded the grounds of irrevocable discord in Indonesian legislation, based at least in part on referral to fiqh books and, indirectly, Egyptian laws. In short, religious courts have given a new definition of "continuous and irreconcilable discord" in Art. 19-F of PP No. 9/1975 and Art. 116-F of KHI No. 1/1991: now, sexual dissatisfaction can be interpreted as a form of "irreconcilable discord" (syiqaq).

The chapter shows how when dealing with uncertainty in the law, judges seek to apply only what the law allows. However, they also strive for flexibility in interpreting the law and draw on a variety of legally relevant resources to do so. When a wife who is sexually dissatisfied files for divorce at a religious court, the judges attempt to identify laws that can serve as the basis for adjudication. They are concerned with the practical challenge of resolving social conflicts, including in the field of divorce. If they can find a way to adopt a legal rule to apply to the lawsuit, they will do so. Judges will adjudicate a case based on the witnesses' and disputants' information by referring to the existing written law and then developing legal arguments to support their decision. They seek a formal ruling within existing Indonesian law to suit the needs, the procedure, and the judicial relevance to correctly carry out the "act of judging" (Dupret and Yakin 2018).

### *Acknowledgments*

I thank Euis Nurlaelawati, Stijn Cornelis van Huis, Nadia Sonneveld, Baudouin Dupret, and Erin Stiles for their comments and feedback on an early draft of this chapter, but any errors are mine. The chapter originated in presentations at the International Society for Islamic Legal Studies (ISILS) in Finland in 2018 and the Law and Society Association in Washington, D.C., in 2019.

## NOTES

1. Later, I asked the judges why they had not asked the woman for more information about her problem. They answered that it is always embarrassing to ask litigants about what happened "in the bedroom," so they did not ask for more information (interview, 2016).
2. I was informed later that she had intentionally failed to attend the hearings because of social, cultural, and religious pressure (interview, 2016).
3. The complete file of case No. xxxx/Pdt.G /2016/PA.xx, section: claims of the plaintiff, 4 pages, 2. The x's indicate removed information to protect the people's identity.
4. John Bowen, who, in the 1980s and 1990s conducted legal anthropology research in Aceh that culminated in his book *Islam, Law, and Equality in Indonesia*, told me that in twenty years of research he never came across a divorce case due to sexual dissatisfaction (personal communication, May 10, 2019).
5. The laws apply to non-Muslims too.
6. *Taklik talak* is a conditional divorce pronounced by the husband following the marriage ceremony in order to protect the woman, if he (1) abandons his wife for two consecutive years, (2) fails to provide a monthly family allowance to his wife for three months, (3) commits physical or psychological violence against his wife, or (4) does not pay attention to his wife for six months (continuously).
7. This argument was developed by Dupret, Bouhya, Lindbekk, and Yakin (2019, 405–436).
8. Since Independence, by Law No. 19/1964 and PP No. 14/1970, the Indonesian judicial system has had four courts: civil, religious, military, and administrative courts.
9. Art. 13 A (1–2) of UU PA No. 50 /2009 and the decision of the Constitutional Court No. 43/PUU-XIII/2015 and Regulation of the Supreme Court No. 2/2017 on Judges' Selection.
10. Secretary of the MARI No. 838/SEK/KP.00.2/08/2017, annex 1, No. 01/Pansel/MA/07 /2017, 4.
11. The Regulations of the Supreme Court: PERMA No. 1, /2008, and PERMA No. 1, /2016.
12. This description is based my ethnographic work in the religious court of first instance of South Jakarta, which is the application of Indonesian legislation (UUP No. 1/1974; PP No. 7/1975; KHI No. 1/1991; UU PA No. 7/1989; No. 3/2006; No. 50/2009) in daily routine work of the religious court. Finally, religious courts are obliged to upload their decisions to the online repository of BADILAG MARI. All decisions by the religious courts have been uploaded to the online repository of the Indonesian Supreme Court since the beginning of the 2000s, and this has been compulsory since 2010 (SEMA RI No. 2010 and SEMA RI No. 2014).
13. According to the Central Bureau of Statistics of the Republic of Indonesia, there are 2 million registered marriages annually: 2,289,648 in 2012; 2,210,046 in 2013; 2,110,776 in 2014; 1,958,394 in 2015; and, according to the MORA marriage registration section, 1.9 million respectively in both 2016 and 2017.
14. The number of divorces is drawn from the 2016 annual report of the BADILAG MARI, but my own calculation is slightly different, at 365,628. Every year, according to the BADILAG MARI, 30 percent of marriages culminate in a divorce petition: 346,480 in 2012; 324,247 in 2013; 344,237 in 2014; and 347,256 in 2015.
15. No. xx/Pdt.G, /2011/PA.xxx., from South Sulawesi.
16. No. xxx/Pdt.G/2015/PA.xx., from Yogyakarta.
17. No. xxx/Pdt.G/2016/PA.xx., from Jakarta.

18. Cases from both men and women had been taken into account to see both perspectives; see De Hart, Sonneveld, and Sportel 2017.
19. No. xxxx/Pdt.G/2010/PA.xxx.
20. No. xxx/Pdt.G/2011/PA.xxx.
21. In other words, the plaintiff and the defendant responded to each other before the court following the procedural rules in the divorce process.
22. No. xx/Pdt.G/2013/PA.xxx.
23. No. xxxx/Pdt.G/2014/PA.xxx.
24. No. xxxx /Pdt.G/2010/PA.xxx.
25. No. xxxx/Pdt.G/2007/PA.xxx.
26. *Najis*, from the Arabic, means unclean or impure, and it is applied for wine, alcoholic drinks, dogs, pigs, and so on. In Indonesia, if a husband or a wife calls their spouse *najis*, it means "You are like those animals [dogs, pigs] so I cannot be with you." It implies saying: 'I dislike you because you are disgusting!"
27. Husbands may choose not to attend judgments out of shame.
28. No. xxx/Pdt.G/2011/PA.xxx.
29. No. xx/Pdt.G/2011/PA.xxx.
30. No. xxxx/Pdt.G/2016/PA.xxxx.
31. No. xxx/Pdt.G/PA.xxx.
32. No. xxx/Pdt.G/2011/PA.xxx.
33. No. xxx/Pdt.G/2011/PA.xxx.
34. This explanation could be found in, for example, the case from North Sumatera, No. xx/Pdt.G/PA.xxx, or case No. xxxx/Pdt.G/2016/PA.xx, from Southeast Sulawesi.
35. No. xxxx/Pdt.G/2016/PA.xx.
36. In the twelve cases presented in this chapter, six decisions referred to the Qur'an 30:21.
37. Ali 2009, 693.
38. This is translated from case No. xxxx/Pdt.G/2014/PA.xxx, but similar reasoning is found, for instance, in cases No. xxx/Pdt.G/2011/PA.xxx, No. xxxx/Pdt.G/2013/PA.xxx, No. xxx/Pdt.G/2011/PA.xxx, No. xxx/Pdt.G/2013/PA.xxx.xx, No. xxx/Pdt.G/2011/PA.xxx, and No. xxxx/Pdt.G/2016.PA.xx.
39. This is translated from case No. xxx/Pdt.G/2014/PA.xxx.
40. In other divorce decisions based on sexual dissatisfaction, the judges have referred to other verses such as the Qur'an 33:49 (Central Java, No. xxxx/Pdt.G/2007/PA.xxx), 4:130 (South Kalimantan, No. xxxx/Pdt.G/2016/PA.xxx.), and 2:227 (West Kalimantan No. xxxx/Pdt.G/2014/PA.xxx; Sulawesi No. xxxx/Pdt.G/2016/PA.xx; East Java No. xxx/Pdt.G/2009/PA.xxx; and Central Java No. xxxx/Pdt.G/2013/PA.xx).
41. No. xxxx/Pdt.G/2016/PA.xxx from Bangka Belitung, No. xxx/Pdt.G/2011/PA.xxx from East Java, and No. xxx/Pdt.G/2009/PA.xxx from Madura.
42. No. xxxx/Pdt.G/2016/PA.xxx from Bangka Belitung, No. xxx/Pdt.G/2011/PA.xxx from East Java, and No. xxx/Pdt.G/2009/PA.xxx from Madura.
43. No. xxxx/Pdt.G/2016/PA.xxx from South Kalimantan.
44. No. xx/Pdt.G/2013/PA.xxx., from North Sumatera.
45. In the twelve cases presented here—as in the overall data set of twenty-nine cases—the judges referred to fiqh books: *Ghāya al-Marām* by Shaikh al-Majdī; *Tuḥfa al-Muḥtāj* by Ibn Hajar al-Haythami; two *qawā'id al-fiqhiyya* (Islamic legal maxims) books (*al-Ashbāh wa*

*al-Naẓā'ir* of Jalāluddīn al-Suyūṭī and *Hāshiya al-'Aṭṭār 'alā Sharḥ al-Maḥallī 'alā Jam'i al-Jawāmi'* of Ibn Mahmūd al-Aṭṭār), and to *Aḥkām al-Qur'ān* by al-Qurṭubi.

46. No. xxxx/Pdt.G /2010/PA.xxx from South Kalimantan.
47. No. xx/Pdt.G/2013/PA.xxx from North Sumatera.
48. No. xxxx/Pdt.G/2010/PA.xxx from South Kalimantan.
49. No. xxxx/Pdt.G/2014/PA.Bgl from Bangil, No. xxxx/Pdt.G/2011/PA.Tbn from Tuban, and No. xxxx/Pdt.G/2011/PA.Plh from Pelaihari.
50. *Fiqh al-Sunna* (2004) is a contemporary fiqh manual authored by an Egyptian jurist al-Sayyid Sābiq (1915–2000).
51. No. xxxx/Pdt.G/2011/PA.xxx from South Kalimantan, No. xxxx/Pdt.G/2016/PA.xxx from East Lombok, No. xxxx/Pdt.G/2013/PA.xxx from Central Java, and No. xxxx/Pdt.G/2009/PA.xxx from East Java.
52. Before these articles, the court referred to Art. 22-2 of PP No. 9/1975, Art. 76-1 and Art. 82 of UU PA No. 7/1989, and No. 50/2009. These articles deal with procedural laws that seek to ensure that the process of the religious court has been followed by listening to witnesses, the plaintiff, and the defendant, seeing proof, trying to reconcile the couple, and similar issues.
53. Art. 19 letter E, PP No. 9/1975 and Art. 116 letter E, KHI 1991.

## REFERENCES


Ali, Abdullah Yusuf. 2009. *The Meaning of the Holy Qur'ān*. Leicestershire: Islamic Foundation.

Bowen, John. 2003. *Islam, Law, and Equality in Indonesia*. Cambridge: Cambridge University Press.

Cammack, Mark E., Helen Donovan, and Tim B. Heaton. 2007. "Islamic Divorce Law and Practice in Indonesia." In *Islamic Law in Contemporary Indonesia: Ideas and Institutions*, edited by R. Michael Feener and Mark E. Cammack, 99–127. Cambridge, MA: Harvard University Press.

Cammack, Mark E., and Tim B. Heaton. 2011. "Explaining the Recent Upturn in Divorce in Indonesia: Developmental Idealism and the Effects of Political Changes." *Asian Journal of Social Science* 39:776–796.

Cammack, Mark E., Lawrence A. Young, and Tim B. Heaton. 2010. "The State, Religion, and the Family in Indonesia: The Case of Divorce Reform." In *Family, Religion and Social Change in Diverse Societies*, edited by Sharon K. Houseknecht and Jerry G. Pankhurst, 175–204. New York: Oxford University Press.

Creutzfeldt, Naomi, Marc Mason, and Kirsten MacConachie. 2020. "Socio-Legal Theory and Methods." In *Routledge Handbook of Socio-Legal Study and Methods*, edited by Naomi Creutzfeldt, Marc Mason, and Kirsten MacConachie, 3–8. Oxon: Routledge.

De Hart, Betty, Nadia Sonneveld, and Iris Sportel. 2017. "New Perspectives on Gender in Shari'a-Based Family Law Studies: Moving Beyond the Women's Issue." *Religion and Gender* 7 (1):45–52.

Dupret, Baudouin. 2006. *Droit et sciences sociales*. Paris: Armand Colin.

———. 2007. "What Is Islamic law? A Praxiological Answer and an Egyptian Case Study." *Theory, Culture and Society* 24 (2), (March): 79–100.

———. 2010. "Droit et sciences sociales: Pour une respécification praxéologique." *Droit et Société* 75:315–335.

———. 2011. *Adjudication in Action: An Ethnomethodology of Law, Morality and Justice*. London: Ashgate.

Dupret, Baudouin, Maurits Berger, and Laila al-Zwaini. 1999. "Introduction." In *Legal Pluralism in the Arab World*, edited by Baudouin Dupret, Maurits Berger, and Laila al-Zwaini, xi–xviii. The Hague: Kluwer Law International.

Dupret, Baudouin, Adil Bouhya, Monika Lindbekk, and Ayang Utriza Yakin. 2019. "Filling Gaps in Legislation: The Use of *Fiqh* by Contemporary Courts in Morocco, Egypt, and Indonesia." *Islamic Law and Society* 26 (3):405–436.

Dupret, Baudouin, and Ayang Utriza Yakin. 2018. "La Praxeologie du droit: Mise en perspective et mis en pratique." In *Etnographies du raisonnment juridique*, edited by Julie Colemans and Baudouin Dupret, 223–242. Paris: LGDJ.

Fluehr-Lobban, Carolyn. 1987. *Islamic Law and Society in the Sudan*. London: Routledge.

Heaton, Tim B., Mark R. Cammack and Larry Young. 2001. "Why Is the Divorce Rate Declining in Indonesia?" *Journal of Marriage and Family* 63 (May): 480–490.

al-Haythami, Ibn Ḥajar. 2016. *Tuḥfa al-Muḥtāj bi-Sharḥ al-Minhāj*. Vol. 3. Beirut: Dār al-Kutub al-'Ilmiyya.

Hisyam, Muhammad. 2002. "The Interaction of Religion and State in Indonesia: The Case of Islamic Courts." In *Islam in the Era of Globalization: Muslim Attitudes towards Modernity and Identity*, edited by Johan Meuleman, 218–230. London: Routledge.

Hurgronje, C. Snouck. 1906. *The Achehnese*. Translated by A. W. S. O'Sullivan. 2 vols. Leiden: Brill.

al-Jazīrī, 'Abd Raḥmān. 1987. *Kitāb al-Fiqh 'Alā Madhāhib al-Arba'a*. Vol. 4. Beirut: Dār al-Fikr.

Lev, Daniel S. 1972. *Islamic Courts in Indonesia: A Study in the Political Bases of Legal Institutions*. Berkeley: University of California Press.

———. 2000. *Legal Evolution and Political Authority in Indonesia*. The Hague: Kluwer Law International.

al-Māwardī, Abū al-Ḥasan 'Aly. 1994. *al-Hāwī al-Kabīr Sharḥ Mukhtaṣar al-Muzannī*. Vols. 9, 10. Beirut: Dār al-Kutub al-'Ilmiyya.

Nakamura, Hisako. 1993. *Divorce in Java: A Study of the Dissolution of Marriage among Javanese Muslims*. Yogyakarta: Gadjah Mada University Press.

———. 2006. *Conditional Divorce in Indonesia*. Cambridge, MA: Harvard University Press, Islamic Legal Studies Program.

Nasir, Mohamad Abdun. 2013. "Islamic Law and Social Change: The Religious Court and the Dissolution of Marriage among Muslims in Lombok, Indonesia." PhD thesis, Emory University.

Nurlaelawati, Euis. 2010. *Modernization, Tradition and Identity: The Kompilasi Hukum Islam and Legal Practice in the Indonesian Religious Courts*. Amsterdam: University of Amsterdam Press.

———. 2013. "Muslim Women in Indonesian Religious Courts: Reform, Strategies, and Pronouncement of Divorce." *Islamic Law and Society* 20 (3):242–271.

Osanloo, Arzoo. 2009. *The Politics of Women's Rights in Iran*. Princeton: Princeton University Press.

Peletz, Michael G. 2020. *Sharia Transformations. Cultural Politics and the Rebranding of an Islamic Judiciary*. Oakland: University of California Press.

Rispler-Chaim, Vardit. 1995. "Hasan Murād Mannā', Childbearing and the Rights of the Wife." *Islamic Law and Society* 2 (1):92–99.

Riyani, Irma. 2020. *Islam, Women's Sexuality and Patriarchy in Indonesia: Silent Desire*. London: Routledge.

Sābiq, al-Sayyid. 1425/2004. *Fiqh al-Sunna*. Cairo: Dār al-Hadīts.

Stiles, Erin E. 2015. "Unsuitable Husbands: Allegations of Impotence in Zanzibari Divorce Suits." In *Gendered Lives of Western Indian Ocean: Islam, Marriage, and Sexuality on the*

*Swahili Coast*, edited by Erin E. Stiles and Katrina Daly Thompson, 245–268. Athens: Ohio University Press.

Tucker, Judith E. 1994. "Muftis and Matrimony: Islamic Law and Gender in Ottoman Syria and Palestine." *Islamic Law and Society* 1 (3):265–300.

van Huis, Stijn Cornelis. 2015. "Islamic Courts and Women's Divorce Rights in Indonesia: The Cases of Cianjur and Bulukumba." PhD thesis, Universiteit Leiden.

———. 2019. "*khul*' over the Longue Durée: The Decline of Traditional *Fiqh*-Based Divorce Mechanisms in Indonesian Legal Practice." *Islamic Law and Society* 26 (1–2):58–82.

Yakin, Ayang Utriza. 2015. "The Register of the Qadi Court '*Kiyahi Pĕqih Najmuddin*' of the Sultanate of Bantĕn, 1754–1756 CE." *Studia Islamika* 22 (3):405–442.

———. 2016a. "The Transliteration and Translation of the Leiden Manuscript Cod.Or. 5626 on the *Sijill* of the Qadi of Banten, 1754–1756 CE." *Heritage of Nusantara* 5, no. 1 (June): 23–76.

———. 2016b. "Undhang-Undhang Bantĕn: A 17th- to 18th-century legal compilation from the qadi court of the Sultanate of Bantĕn." *Indonesia and the Malay World* 44 (130): 365–388.

# 5

# "I Divorced Him but He Said He Has Not Divorced Me"

## Gendered Perspectives on Muslim Divorce in Accra, Ghana

FULERA ISSAKA-TOURE

The title of this chapter is a revealing window into women's experiences of Islamic divorce processes and procedures in Accra, the capital city of Ghana. The statement, "I divorced him, but he said he has not divorced me" was voiced by an interlocutor during my fieldwork, and it reflects the common situation of women who want to leave their marriage but are unable to do so because their husbands do not agree.

Divorce and remarriage are both common and accepted among Muslims in Accra.[1] In classical Islamic law, men and women have different options in divorce. If a Muslim man wants to divorce his wife, he can simply repudiate her. However, if a woman wants to divorce her husband, she must go through a court to request a divorce or she must convince her husband to repudiate her. One form of divorce that a woman may request is *khul'*, which is often understood as a divorce "purchased" by women whose husbands do not want to separate. As many scholars have noted, a common feature of khul' in many countries is that a woman must return or give up her *mahr*—dower or, sometimes, bridewealth—in exchange for repudiation (Mir-Hosseini 2000, 2009, 2015; Ali 2006, 2010; Sonneveld and Stiles 2019).

The practical application of Islamic family law varies across Muslim societies, however. Research in legal anthropology in Muslim communities has indicated that laws—both in theory and in practice—respond to the needs of society. Much of this research has shown that the practical application of laws can alter the theory, in that practical issues on the ground can have a great effect on legal reasoning (Fluehr-Lobban 1987; Hirsch 1998; Stiles 2009).

To understand any form of legal reasoning, including the practical application of Islamic family law, the cultural context must be considered. Such an approach foregrounds the historical trajectories of particular settings that can lead to new interpretations and particular applications of law. Thus, it is enlightening to study Islamic family law not from the angle of legal statutes, but rather from the practical application of the law (Ewing 1988; Haeri 1989; Messick 1993; Tucker 2008 Bowen 1996, 2000; Peletz 2002; Stiles 2009).

Given the gendered inequities in classical Islamic family law (Schacht 1964), it might be expected that women have few options in marriage and divorce. However, a number of studies on Islamic family law in practice have shown that Muslim women contest classical theories of the law. Such research has shown that across cultures, Muslim women are largely not passive recipients of the law but rather active participants in bringing the law to life (Tucker 2008; Hirsch 1998, 2010; Mir-Hosseini 2000; Stiles 2009).

In this chapter, I discuss the various ways in which Muslim women in Accra, Ghana, employ different procedures of divorce. The chapter raises particular questions concerning the tensions that arise between divorce in practice and the rules articulated in Islamic jurisprudential sources. In particular, the chapter seeks to understand broader notions of Islamic law from the "bottom up" (Stiles 2018, 121–123). Erin Stiles's works highlight the ways in which "everyday actors" describe what is legal and differentiate between the authorities who play active roles in dispute resolution (2009, 2018).

This chapter is based on empirical research that was carried out over several months among Muslims of Accra. Data was collected from 2007 to 2008 and 2014 to 2019. The chapter draws on my observations at mediation centers, personal narrations at mediation centers, and informal conversations and interviews with over 120 Muslim women and men. I used English and other languages, including Hausa, in data collection. However, the use of Hausa dominated because it is the most widely spoken language in the various Muslim communities of Accra, which are known as the Zongos. All translations of Hausa are my own. Although my data was gathered from both men and women, the analysis in this chapter derives mainly from female experiences of divorce. Throughout the chapter pseudonyms are used for all interlocutors for privacy reasons.

In Ghana's pluralistic legal framework, Islamic family law is considered part of customary law and is therefore allowed to operate informally, without any direct state supervision; the state only becomes an interested party in the application of customary laws when an aspect of customary law infringes on human rights. Most Muslim marriages are largely concluded customarily, but a few take the form of "ordinance marriage."[2] By law, all marriages—ordinance and customary—must be registered with the state.

In similar fashion, customary divorce procedures are covered under Ghana's customary laws. As such, various legal options for divorce—both customary and common law—are available to Muslims. Muslims can therefore decide on accessing *malamai* (Islamic religious authorities; singular *malam*) or using another method (Opoku 1976; Essien 1994; Wanitzek 1994; Issaka-Toure 2018).

## Divorce Procedures and Muslim Women's Reactions to Divorce

This section discusses locally acceptable forms of *saki*, which is the local term for divorce by male repudiation (in Arabic, *ṭalāq*), and *khulʿ*, the term used by Malamai to describe divorce initiated by women. The section first addresses how saki takes place and women's reactions to repudiations. Then, I discuss divorces initiated by women. In this section, the complications that arise with regard to khulʿ and saki will be made evident.

### *Saki: Male Unilateral Repudiation*

My research shows that although saki is a legally acceptable form of Islamic divorce, Muslim women of Accra do not allow divorce through repudiation to take place without contesting it. Especially if they are not ready for divorce, they will look for ways of preventing repudiations. However, they are not always successful.

In my interactions with and observations of Muslims in Accra, it emerged that repudiation has two forms: written and verbal. A husband may either write or state, "I divorce you," and mention his wife's name. Some husbands may repeat the same sentence three times. My interactions with lay Muslims revealed that in common understanding, stating or writing it only once means such divorce is revocable but stating or writing it three times signifies an irrevocable divorce; this is known locally as *saki uku* or *triple ṭalāq*. Malamai find the former legitimate but question the legitimacy of triple ṭalāq.

Divorce practices among Muslims in Accra are undergirded by gendered power relationships. Muslim men can legitimately repudiate women without any reason, yet despite this fact, Muslim women contest these declarations of divorce on several grounds. For example, Muslim women sometimes consult malamai to intervene on their behalf for reconciliation in cases of saki because they are unprepared for separation. My observations at a mediation center showed that women often find allies in the malamai. Although malamai do not challenge the legality of saki, they often find saki quite hard to accept and try to prevent it. However, they are not always successful at discouraging saki due to the legal impediments they face. The malamai can only attempt to reconcile couples when a woman requests intervention in matters of saki. In some cases the malamai are successful but in others they are not.

In the case of repudiations, only women consult the malamai since they are the ones who seek reconciliation after being repudiated. The experience of a woman I will call Bushira is typical. She sought the intervention of malamai in her repudiation because she wanted to remain in the marriage, though clearly her husband did not. Bushira reported the case to the Ahlu Sunnah Wal Jama'a (ASWAJ), a popular Islamic religious authority in Accra.[3] A meeting was set with her and her husband to start hearing the case. When Bushira presented her case, she claimed that she did not know why her husband was repudiating her and stated that all she wanted was for him to rescind his repudiation.

The sitting malam pleaded on Bushira's behalf and attempted to convince her husband to retract the saki. However, his attempt to reconcile the couple failed and the malam ended the session and scheduled another meeting with hopes that time would help in some ways. At the next session, all attempts by the malam again proved futile. Consequently, the repudiation took effect. As is the local practice, the woman must be given *alkhairi*, a sum of money as farewell gift from the husband.[4] The alkhairi depends on the husband's financial capacity and his will. Bushira's husband suggested an amount that did not satisfy her. After the meeting, Bushira contacted the malam and argued that her husband was wealthier than he claimed. She also argued that she needed more money than what he had offered in order to establish a business. She requested an amount of 6,000 Ghana cedis (around 1,500 USD at the time). On the day of settlement, the husband bargained over the amount and they finally settled on 4,800 Ghana cedis (a little over 1,000 USD) as alkhairi.[5]

A second instance of repudiation involves a woman I will call Salamatu. Repudiated by her husband, Salamatu also reported the saki to the ASWAJ malamai. According to Salamatu, her husband falsely accused her of encouraging their daughter to escape from the husband he had selected for her. Salamatu denied this. She argued that if she had wanted to do so, it would have been when her husband took the daughter out of school at the age of sixteen to marry her off to a relative in a neighboring country. Salamatu said she believed their daughter should have remained in school, but she did not want to have any problem with her husband so she overlooked his curtailment of her daughter's education. After having a child, their daughter left the marriage and came back to Accra. Salamatu said that her husband accused her of forcing their daughter to leave the marriage and thus she believes the repudiation was her punishment. When Salamatu brought the complaint to the malamai, her husband was invited to attend but he did not heed the call. Thus, his repudiation became binding.[6]

### *Women's Responses to Saki*

My interviews reveal that repudiation is clearly considered a legally acceptable form of divorce. The socioreligious practice of saki empowers men and disempowers women, who are ostensibly partners in marital relationships but do not have the same advantages in pursuing divorce. This inequity suggests a weaker position for Muslim women and hence forms the basis for raising the malamai's alarm bells whenever an episode of saki occurs. Salamatu's experience, for example, brings up the important dimension of a child's right to education, which would have been a significant reason for her to prevent her daughter's marriage in the first place. However, the helplessness she felt due to the gendered power relations prevented her from acting.

In Accra, Muslim women's responses to repudiations are characterized by feelings of powerlessness intertwined with both the pain of potential divorce and the hope for reconciliation. It seems clear that some Muslim men utilize their right to repudiate without any concern about the impact on their wives. This places women in a difficult situation since a husband needs to provide no reason for repudiation and can repudiate a wife at any time. As my interviews revealed, the women felt disillusioned by their husbands' decisions and contested them, albeit not always successfully.

Salamatu and Bushira's stories are instructive about the experience of repudiation. First, they point out that husbands can either pronounce or write "I divorce you" without any regard for their wives' opinions or preferences. Second, both cases involve women who were unprepared for divorce. Salamatu's case is an especially poignant illustration, as she believed her husband divorced her because of the part she supposedly played in her daughter's actions. One may infer that both Bushira and Salamatu sought reconciliation because of their emotional investment or unpreparedness for sudden divorce. These women's experiences illustrate the limitations of female agency within the context of repudiation. Clearly, even the financial negotiations allow very little space for women's agency.

Furthermore, stating or writing "I divorce you" three times cripples women's agency and raises concern among the malamai. The women I talked to about their experiences of triple ṭalāq indicated their sense of extreme helplessness even if they consulted a malam. The malamai abhor the practice of triple ṭalāq as un-Islamic and they frequently try to intervene. However, their intervention depends on the decisions of men who engage in such practices. In other words, regardless of whether ṭalāq is spoken or written, it is only the husband who can rescind it. The following cases show that sometimes husbands will do so.

Rabi's husband, who was convinced by a malam to rescind his decision, is a good example. Rabi sought Malam Ushau's intervention in a repudiation she received from her husband. Malam Ushau invited Rabi's husband to see him, and the husband rescinded his decision following the malam's intervention. Rabi's experience indicates that there is always a possibility that husbands will rescind their repudiations.

Memuna's experience of having her husband withdraw a triple ṭalāq through a malam's intervention is also illustrative. Memuna received a verbal pronouncement of triple ṭalāq and sought Malam Fari's intervention. The malam's efforts resulted in Memuna's husband rescinding his decision. According to Malam Fari, although the practice of triple ṭalāq is prevalent among Muslims, is it not properly Islamic. He explains that if ṭalāq appears three times in one session, then it is not an Islamic practice. With this perspective from Malam Fari and further discussions of the reasons for Memuna's husband's triple ṭalāq, an amicable settlement was reached. In Memuna's experience, we see that while husbands' power to exercise triple ṭalāq is consonant with the dominant understanding by lay Muslims, it is not in line with the understanding of Islamic religious authorities (as will be discussed later in the chapter).

Furthermore, men may use saki (repudiation) in two different ways Aside from the popular understanding that it is only husbands who have the power to repudiate, I found that malamai also sometimes use repudiation. In my interactions with the malamai of ASWAJ, I learned that they can employ ṭalāq if a husband refuses to repudiate his wife. This may happen if a malam is absolutely convinced that such a marriage is not workable. This specific situation of saki highlights a broader understanding of the concept beyond common knowledge among Muslims.

### *Divorces Initiated by Women*

The second type of divorce experienced by Muslims in Accra is female-initiated divorce, which is known as khulʿ by the malamai. However, it is vital to clarify that neither women nor malamai use the Arabic term "khulʿ" in the process of hearings or adjudications. Women only want to be divorced through malamai and do not use the term. It was when I sought for clarification after adjudication processes that the malamai mentioned khulʿ and explained it to me. However, my interactions with malamai indicated that they generally use khulʿ as part of their adjudication but that it does not appear literally in proceedings because of the common use of the Hausa generic term *rabuwa*, meaning separation. According to the malamai, an application of khulʿ happens when a woman initiates a divorce. Essentially, malamai in Accra refer to any divorce initiated by a woman as khulʿ.

The following two excerpts from interviews illustrate how and why Muslim women initiate divorce in Accra. According to Salama:

> My husband is very aggressive, and it worsened when he lost his job. I am a seamstress, so I took all the financial responsibilities. He can suddenly break communication without any offence. But since I realized that was his nature, I tried to adjust. He also has the habit of withholding sex. Sometimes we will sleep in the same room for two weeks without sex. He may satisfy himself outside, but I cannot do that since I am a woman. When I complained, he said he was not a dog to be climbing a woman all the time. One night, I wanted to discuss this issue, which was disturbing me with him, [but] he pushed me and I fell on the floor. He then dragged me and said if I did not keep quiet he would beat me. I then managed to run out of the room to an imam [Islamic religious leader] who was our neighbor. This happened at midnight. My parents later came in to settle the issue with his [husband's] parents, but it did not work after their arbitration. That was what happened, and I divorced him through the office of ASWAJ.[7]

Sauratu, of Lapaz, narrated her story as follow:

> This man [indicating her husband] deals in cocaine and he womanizes a lot. Initially, I did not want to marry him, and my mother was also not in favor. I met him in person though. During dating, my fiancé used to tip my father's family; so they pressured me and they did the wedding. He goes out and comes at dawn. When I indicate my displeasure, his response was

> I know what he does. In the first four months of the marriage, he beat me up because of his girlfriend and later brought the police to arrest me because I fought his girlfriend. In the second year of our marriage, I went home [to her own family] four times and it has been continuing. Meanwhile, he accepted my proposal to stop dealing in drugs before the marriage. Now that he is saying I cannot tell him the type of work to do and he cannot stop, I will divorce him. What he does is un-Islamic, and I am not ready to have a share of his deeds in the hereafter. As a wife, I played my role to the best of my knowledge. What I want from ASWAJ is to initiate the divorce process since I am no longer interested in the relationship.[8]

Both interviews reveal that women are aware of the functional application of Islamic divorce laws and know how to follow those procedures. This knowledge gives women the ability to be active participants in the practical application of Islamic family law. When they initiate divorce, Muslim women are in a legally unquestionable position because seeking divorce is legally permissible according to Islamic jurisprudential sources and local Muslim practice. The experience of Salama and Sauratu also indicates that Muslim women are active parties in negotiating marriage and divorce.

Still, unlike saki, if a Muslim woman does not have a convincing reason for initiating divorce, she will not do so. Both Sarautu and Salama had unambiguously convincing claims against their husbands that enabled them to win their cases. Both cases involve ethical concerns of Muslim women, but they differ in key ways. Salama's complaint had to do with sex, an important factor in an Islamic marriage. When a husband withholds sex from his wife, it becomes an issue of particular concern in a marriage and a valid reason for seeking divorce according to the malamai, much like the physical abuse and extramarital relationship that Salama described (for parallels on sexual dissatisfaction in Indonesia, see Yakin's chapter in this volume). Her case indicates his failure to maintain her, which is another permissible reason for divorce.

Sauratu's ethical concern deals with her husband's drug dealing. She describes it as "un-Islamic" because it causes harm to others and raises issues of safety. Safety in this sense applies both personally for Sauratu as an individual and, as I gathered in the field, for other families who might experience abuse from drug dealers. Sauratu's grievance underscores the breach of trust and insecurity she felt when her husband refused to give up dealing drugs and even caused her arrest when she confronted his girlfriend.

Both women's stories show that there are various levels of negotiating marital issues. Both women went through series of procedures: they first sought family interventions before initiating divorce with the malamai. It is important to reiterate that the women did not mention the term *khul'*. My research indicates that the term is not part of Muslim women's common knowledge and was only used by malamai when I asked for an explanation of their arbitration procedures. This demonstrates how contexts impact the understanding of concepts.

Furthermore, the explanation of khulʿ given by the malamai is very broad. This means that there could be complications in how khulʿ is used because there is no standard understanding among either malamai or women for women who initiate Islamic divorce. Women's strategies for divorce are in the next section for the insight they can provide on the theoretical debates about khulʿ.

## Women's Disadvantage in Divorce and the Power of the Malamai

The cases of repudiation and female-initiated divorce illustrate power imbalances in Muslim marital relationships that do not go unnoticed by the malamai. Ghanaian understandings of Islamic divorce law disempower women by only permitting them access to divorce through the malamai's mediation. The malamai are clearly concerned with the male prerogative in divorce and the use of saki in particular. And as we have seen, neither Muslim women nor the malamai leave their power unchecked.

A Muslim woman's relatively weak position in marital bargaining is evidenced in her negotiations of reconciliation after saki and in negotiating the farewell money. Muslim women's insecurity in marital relationships is based in the ease with which a husband can easily write or pronounce the words, "I divorce you." When the divorce pronouncement is confirmed, the husband is usually the sole determiner of the amount of the farewell money. The link between pronouncing "I divorce you" and determining the amount of the farewell money illustrates women's weaker position in relation to divorce. Indeed, the farewell money can actually deprive women of some material gains since husbands have greater say in the amount despite the space for women to negotiate.

Furthermore, women are often not ready for divorce when they are repudiated, and there are emotional consequences from this experience. My field research shows that despite the pain of repudiation, both women and the malamai accept that "that is how things are done." In other words, the prevailing perspective is something to the effect that the law is the law and no one can do anything about it. The cases indicate the difficulty for Muslim women who face repudiation since it may happen without any apparent reason. As women often articulated to me in informal conversations in the field, men marry women and they can divorce women.

However, Muslim women's consultation of malamai complicates the question of power. First, women contest men's power when they seek the malamai's intervention to encourage their husbands to rescind repudiation. Second, Islamic religious authorities contest the male power of saki by encouraging reconciliation, even though they are not always successful. The malamai's crucial intervention serves as a form of check on the male abuse of power vis-à-vis repudiations in

Islamic family law. This can be seen in Malam Fari's intervention, which resulted in bringing about a reconciliation between Memuna and her husband.

The cases presented in this chapter demonstrate how in Accra power is vested in the hands of the malamai. However, a Muslim's submission to the authority of the malamai is voluntary, not mandatory. Hence, Salamatu's husband could refuse to heed their call. This quandary indicates the difficulty the malamai face when the issue of men's power to repudiate arises. As the malamai perceive this male privilege to be sacrosanct, they can only use their powers of persuasion in encouraging reconciliation.

Ghana's legally pluralistic context further complicates the difficulties the malamai face. A Muslim's decision to resort to the malamai is not a state-sanctioned legal duty but rather a voluntary and socioreligious act. As such, the malamai cannot compel the parties—either the complainant or the respondent—to heed their call or abide by their decisions. Women often make the personal decision to report cases to the malamai, but some Muslim men decide not to submit themselves to the malamai's call, and hence their repudiations are deemed valid. Despite this reality, the malamai appear to hold a very respectable position in Accra's Muslim communities, and in a sense they are the vehicles that keep communities in constant change because they enable Islamic family law to function.

My field research revealed that it is nearly always women who seek the assistance of the malamai in divorce matters. In the communities, women's propensity to bring the matters before the malamai is often interpreted by some malamai and some husbands as a mark of impatience and emotionalism. However, women who find themselves dealing with saki or khulʿ do not perceive themselves as either impatient or emotional. Rather, they consider seeking help from the malamai to be a valid response to the legal predicament in which they find themselves.

## "Structural Divorce" and "Marriage on Top of Marriage"

This section discusses a particular kind of contested divorce procedure that Muslim women resort to in Accra. I will reference what Erin Stiles has termed "structural divorce" (2005), a concept emanating out of her ethnographic study of Muslim women's use of Islamic courts in Zanzibar, East Africa. Discussing structural divorce and its use in the Accra context, which an interlocutor called marriage on top of marriage, will aid in advancing this chapter's arguments about female divorce procedures and the broader ways in which women seek redress beyond established understanding of female-initiated divorce, such as khulʿ. The practice of marriage on top of marriage signals Muslim women's contestations of and resistance to the terms of divorce and remarriage in Accra.

In Stiles's work on legal reasoning in Zanzibar, she uses the term "structural divorce" to indicate situations in which an official divorce has not occurred but women assume it has taken place because certain structural actions that typically accompany divorce have occurred (2005, 588–591). I employ this concept to illuminate the manner in which divorces in Accra have occurred through unconventional or unofficial procedures yet ended in marriage on top of marriage, or in effect, remarriage without an official divorce. Within the context of this study, an "official" divorce denotes going through the socially acceptable procedure.

I will argue that in Accra, although local understandings of Islam do not legally sanction marriage on top of marriage, people in the community recognize this as a legitimate process. In such cases, women who have not gone through the legally acceptable procedure of Islamic divorce, but rather divorced their husbands through cultural assumptions of divorce, have then remarried them.

As Stiles indicated, there are certain social practices in Zanzibar that show the status of a woman's divorce, regardless of whether she has evidence of a repudiation. This could be the point when a woman is told by her husband to move from her matrimonial home to her parents' home—to "go home"—or when he throws her belongings out of the matrimonial home (2005, 582). In Zanzibar, then, women interpret certain structural elements of divorce as evidence of a male repudiation. In Accra, the significance of a wife being told to "go home" is also very important. However, here I focus on women's actions that indicate female-initiated divorce.

In Accra, the phrases "she has gone home" or "I have gone home" carry a great deal of meaning in relation to women's divorce procedures. The former indicates others' designation of a woman's voluntary desertion of her matrimonial home while the latter is used in a woman's own narration of her experiences or action of abandoning her matrimonial home. Another designation commonly used is *hijra*.[9] Hijra means to flee from a husband's home. The use of "hijra," "she has gone home," or "I have gone home" have the same ramification when used in relation to women's divorce procedures and indicates a woman's intention to divorce her husband. Initially, a woman's hijra is surrounded by shame and secrecy. Usually, the men feel ashamed for not meeting social expectations while the women suffer shame because returning home has many unspoken implications, such as the implication that she was neither patient nor courteous enough to keep the secrets of her home.

Hijra can occur in instances of a husband's desertion or his maltreatment of his wife. For example, after twelve years of marriage, Naima went home for the first and last time after an episode of physical abuse. In other instances, women return home due to their husbands' inadequate care for them and the home. Nadia, for example, spoke of her experience of "going home" because her husband did not give her the emotional and financial care she expected.[10] In such circumstances, women return to their natal family homes or, when they are financially capable, they move into their own apartments.

Sometimes a husband pursues his wife through family elders and talks of possible reconciliation begin. If a wife insists that she will not return to the matrimonial home, there could be a settlement on verbally agreed terms or a divorce. Elders of the families of husband and wife lead such talks but the parents of the couple are not usually directly involved. When elders attempt reconciliation, both parties discuss their grievances. If a solution is found, the woman will return to her husband. In instances where an amicable settlement cannot be found and a woman insists on divorce while her husband refuses, then she will continue to stay with her natal family or on her own. After waiting for a while, a husband may eventually give in to his wife's demands and repudiate her. Alternatively, a woman may choose to go through the divorce procedures with the malamai that were described in the previous section. In other cases, however, the community simply assumes that a woman is officially divorced and can remarry if she decides to do so. However, as we shall see, in such cases problems may arise.

The cases of Baba, Sadik, and Samia illustrate a "structural divorce" that ended in a marriage on top of marriage. Baba had one wife, Samia, during my early interactions with him. However, during my later interactions with him it emerged that he had married a second wife. Before marrying Baba, Samia had been married to Sadik for over fifteen years; Samia and Sadik did not have any children. At one point in their relationship, Sadik traveled abroad and, because of legal troubles, he was detained in prison. After a few years of waiting, Samia decided to "go home." She went home and settled for a while, and then she met Baba and married him. A few months into the marriage, Sadik reappeared and maintained that he had not divorced Samia and so Baba should release her to come back to him. He made all possible attempts through Islamic religious authorities and other family elders, but his efforts were to no avail and he finally gave up.[11]

I gathered from the family elders that Samia went home on grounds of desertion. They specifically indicated that from the time she went home, she stayed for some time without any contact from Sadik. As a result, they understood divorce to have taken place and she was able to move on with her life. Even if she eventually heard from Sadik and refused to reconcile with him, her action would still be considered legitimate.

Moreover, the malam who handled Samia's case indicated to me that according to a prophetic tradition, a woman who is deserted by her husband for a period of three months has every right to divorce him. Therefore, although Samia's divorce happened in a different way, it was akin to khulʿ from the perspective of the malam. Furthermore, such cases must be understood in relation to their own circumstances and each case has its own merit. There are thus different dimensions of legal reasoning that include the circumstances of each case, and cultural assumptions play a vital role in legal reasoning. This is a clear indication of a circumstantial understanding of khulʿ.

Notably, the malamai conduct these marriages on top of marriages just like any other marriage. During my fieldwork I encountered similar cases. In another case of "going home," Zainab waited for several years for her husband to return from abroad. In the meantime, she got pregnant and went home thereafter. Although these two cases relate to husbands' absences and, in the case of Zainab, a pregnancy, it by no mean suggests that going home has to do with childbearing and husbands' absence. There are numerous instances in which other reasons—including a woman's lack of interest in her husband—have culminated in going home. Also, sometimes going home is involuntary, as a husband may ask his wife to go home and, just like what Stiles described in Zanzibar (2005, 591), in Accra this is also considered a sign of repudiation.

The phrases "hijra," "I have gone home," and "she has gone home" have the same meaning and are usually related to a woman's protestation of something in her marriage or her declaration of an intent to divorce. I have noticed that these situations usually result from the husband's deviation from socially accepted practices in marriage. When men fall short of marital expectations, women will protest by "going home."[12] In some instances, however, certain other events could be a factor in women's going home, as we saw in Zainab's case.

A woman's hijra is initially surrounded by shame and secrecy for both husband and wife. This sometimes leads to a woman keeping her hijra private in the early stages. Nonetheless, this atmosphere of shame indicates the existence of expected standards that must be met by both parties in a marriage. Men are expected to care for their families emotionally and financially and women are expected to stay calm and persevere in the marriage. Women often find perseverance burdensome if their husbands are not meeting their expectations, such as providing for the family.

Such social expectations also serve as the way in which the Muslim communities in Accra attempt to socially police married couples. In a sense, marriage in the context of the Muslim communities in Accra, like other communities across Ghana, is not between two individuals but rather is communal. Thus, for families that came together to contract the union, the instance of going home reflects poorly on both families because it is not simply an individual affair.

I propose that going home is a kind of silent protest by women that actually speaks volumes and makes women's voices louder. Women usually have the benefit of family support when marital grievances arise, which can lead to separation. Although the possibility of reconciliation is a means of dealing with the public shame of going home, women often demonstrate their objections to mistreatment by their husbands by refusing reconciliation. Indeed, this factor contributes to marriage on top of marriage. If men are unwilling to release them through divorce, then women may feel that they have the right to move on with their lives by simply remarrying.

I argue that going home is both a symbolic construct and a voluntary female behavior that contests male power and privilege in divorce. It is a particular kind of female reaction to Islamic family law on gendered terms. This is very clear in Samia's case, which concluded in marriage on top of marriage. Despite the fact that her marriage to Baba was legitimized by Malamai, it was legally challenged by her former husband, Sadik.

At this juncture, it is critical to question the legality of marriage on top of marriage. When I posed this question to the malamai and in informal conversations with lay Muslims, I did not get one straightforward answer. Rather, people often responded by making a rhetorical point about *zinā* (fornication or adultery). In other words, if a woman "goes home" she could end up in an illicit sexual relationship—zinā—so marriage on top of marriage is preferable. In general, both malamai and lay people felt it was better to remarry than to fornicate. This position validates going home as a particular kind of lawful divorce. Furthermore, the malamai used this argument to legitimate such marriages. In other words, zinā is a sin while marriage on top of marriage is lawful.

As such, the malamai who argue that marriage is better than zinā ultimately present us with a thought-provoking perspective on understanding Islamic family law on divorce. Women did not consider their actions unlawful according to Islamic law. Rather, they emphasized their needs and the nature of God's justice. This response from Muslim women demonstrates how female agency can sometimes bend legal or religious interpretations to their benefit. Studying divorce practice on the ground highlights a particular mode of understanding and applying Islamic divorce law.

However, in some cases, structural divorces did not end in marriage on top of marriage but rather in a dispute over whether a woman is married or divorced. Larmie's experience illustrates this situation. Larmie was married to Abu, but eventually she went home for a prolonged period; Abu did not follow her or ask her to return to the matrimonial home. Larmie became involved with another man, which almost resulted in marriage. However, someone informed the other man that Larmie was not legally divorced, and as a result he withdrew his marriage proposal.[13]

Larmie's experience underscores the ambivalent situations in which women can find themselves when initiating divorce. It is critical to understand that gender plays a significant role in the divorce process. Whereas men can pronounce or write, "I divorce you," women are expected to go through a legal process. However, some women, such as Larmie, go through some form of structural divorce, which may or may not be successful in changing their marital status.

Although these social practices of divorce can result from husbands asking their wives to go home, which would signify repudiation, it is important to make clear that this cultural understanding of Islamic divorce is particular to this context. In this case, "I have gone home," "she has gone home," or "hijra" indicate the local understanding of female-initiated divorce. Going home is understood as the first sign of female-initiated divorce in that it signals a woman's intention to divorce. Although there are sometimes verbally agreed-upon terms between the family elders of the couple intended to bring about reconciliation, a women's intention to divorce is made clear by her actions. Moreover, husbands' treatment of wives is a typical yardstick of women's marital dissatisfaction. In this regard, husbands' lack of commitment to certain expectations of marriage, such as providing for the family, results in female resistance.

## Conclusion

This chapter is a modest empirical contribution to the study of Islamic divorce law. I have attempted to juxtapose the theory of the law with the application of the law. To this end, the chapter presents an argument about the different levels of power relationships with regard to divorce in Accra. It is evident that while Muslim women in Accra understand and accept gendered differences in divorce law, they also contest these inequities in diverse ways.

The chapter examined male- and female-initiated divorce. While the former, saki, seems clear cut and straightforward, the latter frequently is not. In particular, Muslim women do not usually use the term khulʿ; rather, it is the malamai who identify certain types of divorce as khulʿ. While women are typically expected to go to the malamai if they want a divorce, Muslim women also declare the intention to divorce by action—going home—and sometimes achieve a divorce through this action.

Contextualizing female-initiated divorce through female resistance and contestation heightens our understanding of Muslim divorce processes. The idea of female-initiated divorce comes to the fore in this chapter in two ways: going home, or hijra, and obtaining divorce through a malam. Although the procedures define contestation and resistance in different ways, they are both forms of female-initiated divorce. One, requesting divorce from the malamai, is in conjunction with broader understandings of Islamic divorce law; the other, going home is a locally contextualized form. The particular practice of female-initiated divorce through action, going home, or "hijra" is specific to Muslims in Accra.

Islamic family law on divorce is also being contextualized in the ways in which Muslim women respond to the cases of repudiation, or saki. Muslim women's contestations of saki indicate the precarious legal position in which they find themselves. Yet these women still have confidence in the negotiations of Islamic religious authorities to bring about reconciliation.

The idea of power in the application of Islamic family law is also highlighted through the works of Islamic religious authorities. Such authorities are simultaneously powerful and not powerful. The malamai's power lies in their authority to issue divorces to Muslim women without any recourse to men. However, they have no power to overturn men's repudiations. Furthermore, Islamic law on divorce appears to be malleable, a flexibility established through legal reasoning, such as malamai contracting marriage on top of marriage. Islamic religious authorities' power to legitimize marriage on top of marriage renders men's power of repudiation questionable in such instances.

The chapter also illustrates local understandings of khulʿ.[14] For the malamai, khulʿ appears to mean any divorce initiated by a woman. However, the malamai do not agree on any clear position on khulʿ procedure, which can result in tension. Samia's case clearly shows the tension that arises between a dominant practice of female-initiated divorce process, going through a malam, and going home, which is a cultural assumption of divorce. While the malam and Samia's family elders concurred that Samia's action was tantamount to divorce, her husband, Sadik, did not have that perception. In fact, the malam indicated that Samia's action was khul'. Finally, the chapter also adds a perspective to studying law from the experiences lay people—the people it is meant for. This has to do with how law appears differently in understanding and application. At the end, therefore, this raises a concern on how to study law: whether from a law-on-the-books perspective or from the perspective of local legal reasoning and understanding.

## NOTES

1. Accra is the capital of Ghana, a secular multifaith and multiethnic country located in West Africa. It has a population of approximately 25 million people according to the 2010 census. In terms of religious demographics, 71.2 percent of the population profess Christianity, followed by 17.6 percent of Muslims, of whom live in Ghana. Other religious expressions, including African traditional religions, constitute the rest of the population The Maliki school is the dominant legal school. Prominent religious groups include the Tijaniiya Sufi order and Salafi-Wahabi group popularly called Ahlu Sunnah. For more on this, see Nyarko 2012 and Essien 1998.
2. Ordinance marriage is a particular kind of legal provision of marriage, which states that a marriage is strictly monogamous. For a detailed discussion of marriage practices in Ghana, see Issaka-Toure 2018.
3. The ASWAJ (also called Ahlu Sunnah) is a Salafi-Wahabi nongovernmental organization, which created a counseling and arbitration unit to mediate marital and familial issues. It was indicated to me that it became necessary for them to do so when people chose to apply for relief to a customary group or law instead of the state's judicial system and persisted in reporting such cases to them. ASWAJ is not a court and so their procedures vary. Unlike court cases, each of which is numbered, here the cases are only written on files with the names of the complainant and kept for the records of the ASWAJ office.
4. The literal meaning of *alkhairi* is "gift." In this context of divorce, alkhairi has a deeper connotation, as it refers to the farewell gift to the woman following repudiation. It is intended to help the woman resettle financially. However, because only husbands decide the amount, it does not always achieve this purpose. My research also found that this practice emanates from a prophetic tradition that urged husbands to give a gift their wives on divorce.
5. Interview, Hajj Garba, ASWAJ office, Nima, Accra, May 18, 2015. Interviewed in English by the author.
6. Informal discussion in Hausa, Nii Boye Town, Accra, August 17, 2008.
7. Interview, ASWAJ office, Nima, Accra, June 19, 2008. Interviewed in Hausa and translated by the author.
8. Interview, Lapaz, Accra, November 13, 2007. Interviewed in Hausa and translated by the author.
9. The term *hijra* has Arabic roots and means "to migrate." In this context, it has been adapted to describe women leaving their matrimonial homes.
10. Matrimonial residences are largely provided by the husbands themselves or through assistance from their natal families. It is only in a few cases that matrimonial residences

are provided either by a woman herself or through the assistance of her natal family. In this context, the male provision of the matrimonial residence explains going home or hijra. This last sentence is not specific.

11. This observation occurred when I went to the field in 2016 and realized that Baba, whom I had met earlier with one wife, had married a second.
12. The observation was made during my several field research periods, and such statements were frequent during the discussions in Hausa.
13. This information was gathered via informal conversation by the author in English with Larmie, Madina, Accra, November 28, 2019.
14. This is an interesting addition to comparative studies of khulʿ such as that in Sonneveld and Stiles 2019.

## REFERENCES


Ali, K. 2006. *Sexual Ethics and Islam: Feminist Reflections on Qur'an, Hadith, and Jurisprudence.* Oxford: Oneworld.

———. 2010. *Marriage and Slavery in Early Islam.* Cambridge, MA: Harvard University Press.

Bowen, J. R. 1996. "Religion in the Proper Sense of the World: Law and Civil Society in Islamist Discourse." *Anthropology Today* 12:12–14.

———. 2000. "Consensus and Suspicion: Judicial Reasoning and Social Change in an Indonesian Society, 1960–1994." *Law and Society Review* 34:97–128.

Essien, V. 1994. "Sources of Law in Ghana." *Journal of Black Studies* 3:246–262.

Ewing, K. 1988. *Shari'at and Ambiguity in South Asian Islam.* Berkeley: University of California.

Fluehr-Lobban, C. 1987. *Islamic Law and Society in the Sudan.* London: Frank Cass.

Haeri, S. 1989. "Ambivalence toward Women in Islamic Law and Ideology." *Middle East Annual* 5:45–67.

Hirsch, S. F. 1998. *Pronouncing and Persevering: Gender and the Discourses of Disputing in an African Islamic Court.* Chicago: University of Chicago Press.

———. 2010. "State Intervention in Muslim Family Law in Kenya and Tanzania: Applications of the Gender Concept." In *Muslim Family Law in Sub-Saharan Africa: Colonial Legacies and Post-Colonial Challenges*, edited by S. Jeppie, E. Moosa, and R. Roberts, 305–323. Amsterdam: Amsterdam University Press.

Issaka-Toure, F. 2018. "Marriage Practices: Ghana." In *Encyclopaedia of Women and Islamic Cultures.* General Editor Suad Joseph. Http://dx.doi.org/10.1163/1872-5309_ewic_COM_002146.

Messick, B. 1993. *The Calligraphic State: Textual Domination and History in a Muslim Society.* Berkeley: University of California Press.

Mir-Hosseini, Z. 2000. *Marriage on Trial, a Study of Islamic Family Law: Iran and Morocco Compared.* London: Tauris.

———. 2009. "Classical Fiqh, Contemporary Ethics and Gender Justice." In *New Directions in Islamic Thought: Exploring Reform and Muslim Tradition,* edited by K. Vogt, L. Larsen, and C. Moe, 77–88. London: Tauris.

———. 2015. "Muslim Legal Tradition and the Challenge of Gender Equality." In *Men in Charge? Rethinking Authority in Muslim Legal Tradition,* edited by Z. Mir-Hossein, M. Al-Sharmani, and J. Rumminger, 13–43. London: Oneworld.

Nyarko, P. 2012. *2010 Population and Housing Census: Summary of Final Results.* Ghana Statistical Service.

Opoku, K. 1976. *The Law of Marriage in Ghana: A Study in Legal Pluralism.* Hamburg: Alfred Metzner Verlag.

Peletz, M. 2002. *Islamic Modern: Religious Courts and Cultural Politics in Malaysia.* Princeton: Princeton University Press.

Schacht, J. 1964. *An introduction to Islamic law.* Oxford: Clarendon Press.

Sonneveld, N., and Erin Stiles. 2019. "Khul': Local Contours of a Global Phenomenon." *Islamic Law and Society* 26 (1–2):1–11.

Stiles, E. 2005. "'There Is no Stranger to Marriage Here!': Muslim Women and Divorce in Rural Zanzibar." *Africa* 75 (4):582–598.

———. 2009. *An Islamic Court in Context: An Ethnographic Study of Judicial Reasoning.* New York: Palgrave MacMillan.

———. 2018. "Legal Pluralism from the Ground Up: Marital Disputing in Zanzibar." *Irvine Law Review: Law and Social Science Issue* 8:101–123.

Tucker, J. 2008. *Women, Family, and Gender in Islamic Law.* Cambridge: Cambridge University Press.

Wanitzek, U. 1998. "Bulsa Marriage Law and Practice: Women as Social Actors in a Patriarchal Society." In *Sovereignty, Legitimacy and Power in West African Societies: Perspectives from Legal Anthropology*, edited by E. A. B. v. R. van Nieuwaal and W. Zips, 119–171. Hamburg: LIT Verlag.

# 6

# Undoing Marriage in Lebanon

## Divorce within and beyond Family Courts

JEAN-MICHEL LANDRY

Munira and I were sitting outside Café Casperi, an unpretentious restaurant named after the protagonist of the 1960 Paramount Pictures cartoon *Casper the Friendly Ghost* and located on the western fringe of the Beiruti working-class neighborhood *Ṭarīq al-Jadīda*.[1] The area's predominantly Sunni population and the escalating tensions between Sunni and Shiʿi militants at the time (July 2013) made the place an improbable location to discuss the technicalities of Shiʿi divorce. Munira made that observation on my arrival at the café, a few weeks after we met in Beirut's Shiʿi family court. While tea and sweets were served, she explained that even though she had spent countless hours in Shiʿi courts, she is a Sunni Muslim. She practices Islam in accordance with the Sunni tradition and is registered as a member of the Sunni sect (*ṭāʾifa*).[2]

Munira became entangled in the labyrinthine system of Shiʿi family law in 1991, when she married a fellow Lebanese (whom I call Walid) who is registered as a Shiʿi citizen. Soon thereafter, she and Walid moved to Kuwait. The couple had two children abroad. In 2000, they relocated to Lebanon, and she flew to Beirut with the kids. Walid was supposed to follow shortly but he repeatedly delayed his return. When he finally arrived in Lebanon, it was to explain that he had married another woman, with whom he wished to live permanently in Kuwait. He agreed to divorce Munira under one condition: that she give him the house she inherited from her father. She refused. Walid promised that she would never get a divorce and returned to Kuwait. When I met Munira in February 2013, she had already spent three years trying to obtain a divorce in order to be able to remarry one day. From Kuwait, Walid hired a lawyer who made every possible effort to prevent Munira from ending their marital relationship. When I left Lebanon, she had not yet been able to break the bond of marriage.[3]

Though complex, Munira's story exemplifies the material challenges and institutional opacity that many Lebanese women face when their marriages turn sour. This chapter will return to her quest, but only after having examined the legislation and regulations governing the legal treatment of divorce in the three regimes of Islam-based family law (Sunni, Shiʿi, and Druze) operating in Lebanon. Although some of these legal systems make it easier than others for wives to obtain a release from a dysfunctional marriage, I show that ending such marriages often translates into long, costly, and uncertain legal journeys. Religious norms are not solely responsible for the hardship Muslim women encounter along this journey; several patterns of gender inequality associated with Islam-based divorce also find their roots in secular legal practice. I begin by reviewing the legislation applicable to shariʿa-based divorce in Lebanon today. I argue that although the state has often refrained from intervening in the domain of divorce, this situation does not signal a lack of regulation but rather constitutes a particular mode thereof. The following two sections provide an ethnographic perspective on how divorces are performed in Islamic courts. The chapter's final section analyzes a form of divorce exclusive to Shiʿi Muslims, which is granted by clerics working outside Lebanese family courts.

What follows is based on multiyear ethnographic and archival research. It draws on recent anthropological scholarship but also on a multitude of empirical sources, including interviews with family judges (all male), litigants, shariʿa scholars, lawyers, court personnel, and legal activists. I also draw on a compilation of more than one hundred decisions issued by Sunni and Shiʿi family courts. Between 2012 and 2014, I followed the judicial unfolding of countless stories about divorce, both in Shiʿi first-instance courts and in the High Court; I attended hearings, examined court decisions, and talked with judges, lawyers, and litigants. Conversation with judges helped me reconstruct the framework of assumptions, constraints, and possibilities within which they adjudicate divorce matters, and speaking with lawyers and litigants enabled me to appreciate the social, gendered, and material inequalities underpinning many of these family-law disputes.

## Laissez-Faire Secularism

Katherine Lemons's *Divorcing Tradition* (2019) provides a useful framework for conceptualizing the connections between the different kinds of Muslim divorce that are pronounced in Lebanon today. Lemons argues that the judicial regulation of Islamic divorces is vital to secularism, which she understands as an attempt to maintain "an appropriate relationship between religion and politics" (7). She grounds her argument partly on an analysis of state interventions meant to limit Muslim husbands' privileges in India. In 1985, for instance, the Supreme Court of India forced a wealthy lawyer to pay maintenance fees to his ex-wife even after the three-month waiting period (*ʿidda*) during which he must provide for her. In 2016, the same court banned the irrevocable divorce known as triple-ṭalāq on the grounds that it violates the principle of equality before the law. The Supreme Court went further in 2017 by making it a crime for a Muslim husband to say "I divorce you, I divorce you, I divorce you" to a wife (either in oral or written form), which makes the divorce irrevocable.[4]

The connection between Islamic divorce and secularism is no less vital in Lebanon, but it occurs in other sites: the Lebanese postcolonial state has been much less proactive than its Indian counterpart in reforming divorce legislation. As the home of fifteen different regimes of family law (three of which are based on Islam), Lebanon is often construed as a remarkable instance of legal pluralism. Indeed, few nation-states accommodate such a wide spectrum of judicial diversity. But Lebanon is also unique for its laissez-faire approach to family-law affairs, and to divorce matters in particular. Not only is triple-ṭalāq allowed and relatively frequent in Lebanon, but parliament has so far refrained from adopting any of the legal measures enacted by other countries to bolster the capacity of Muslim women to end a marriage.

A cursory look at the reforms carried out by other Arab states since the mid-twentieth century helps highlight the contrast. In 2000, Egypt and Jordan reconfigured a particular type of divorce (*khulʿ*) so that it allows wives to terminate their marriage at will and without demonstrating the husband's responsibility in the union's failure (Sonneveld and Stiles 2019, 3–5).[5] Sunni and Shiʿi women can also obtain a khulʿ divorce in Lebanon, but here they cannot pursue this option without the consent of their husband. Other countries modified legislation to extend the husband's financial obligations toward the divorcée beyond the three-month maintenance period (ʿidda) and the payment of the dower (*mahr*). In the second half of the twentieth century, these postdivorce compensations have become a "standard feature of statutory law in the [Arab] region"—except in Lebanon (Welchman 2007, 126). A third strategy to mitigate the husband's prerogatives has been to establish family courts as the proper location for divorce. Egypt, Yemen, Tunisia, Iraq, and Morocco have deployed different means to make divorce a judiciary procedure (122–125). Lebanese Sunni and Shiʿi men can have their divorce certified by judges, but nothing prevents them from repudiating a wife without the intervention of judicial authorities.

It is tempting to understand Lebanon's reluctance to amend divorce laws as evidence that the country is governed by a weak or nonsecular state. A number of influential scholars have pursued this line of thought. Some have argued that the Lebanese state has lost control over some of the most unjust laws enforced on its territory (El-Khazen 2000; Rotberg 2004). Others have maintained that the country is split by a "dual legal system" encompassing a secular-law system enforced by the state and a family-law system "left entirely in the hands of the ʿulama'" (Thompson 2000, 114).

The problem with this approach is that it conceals the fact that Islam-based family courts are not autonomous legal institutions but rather creatures of the secular state, which are funded by the Ministry of Justice and enabled by the country's parliament. In Lebanese family courts, as elsewhere in Lebanon, the religious and the secular are closely intertwined. Therefore, rather than understanding the state's reluctance to intervene in divorce legislation as a lack of secular regulation, I find it more productive to follow Antonio Gramsci (1971, 160) in approaching non-intervention as "a form of state regulation" in its own right. Upholding the current laws against the demands for reform articulated by activists is not to refrain from regulating marital life but rather to insist on regulating it in a particular way.[6] Although this form of regulation is partly based on religious precepts, it also derives its legal force from secular norms, procedures, and apparatuses.[7]

I will come back to the question of secularism in the conclusion. For now, let us briefly review the frame in which most Muslim divorces are adjudicated in Lebanon. Numerous laws governing family matters today are taken from the 1917 Ottoman Law of Family Rights (OLRF), which was drafted by the modernizers of the Ottoman Empire and upheld by the French officers who ruled the country until 1943. The OLRF regulates divorce in three ways. First, Section 110 stipulates that men must inform the court after they have divorced a wife. Although no sanction is attached to this law and many bypass it, it nonetheless helps bring Muslim divorce under the jurisdiction of the courts. Second, Section 104 prohibits judges from recognizing divorces that are pronounced under conditions of intoxication or coercion. Third, and most important, the OLFR includes a type of juridical divorce called *tafrīq* (separation) that can be initiated by women seeking to terminate their marriage: section 132 stipulates that both women and men can petition the courts to ask for tafrīq on grounds such as adultery, long-term imprisonment, or insanity. In a rare case of intervention in divorce legislation, the Lebanese postcolonial state expanded these grounds in 1962 to include physical or verbal abuse and discord (Al-Zayn 2003, 74–75). It also excluded Druze Lebanese from the purview of the OLFR. Even though Lebanon is often described as the only country that continues to enforce the OLFR, it only applies fully to Lebanese couples who married in Sunni courts. Tafrīq, as a result, is unavailable to women like Munira.

## Abstract Equality and Concrete Bureaucracy: Druze and Sunni Courts

The mostly rural and relatively small Druze community (6 percent of the country's population) forms an exception to the laissez-faire approach that has characterized Lebanon since its colonial founding.[8] Although subject to the OLFR during the French Mandate (1926–1943), Druze Lebanese reformed divorce procedures in 1948 when drafting their family code. The Ottoman law does not question the husband's ṭalāq prerogatives; it only limits them. Druze leaders moved further by granting equal divorce rights to the men and women of their ṭā'ifa (sects). The architects of the 1948 Druze law also prohibited out-of-court ṭalāq and forbade ex-spouses to remarry under the community's family law. Divorced Druze couples wishing to remarry must convert to one of the other state-recognized sects or arrange a marriage abroad.

Druze women, as a result, cannot be repudiated by triple-ṭalāq. Like other Muslim Lebanese, however, those wanting to terminate their marriage must undergo a lengthy mediating process involving adjudicators appointed by the court and tasked with saving the marriage. The difficulty facing anthropologists interested in Druze divorce is that the ṭā'ifa's courts are virtually impossible for nonmembers to access. Fortunately, we can learn from the work of Lubna Tarabey (herself a Druze), who conducted fieldwork in Druze courts. Her *Family Law in Lebanon: Marriage and Divorce among the Druze* (2013) provides valuable insights into the working of religious courts and the transformations affecting the Druze family structure today.

Tarabey put great emphasis on the fact that Druze divorce law places both sexes on an equal footing. Her findings, however, call attention to the abstract nature of the equality built into family law. Even though Druze women enjoy the right to divorce, Tarabey observes that those who exercise their right often face opprobrium within the community. Women "who approach courts [for divorce]," she notes, "find themselves forced to deal with public humiliation" (172). Beyond divorce, she shows that legal reforms have not dislodged fathers, brothers, and husbands from their position of authority within the household. Tarabey is nonetheless careful to note that these patterns of inequality are not exclusive to the ṭā'ifa; they pertain to the Lebanese society as a whole. Her observation that younger generations of Druze Lebanese are more likely to petition for divorce also echoes larger societal trends: the national divorce rate increased by 30 percent between 2003 and 2013 (158).

Druze divorces are also more prevalent in urban settings. Tarabey affirms that women living in cities are more inclined to turn to family courts to resolve their marital conflict than their coreligionists from the countryside (118). This finding leads her to make the interesting claim that in cities like Beirut, the Druze court system "fulfills the role of the family in the villages" (119). How do judges assume this role? And can this also be said of secular courts? Tarabey provides an insider view into the treatment of Druze marital affairs but she does not engage with these questions. More unfortunate is the lack of ethnographic attention that she gives to the mediation process, which can hinder a wife's ability to release herself from a dysfunctional marriage. To see how judges and litigants approach this crucial phase of the divorce process, we must turn our attention to Sunni and Shi'i Muslim courts.

UNLIKE THE DRUZE, Sunni and Shi'i citizens (representing 86 percent of Lebanon's Muslim population) must cope with men's exclusive right to terminate a marriage at will, without cause, outside the courtroom, and sometimes even without notifying their wives. Given the Lebanese parliament's laissez-faire approach to religious divorce, the only Sunni and Shi'i women capable of ending their union unilaterally are those who took the trouble of adding to their marriage contract a clause giving them a right to divorce. A recent study, however, suggests that fewer than 2 percent of Muslim marriage contracts include such a clause (Geagea, Makhlouf, and Fakih 2015, 18). I saw several couples refuse to add this clause, whose inclusion necessarily forces brides and grooms to consider the possibility that their not-yet-celebrated union may actually be dysfunctional. Like most young couples in the world, the vast majority of Lebanese couples do not set up the terms of their potential divorce when getting married. What follows therefore focuses on the 98 percent of couples who have not anticipated divorce in their marriage contract. Wives involved in these unions cannot, strictly speaking, divorce their husband.

Women approaching Sunni family courts are nonetheless better equipped to end defective marriages than their Shiʿi fellow citizens. Remember that Munira, the woman whom I described at the beginning of this chapter, said that her quest would have been much easier had she married a member of the Sunni ṭāʾifa. Women can dissolve their union with greater ease in Sunni courts since, in matter of divorce, they are subject to a version of the OLFR enabling them to request a juridical separation (a tafrīq). The path leading to tafrīq, however, is so lengthy, costly, and bureaucratic that it discourages many Lebanese from terminating unhappy marriages (Geagea, Makhlouf, and Fakih 2015, 43–49). What slows tafrīq procedures is that both spouses involved in the lawsuit must undergo an arbitration process whose aim is not to reach a divorce agreement but rather to reconcile the couple and save the marriage. The Sunni and Shiʿi judges with whom I worked were quick to extol the benefits of reconciliation and always proud to ground their predisposition in Islam. "We live in a culture of divorce," an appeals judge once said to a separating couple. "I know you have problems but . . . remember that there are things that improve with time."[9]

"A reconciliation or an agreement is always preferable," said another judge to a woman seeking divorce in court. "But I don't want an opinion," she retorted; "I want a legal decision."[10] In a flash her response encapsulates the view held by many unhappy wives that the family courts' insistence on reconciliation hinders their ability to end a marriage. As part of arbitration sessions, women going against their husband's will are indeed asked to prove that they suffer harm or are compelled by their husbands to perform prohibited acts (e.g., sodomy). However, the intimate nature of marital life makes it difficult, if not impossible, to muster evidence of harm unless medical or police documents are available.

Although I did not have a chance to observe these arbitration sessions firsthand, Morgan Clarke's monograph (2018) provides a unique view into the maze of bureaucratic requirements that punctuate the path to tafrīq. His *Islam and Law in Lebanon* documents the seemingly technical, yet often decisive, steps through which a couple must go in order to effect a judicial separation. Clarke remarks that securing a tafrīq is an expensive quest (costing around $400 U.S.) and that numerous women end up opting for a khulʿ, a legal arrangement in which the wife must forfeit at least some of her financial rights (see also Geagea, Makhlouf, and Fakih 2015, 46). The cost and duration of tafrīq proceedings nonetheless represent only a fraction of what Shi'i women must spend to extricate themselves from dysfunctional relationships.

## Uncodified Matter: Divorce in Shi'i Courts

Munira would have preferred to deal with a Sunni court. She was aware that tafrīq procedures are tiresome but argued that it would have taken her less than a year to terminate her marriage had she married a Sunni Muslim. Yet Walid, her husband, is registered as a Shi'i citizen. And the OLRF, which authorizes tafrīq, is not fully binding on Shi'i Lebanese husbands, their spouses, or their children. Section 242 of the Lebanese Law on Shari'a Courts enables judges to circumvent the ORLF and adjudicate family affairs according to "the Shi'i legal school." Yet the law does not spell out what the rules of the Shi'i school are. In an interview with me, one Shi'i judge added a poetic twist to this legal situation: "Shi'i law is not in a book," he told me, pointing to the left side of his chest; "It's in the judge's heart; it's in my heart."[11]

The result of this situation is that very few Lebanese know which shari'a norms govern the family life of Shi'i citizens. In matters of divorce, Shi'i legal scholarship is rather consensual; most current debates revolve around a specific type of divorce known as *ṭalāq al-ḥākim* (divorce by the judge), to which I will return shortly. For now, two features of Shi'i divorce are of special interest here. First, unlike their Sunni counterparts, Shi'i judges and scholars do not recognize the triple-ṭalāq as a valid divorce. Second, and most important for our purpose, unlike their Sunni and Druze fellow citizens, Shi'i women cannot extricate themselves from a marriage without their husband's consent or the help of a shari'a scholar. The following stories of two couples exemplify these features and illuminate some of their implications.

Nisrine was thirty-five years old when I first met her in 2013. She is not a committed practitioner of Islam but nonetheless married Kamil under Shi'i family law (no civil marriage exists in Lebanon).[12] They have two children and had just bought a house when their relationship started spiraling downward. Back in October 2011, the couple had had a particularly bitter phone conversation. Before hanging up, Kamil told Nisrine that he would not let her come back home that evening. She should sleep at the parents' house, he said. While Nisrine was staying with her parents, he declared (also over the phone) that he would divorce her. A lawyer close to her family advised Nisrine to bring the matter to court to ensure she received the financial support to which she was entitled.

On the lawyer's recommendation, Nisrine filed a demand for maintenance (*nafaqa*) against Kamil. The plan, however, backfired dramatically. Kamil grew furious, hired a lawyer, and found out that the most effective way to retaliate was to stay married. To defuse the conflict, the two lawyers held a meeting outside the court, after which Nisrine learned that Kamil would not divorce her unless she gave him 10,000 USD. She made it clear that she could not afford to pay such an amount.

Kamil, then, switched tactics: in response to the maintenance petition, he requested that Nisrine be brought back under his authority (a request call *musākana*). Nisrine tactically agreed to move back to the family house, aware that Kamil was only trying to save time and did not wish to live with her anymore.

It was at this juncture, on April 16, 2013, that I encountered Nisrine's case in court. The legal dispute was already eighteen months old. The judge (whom I will call Shaykh Ali) was reminding them that they had been fighting for a year and a half and remarked that their relationship must be deeply flawed as a result. "Divorce might be the best option for everyone," he suggested.[13] He invited the couple to come back the day after, suggesting (without much optimism) that the next twenty-four hours might be their last chance to resume marital life.

The following day, in his office, Shaykh Ali carefully avoided saying the word "divorce" in front of Kamil and Nisrine. Pragmatically, he chose to address all the usual points of contention associated with divorce and postdivorce life: child custody, dower (mahr) payment, child maintenance, choice of the children's school, and so on. After an hour of discussion, Nisrine had agreed to forgo her mahr and all the postdivorce matters were settled. Thus Kamil found himself in a situation where he could hardly refuse to divorce Nisrine through khulʿ. Since tafrīq is not available to Shiʿi Lebanese and given that khulʿ remains the prerogative of the husband in Lebanon, Kamil could have resisted. However, when sitting in front of a judge who was encouraging him to divorce and in a situation in which most contentious issues has been resolved, Kamil agreed. Shaykh Ali never formally recommended that he divorce Nisrine; he simply asked him to pronounce the standard divorce formula ("*anti ṭāliq*") distinctly, so that all syllables were clearly audible. He also suggested that Kamil look Nisrine straight in the eye, but that was more than Kamil could bear. Shaykh Ali did not insist, and Kamil divorced Nisrine.[14]

Islamic judges seldom encourage divorce. Nisrine lost vast sums of money (including her mahr) trying to terminate her relationship with Kamil, but her journey into Shiʿi family law ended with the best of her limited options. Three other features of this story also deserve our attention. First, note that while divorce was the issue behind Nisrine and Kamil's dispute, none of the legal actions they took actually touched on this question. She sued him for maintenance, and he responded by requesting that she stay home. What is left for the archives—and for the historian—is a petition for maintenance solved through divorce rather than a Shiʿi Lebanese woman's attempt to end a marital relationship without giving in to her husband's financial blackmail. An uninformed researcher is indeed likely to be taken aback by the number of maintenance cases filed in Shiʿi courts. As this story—and the next one—shows, numerous maintenance claims have actually little to do with maintenance: in a legal system where women can neither file for ṭalāq nor demand tafrīq, petitions for maintenance become a strategic tool through which Shiʿi Lebanese wives can (sometimes) ransom themselves out of a relationship.

Also worth noting is the role of lawyers. Bringing Muslim divorce under the authority of state courts has been an important strategy devised by Arab modernizers to limit the husband's ṭalāq prerogatives (Tucker 1996). Requesting divorce in a judicial setting, however, often leads spouses to deal with lawyers, who always increase the proceedings' cost. In retrospect, Nisrine regrets having hired a lawyer. "At first," she said, "my husband was willing to divorce me without [a] problem." When two lawyers got involved in the process, they made her wait a year and a half and pay 3,000 USD. The third important feature of this story is that the judge succeeded in convincing Kamil to divorce his wife. The significance of this aspect will become clearer as we examine Munira's judicial journey, to which I now return.

IN 2013, after three years of proceedings, Munira had not yet succeeded in ending her marriage. Recall that Munira grew up as a Sunni citizen and became entangled in Shi'i family law through her marriage with Walid. Given the tensions arising between the Sunni and Shi'i sects at the time of our meetings, Munira could have easily accused the Shi'i judiciary of mistreating her on account of sectarian difference—but she did not. Rather, her remarks transgress the religious divide and highlight the secular nature of several obstacles discouraging women from ending their marriage.

The first time Munira entered the court, it was simply to know what options were available to her. The judge she met informed her that undoing a marriage under Shi'i family law was difficult but not impossible provided she first sued her husband for maintenance. Like Nisrine, then, Munira filed a case of maintenance against Walid. "From that day onward," she remarked, "I had to go to the court once every twenty days. . . . I am not working while at the court; each time, I have to make arrangements. And each time, going to the court costs me at least 4,000 Lebanese pounds [2.64 USD], which is the price of a [loaf of] bread."[15] I have already stressed that getting out of a defective marriage is an expensive endeavor in Lebanon. Clarke (2018, 165) estimates the fees associated with tafrīq at around 330 USD. The path to Shi'i divorce is lengthier, more expensive, and less predictable. Lawyers estimate that it often cost up to 5,000 USD in lawyers' fees.[16]

However, Munira's story suggests that her material situation affected her capacity to break the bond of marriage in yet another way. "I am going to court every twenty days," she told me, "but my husband does not; his lawyer takes care of everything for him." Although placing Islamic divorce under the jurisdiction of family courts has helped women secure postdivorce alimony payments, it also encourages litigants to hire lawyers.[17] And insofar as lawyers are expensive and legal aid is virtually nonexistent, those who cannot afford their help are severely disadvantaged.[18] With the help of his lawyer, Walid used the same strategy against Munira that Kamil used against Nisrine: he responded to Munira's maintenance request by requesting that she live in his house. Since he was living abroad, however, he had to prove that he could fly the whole family to Kuwait, house them, and provide visas for Munira and the children.

Though she was unable to afford a lawyer, Munira received an initial favorable judgment. On April 16, 2013, the judge ruled that Munira (and the children) were entitled to receive maintenance payments. I was in court that day. In delivering his judgment, the judge remarked that according to the Kuwaiti embassy, Walid had not requested visas for his wife and children. That was enough to convince the judge that Walid no longer wanted to live with Munira. However, two months later she received a letter informing her that Walid had appealed the case to the Shi'i High Court. I was able to follow Munira's dealings with the High Court, where she was helped by a lawyer whom I had befriended a few months earlier and who had agreed to work pro bono for her. When I left the country, it was increasingly obvious that Munira would never receive any maintenance payment from Walid. But let us not forget that maintenance was not what she was after: Munira wanted to remake her life and, ideally, find a new husband. Doing so, however, required her to be divorced first. The judge she met before petitioning the court encouraged her to file a maintenance case, since a wife who does not receive support from her husband is entitled to request that an erudite Shi'i scholar divorce her unilaterally. It is to this type of divorce that I now turn.

## Neglectful Husbands and Floating Signifiers: Divorce beyond the Courts

Thus far, I have considered the mix of opportunities and obstacles that divorcing Lebanese women encounter in Sunni, Shi'i, and Druze courts. Tarabey (2013) noted that all divorces among Druze are enacted in courts, and I am not aware of Sunni authorities handling divorce cases outside the sect's family courts. Yet each year, numerous Shi'i Lebanese women initiate divorce proceedings in the margins of state-sponsored courts. Many face a situation similar to Munira's: they cannot end their marriage against their husband's will. The Shi'i legal tradition includes a special form of divorce that can help wives terminate their marriage unilaterally. Ṭalāq al-ḥākim (divorce by the judge) is more often performed by independent scholars than by judges. To become valid in the eyes of Lebanese law, however, these divorces need to be ratified by one of the thirty-two official Shi'i judges. Ṭalāq al-ḥākim thus provides an instructive counterpoint to divorces pronounced in courts. Its hybrid status (pronounced by scholars and confirmed by judges) casts into relief what adjudicating Islamic divorce through state-defined procedures entails for those who are subject to them.

Nisrine and Munira had been told that several Shi'i scholars could help them dissolve their marriage. Neither of them, however, harbored illusions about ṭalāq al-ḥākim: both knew that judges can (and frequently do) challenge a learned scholar's decision to break a marital union, in which case the marriage remains legally intact. Part of what makes ṭalāq al-ḥākim such an unstable judicial decision is the lack of consensus among Shi'i scholars on the conditions that warrant an intervention in a couple's marital affairs. Shari'a interpreters agree that properly trained scholars can divorce a woman whose husband has disappeared for more than four years. But can a Shi'i scholar end a wife's marriage if her husband is imprisoned for life? Can a husband lose his wife to divorce for refusing to provide her with maintenance? These issues are matters of scholarly debate today (see Maghniyyah 1997, 65–70).

What also complicates matters is the fact that the validity of such divorce ultimately depends on the reputation of the scholars who pronounced it. In theory, only an accomplished Shi'i scholar (*mujtahid*) can serve as ḥākim and dissolve a marriage against the husband's will (Maghniyyah 1997, 69). In Islamic parlance, the term mujtahid describes a legist erudite enough to extract from the scriptures a set of precepts helping the faithful to navigate contemporary life. In today's Lebanon, however, the word has come to function as a "floating signifier"—namely, a term that absorbs more meaning than it emits and, as a result, conveys highly variable significations.[19] No consensus holds among Shi'i Lebanese, for instance, as to whether the country hosts one of these erudite scholars. Family judges often argue that some of their colleagues achieved the rank of mujtahid in the past but that no one deserves this title nowadays. Influential figures such as Muhammad Hussein Fadlallah (1935–2010) and Mohammad Mahdi Shamseddine (1936–2001) are remembered as mujtahids by many, but some people claim that they do not deserve the title. To muddy the water still further, secular judges who actively interpret the Lebanese legislation (rather than merely applying it) are often portrayed as mujtahids.[20]

Though it is riddled with ambiguities, ṭalāq al-ḥākim remains the only option for Lebanese women struggling to extricate themselves without their husband's consent from a marriage contracted under Shi'i law. To this day, most divorces pronounced by a ḥākim take place outside the courts, in the office of an influential scholar or the scholar's representative (*wakīl*). All the cases of ṭalāq al-ḥākim that I saw pending ratification in court came from the Higher Shi'i Islamic Council (HSIC) or from Fadlallah's office. Although I was not able to observe how the HSIC handles requests for ṭalāq al-ḥākim, the adviser to the council's vice president explained to me that these divorces are performed according to rules established by the most authoritative Shi'i scholar living today, Ali al-Sistani.[21]

By contrast, the divorces bearing the signature of Fadlallah (or his representative) are based on Fadlallah's own jurisprudence. Since 1990, all demands for shari'a-based pronouncements filed with this influential scholar have been processed directly at his judicial office. Fadlallah acted as ḥākim until his death in 2010. In the following years, demands for ṭalāq al-ḥākim filed at Fadlallah's office were sent to (and eventually signed by) Mahmood Hashemi Shahroudi, an erudite Iranian scholar who cooperates with the judicial office to fill the jurisprudential void left by Fadlallah's death.[22]

Shaykh Hassan, the cleric serving as Fadlallah's representative at the office, took care to clarify that while many people regard him as a judge, his role comes closer to that of an arbiter. "People come here and explain their problem; I help them reach an agreement. Unless their agreement runs counter to the shari'a,

I endorse it with my signature. This is the ideal scenario," remarked the shaykh.[23] When the parties fail to agree, however, the path toward a solution is much less straightforward. "The decisions coming out of this office," Shaykh Hassan continued, "are shari'i [conform to the shari'a] but not *qānūnī* [legally valid]." Cases of ṭalāq al-ḥākim enable us to explore the gap between these two legal conditions. During one of our meetings, the informal judge showed me a folder containing the story of a Shi'i woman trying to end her relationship with her husband. Once he has garnered the necessary documentation, met with the spouses, and evaluated the situation, Shaykh Hassan can recommend a scholar to serve as a ḥākim and overturn the will of a husband refusing to divorce his wife. Petitions for ṭalāq al-ḥākim are free of charge, processed without lawyers, and generally faster than in courts.

Munira and Nisrine both knew that Fadlallah's judicial office helps Shi'i Lebanese wives sever ties with uncooperative husbands. Yet they were also aware that state-sponsored family courts almost always refuse to validate the divorces pronounced by this extralegal office. "Of the forty-six divorce pronouncements [ṭalāq al-ḥākim] issued by this office since I began working for this office [in 2001], only one has been officialized; all others were dismissed in court," the unofficial judge told me in 2013.[24] The fact that shari'a-based pronouncements on divorce made by the country's most influential Islamic scholar are disregarded by family judges is not lost on Shi'i Lebanese embroiled in family disputes. "You can go see Fadlallah," a woman told me at the Shi'i court, "but you will soon realize that the trash cans of this tribunal are filled with decisions issued by Fadlallah's office."[25]

The image of trash cans filled with decisions made by Shi'i clerics forces us to ask how and why courts prevent these extrajudicial divorces from taking effect. First-instance judges are responsible for ratifying out-of-court ṭalāq. Divorces performed against the husband's will (such as ṭalāq al-ḥākim) are subject to close scrutiny. "The first step," a judge explains, "is to know who pronounced the divorce. The ḥākim must be a mujtahid, [and mujtahids] are well-known figures, so if I don't know who divorced the couple, it raises the red flag."[26]

Each judge, he explains, must then look into the moral and scholarly reputation of the ḥākim. A lawyer who was experienced with Shi'i law corroborated the fact that out-of-court divorces open the doors to cases of corruption. He cited the case of a wife who paid 40,000 USD to a scholar to be divorced only to learn a few months later that the Shi'i court refused to ratify the divorce. "The problem," this lawyer continued, "is that far too many clerics pretend to be a mujtahid, and pronouncing a ṭalāq al-ḥākim is an effective way to claim that status."[27] Issuing a ṭalāq al-ḥākim is in this sense a "double performative" (Miller 2002): by pronouncing it, a scholar divorces a couple, and since only a mujtahid can execute this judicial act, the scholar simultaneously institutes himself as a mujtahid. The head of Fadlallah's office also observed that several other Lebanese scholars posturing as mujtahids do not actually have the credentials to handle cases of ṭalāq al-ḥākim with the care that such a momentous practice requires.

None of the judges with whom I worked suggested that Fadlallah's office was corrupt. However, some of them raised doubts about Fadlallah's status of mujtahid. That influential members of the Shi'i judiciary consider that he was no mujtahid—and therefore not entitled to impose a divorce—helps explain why family courts refuse to endorse the divorces pronounced by his office. Clarke (2018, 292) argued that the question actually goes beyond the case of Fadlallah; he suggests that Lebanese family courts "efface" the authority of influential Shi'i scholars. Insofar as Shi'i judges also dismiss the legal pronouncements of many other scholars, his analysis seems correct to me.

But why do family judges act in this way. Why do they undo what has been accomplished by scholars working in the same legal tradition? Clarke noted that feelings of envy and rivalry may explain why certain judges refuse to endorse the divorces pronounced by Fadlallah and others. This explanation aligns with my own observations but it also worth mentioning that the High Court's is currently attempting establish itself as the exclusive provider of ṭalāq al-ḥākim. One of the most important recent developments regarding Shi'i divorce in Lebanon is the High Court's endeavor to bring all procedures of ṭalāq al-ḥākim under its roof.[28] Unlike cases of divorce confirmation, demands for ṭalāq al-ḥākim filed in family courts are handled by the High Court, since its president is the only judge authorized to pronounce such divorces. In an interview with me, the president clarified that he too is entitled to impose divorce on neglectful or absent husbands in his capacity as representative of Ayatollah Ali Al-Sistani. "The High Court . . . comprises three judges," he explained, "but in cases of divorce, I am the only one concerned, because only I can act in the Ayatollah's behalf."[29]

Shi'i family judges claim that these developments promise to accelerate and simplify the treatment of ṭalāq al-ḥākim cases in the country. Yet some of the observations made in this chapter should raise skepticism. Pleading one's case before the Shi'i High Court is a much more laborious endeavor than soliciting the help of Fadlallah's legal office. Interactions occurring at the High Court are regulated by a detailed code of procedures and are often truncated to save time: the Court can process up to fifty cases in a single day. By contrast, the clerics presiding over Fadlallah's office take no more than four appointments per day, which allows them to give more time and attention to the petitioners. And while Fadlallah's office follows a shari'a-based protocol, it is not subject to the 345 points of procedure that govern the family court's proceedings, which often make them unintelligible to ordinary litigants.

More important, perhaps, is the place that lawyers assume in these two forums. Whereas they are not admitted in Fadlallah's office, their presence is mandatory at the High Court. Litigants cannot engage with the High Court or request a divorce directly; they must do so through the mediation of a professionally trained lawyer. An analysis comparing the treatment of ṭalāq al-ḥākim inside and outside the Shi'i High Court would enable us to appreciate the impact of bringing these divorces within the orbit of state law. Although it is too early to pursue such an analysis (the High Court has only treated a limited number of cases thus far), we can nonetheless foresee that it would cast a valuable light on the work performed by the secular legal procedures through which family judges adjudicate divorce cases.

## Conclusion

Over the last decade, research on the secular has gained considerable momentum in the critical humanities and social sciences. The different regimes of religion-based family law cohabiting in the postcolonial world have proved crucial sites for understanding how certain religious traditions have been reconfigured into instruments of secular rule (Agrama 2012; Asad 2003; Lemons 2019; Mahmood 2015). In Lebanon, however, research on secularism and that on family law have followed two distinct trajectories. Scholars interested in the secular have focused on the networks of activists and civic movements upholding secularism [*laïcité*] as a political ideal (Badry 2014; Mikdashi 2014). Meanwhile, those of us pursuing ethnographic research in family courts have raised questions of statecraft, ethics, gender, or the family (Clarke 2018; Ghamroun 2016; Landry 2019). Raja Abilamma (2018) is to my knowledge the only scholar who has brought these two lines of inquiry together by approaching family law (more specifically marriage) as a lens through which to understand Lebanese secularism.

This chapter did not tackle the question of secularism directly; it nonetheless established Lebanese family courts (Sunni, Shiʿi, and Druze) as fitting loci to grasp how shariʿa-derived norms are enforced in a secular legal framework. The preceding pages brought into focus the challenges that many Lebanese Muslims face in trying to extricate themselves from an undesirable marriage. Islamic norms play an undeniable role in this predicament. A cursory glance at the legislation such as the OLFR and jurisprudence on divorce would suggest that Lebanese regimes of Islam-based family law discriminate against women.

What an ethnographic approach to divorce shows, however, is that some of the hardship involved in ending an unhappy relationship cannot be understood as resulting from Islam. Concerns about the protracted nature of the judicial process leading to tafrīq, the court fees, the difficulty of proving physical harm, the required assistance of a lawyer to appeal a court decision, the rates charged by lawyers, and the severe lack of legal aid, all of which were mentioned by the protagonists of this chapter, cannot be traced directly back to the shariʿa tradition. Their genealogy is also rooted in the distinctively secular arrangement of space, procedures, and knowledges through which Islam-based precepts are enforced in contemporary Lebanon and other regions where the shariʿa tradition has been reshaped into family law.

Understanding secularism, we are thus reminded, demands more than simply examining how modern states intervene in religious affairs. I have underscored that unlike other Muslim-majority countries, Lebanon has been particularly reluctant to modify the rules of Islamic divorce. Some would argue that this legislative laissez-faire proves that the Lebanese state is not truly secular. In an effort to add nuance to this analysis, this chapter has called attention to the story of Munira, Nisrine, and other Muslim Lebanese women to show that family courts governing matters of divorce enforce religious and secular norms simultaneously. The question of whether the Lebanese state is truly secular is far beyond the scope of this chapter.[30] But as I close, I want to stress that further research into Islamic divorce would not only illuminate some of the points raised in this chapter, it would also contribute to forging new pathways into studying what secularism enables and what it disables.

### *Acknowledgments*

This essay could never have been written without the contribution of my Lebanese interlocutors, whose names I anonymized in this chapter. I also would like to thank Saba Mahmood, Wendy Brown, Charles Hirschkind, and Katherine Lemons for generous help at numerous stages of this research. And I am also grateful to Rula Jurdi Abisaab, Fabienne Boursiquot, Erin Stiles, Ayang Utriza Yakin, and Marie-Claire Foblets for their engagement with my argument. Ethnographic research was made possible by the Trudeau Foundation, the Canadian Social Sciences and Humanities Research Council of Canada, the Institut Français du Proche-Orient, and the Orient Institute-Beirut. The Max Planck Institute for Social Anthropology (Halle) provided me with a home and a fantastic network of interlocutors during the writing phase of this research.

### NOTES

1. To ensure anonymity, all protagonists have been given pseudonyms.
2. Religious convictions do not always align with sectarian affiliations (transmitted through patrilineal descent). On this, see Joseph 2000.
3. Lebanese women, interview by the author, Beirut, July 2013.
4. Although the state is behind these three legal initiatives, Lemons emphasizes that non-state Islamic forums also contribute to the making of Indian secularism.
5. Women seeking khul' must pay a compensation to their husband, often a portion of the dower.
6. On these demands, see Berry 2002 and Ghamroun 2016.
7. See Landry 2016, 2019.
8. The figures cited in this chapter are taken from U.S. Bureau of Democracy, Human Rights, and Labor 2017.
9. High Court Session, Beirut, December 2013.
10. High Court Session, Beirut, June 2013.
11. Shi'i judge, interview by the author, Beirut, December 2012.
12. Lebanese women (pseudonym: Nisrine), interview by the author, Beirut, July 2013.
13. Court session, Beirut, April 2013.
14. Divorce proceedings in a judge office, Beirut, April 2013.
15. Lebanese women (pseudonym: Munira), interview by the author, Beirut, July 2013.

16. Author's correspondence with Lebanese lawyers, July 2019.
17. While many observers, activists, and even judges recognize that a lawyer can made a difference in first instance courts, litigants are allowed file a case without the help of lawyer. However, litigants must be represented by a lawyer to bring their case to the High Court.
18. On legal aid in Lebanese family courts, see Geagea, Makhlouf, and Fakih 2015, 38, and Sibāʿi 2013.
19. On the notion of "floating signifier," see Lévi-Strauss 1950, 63. See also Clarke's 2018 observations on the use of the term *mujtahid* in contemporary Lebanon (2018, 282–283).
20. See, for instance, Al-Liwa 2019. For parallels in Pakistan, see Giunchi's chapter in this volume.
21. Advisor to the HSIC vice president, interview by the author, Beirut, February 2013.
22. Although Shiʿi Muslims are traditionally required to follow the shariʿa-based pronouncements of a living scholar (also called *marjaʿ*), Fadlallah authorized his followers to continue to abide by his jurisprudence even after his passing. Shahroudi agreed to cooperate with judicial office to provide Fadlallah's followers with divorce pronouncements (ṭalāq al-ḥākim) issued by a living scholars. On Fadlallah's legal authority after his death, see Deeb and Harb 2013.
23. Head of M. H. Fadlallah's judicial office, interview by the author, Beirut, December 2012.
24. Fadlallah's representative at the judicial office, interview by the author, Beirut, July 2013.
25. Lebanese litigant, interview by the author, Beirut, December 2012. This litigant was aware that Fadlallah had passed away at the time of the interview. By "Fadlallah" ("you can go see Fadlallah"), she meant Fadlallah's office, as the rest of the sentence makes clear.
26. Family judge, interview by the author, Beirut, July 2013.
27. Lebanese lawyer, interview by the author, Beirut, July 2013
28. This is not a new law, but rather an attempt by the Court president to establish the Shiʿi High Court as the country's exclusive forum where demands for *ṭalāq al-ḥākim* are treated. Other modifications are, apparently, under consideration. See Shbārū 2019.
29. President of the Shiʿi High Court, interview by the author, Beirut, December 2013.
30. On the question of whether states are secular, see Agrama 2012, 29–36.

## REFERENCES


Abilamma, Raja. 2018. "Contesting Secularism: Civil Marriage and Those Who Do Not Belong to a Religious Community in Lebanon." *PoLAR: Political and Legal Anthropology Review* 41:148–162.

Agrama, Hussein. 2012. *Questioning Secularism. Islam, Sovereignty and the Rule of Law in Modern Egypt.* Chicago: University of Chicago Press.

Asad, Talal. 2003. *Formations of the Secular. Christianity, Islam, Modernity*, Stanford: Stanford University Press.

Badry, Roswitha. 2014. "Secularism as a National Stance." *Hemispheres* 29, (3):27–45.

Berry, Moulouk. 2002. "Radical Transitions: Shifting Gender Discourse in Lebanese Muslim Shiʿi Jurisprudence and Ideology." PhD diss. University of Michigan.

Clarke, Morgan. 2018. *Islam and Law in Lebanon. Sharia within and without the State.* Cambridge: Cambridge University Press.

Deeb, Lara, and Mona Harb. 2013. *Leisurely Islam. Negotiating Geography and Morality in Shiʿite South Beirut.* Princeton: Princeton University Press.

El-Khazen, Farid. 2000. *The Breakdown of the State in Lebanon, 1967–1976*. Cambridge, MA: Harvard University Press.

Geagea, Nayla, Youmna Makhlouf, and Lama Fakih. 2015. *Unequal and Unprotected. Women's Rights under Lebanese Personal Status Laws*. New York: Human Rights Watch.

Ghamroun, Samer. 2016. "Effets d'État: Les juges des enfants, les tribunaux de la charia et la lutte pour la famille libanaise." PhD diss., École Normale Supérieure Cachan.

Gramsci, Antonio. 1971. "The Modern Prince." In *Selections from the Prison Notebooks*, edited by Geoffrey Smith and Quintin Hoare, 125–205. New York: International Publishers.

Joseph, Suad. 2000. "Civic Myths, Citizenship, and Gender in Lebanon." In *Gender and Citizenship in the Middle East*, edited by Suad Joseph, 107–136. Syracuse: Syracuse University Press.

Landry, Jean-Michel. 2016. "The Practice of Shi'i Jurisprudence in Contemporary Lebanon." PhD diss., University of California, Berkeley.

———. 2019. "Dialectic of *Ijtihad*. Reforming Family Law in Contemporary Lebanon." *Comparative Studies of South Asia, Africa and the Middle East* 39 (3):361–373.

Lemons, Katherine. 2019. *Divorcing Tradition. Islamic Marriage Law and the Making of Indian Secularism*. Ithaca: Cornell University Press.

Lévi-Strauss, Claude. 1950. "Introduction à l'oeuvre de Marcel Mauss." In Marcel Mauss, *Anthropologie et Sociologie*, ix–lii. Paris: PUF.

Al-Liwa. 2019. "Nādī qaḍāt unban karm ra'īs al-shūrā as-sābiq al-qāḍī as-salāma." May 8.

Maghniyyah, Muhammad Jawad. 1997. *Divorce: According to Five Schools of Islamic Law*. Teheran: ICRO.

Mahmood, Saba. 2015. *Religious Difference in a Secular Age: A Minority Report*. Princeton: Princeton University Press.

Mikdashi, Maya. 2014. "Sex and Sectarianism. The Legal Architecture of Lebanese Citizenship." *Comparative Studies of South Asia, Africa and the Middle East* 34, (2):279–293.

Miller, Hillis. 2002. *Speech Acts in Literature*. Stanford: Stanford University Press.

Rotberg, Robert. 2004. *When State Fail. Causes and Consequences*. Princeton: Princeton University Press.

Shbārū, Asrār. 2019. "'Ayn 'alā daftar shurūṭ ītmām 'aqad az-zawāj fī al-maḥākim al-ja'fariya . . . hal min jadīd?" *Al-Nahār*, July 30.

Sibū'i, Nirmīn. 2013 "Kīf tū'min niqāba al-muḥāmiyin fī bayrūt al-ma'ūna al-qaḍā'iya?" *Al-Mufakira Al-Qānūniya*, December 3.

Sonneveld, Nadia, and Erin Stiles. 2019. "Khul': Local Contours of a Global Phenomenon." *Islamic Law and Society* 26 (1–2):1–11.

Tarabey, Lubna. 2013. *Family Law in Lebanon. Marriage and Divorce among the Druze*. London: Tauris.

Thompson, Elizabeth. 2000. *Colonial Citizens. Republican Rights, Paternal Privileges, and Gender in French Syria and Lebanon*. New York: Columbia University Press.

Tucker, Judith. 1996. "Revisiting Reform: Women and the Ottoman Law of Family Rights, 1917." *Arab Studies Journal* 4 (2):4–17.

———. 2008. *Women, Family, and Gender in Islamic Law*. Cambridge: Cambridge University Press.

U.S. Bureau of Democracy, Human Rights, and Labor. 2017. "Lebanon 2015 International Religious Freedom Report." U.S. Department of State. https://2009-2017.state.gov/documents/organization/256489.pdf.

Welchman, Lynn. 2007. *Women and Muslim Family Laws in Arab States*. Amsterdam: Amsterdam University Press.

Al-Zayn, Arif Zayd. 2003. *Qawānin wa Nuṣūṣ wa Aḥkām al-Aḥwāl al-Shakhṣiya wa Tanẓīm al-ṭawā'if al-Islāmiya fī Lubnān*. Beirut: al-Halabi.

# PART THREE

# Islamic Divorce in the Context of Global Patterns of Mobility, Upheaval, and Changing Household Economies

# 7

# Islamic Renewal, Muslim Divorce, and Gender Relations in Mali

DOROTHEA SCHULZ AND SOULEYMANE DIALLO

In urban Mali, divorce has become a frequent and hotly debated subject of everyday conversations among friends and peers, and the topic is also repeatedly addressed in Friday *khutbas* (sermons), Sunday church services, televised talk shows, and talk radio programs. People's complaints about rising divorce rates point to a real-time development, yet it seems that their apprehensions also reflect broader socioeconomic and institutional reconfigurations.[1]

The factors that are most striking about the widespread condemnation of divorce are, first, the readiness to blame women for the increasing divorce rates; second, the interpretation of the development as proof of the erosion of the moral fabric of Malian society; and third, the explanation of rising divorce rates as the result of people's refusal to comply with "Islamic values." People's tendency to refer explicitly to Islam when arguing for or against divorce is a relatively new phenomenon in Mali. Neither colonial nor postcolonial state law ever incorporated Islamic regulations and Mali has a strong legacy of the French Code Civil and principle of secularism (*laicité*).[2] Even judges and other legal experts increasingly refer to Islam or Islamic values when they justify their decision to grant a divorce.

That Islam increasingly forms the key reference point in debates on public order and the regulation of personal relations can be related to a broader Islamic awakening that started in Mali's urban areas in the late 1970s and since then has gained momentum in many rural areas as well (Hock 1998; Schulz 2008, 2012; Holder 2018). Islam's growing political weight is evident in the way various Muslim militant groups in Mali's northern triangle challenge the central state, and also in the mounting public visibility of Muslim interest groups in the capital city of Bamako and throughout the urban South. Since the late 1980s, public support has increased for Muslim groups and leaders who claim that "Islam" is an integral element of Mali's "cultural traditions" and call for an ordering of social relations according to Islamic precepts (Schulz 2010a, 2010b; Schulz and Diallo 2016). The capacity of these organizations to mobilize widespread street opposition and public protests has hindered state efforts to eliminate inconsistencies within the Malian legal-judicial system, align locally diverse customary and "Islamic" legal rules with constitutional law, and render Mali's legal system consistent with international legal standards.

The new family law (Code Malien des Personnes et de la Famille du Mali) is a striking illustration of how mounting Muslim political influence has impinged on law making. This growing assertiveness by Muslim activists can be seen as a response to a globalizing discourse of human rights and gender equality by Muslim opponents of family-law reform in Mali. The new family law was approved in 2011 after decades of struggle between a coalition of state officials, politicians, and women's rights activists on one side and Muslim interest groups and religious authorities on the other. However, in May 2018, the African Court on Human and Peoples' Rights (ACHPR), in a ruling on the case of *Association for the Advancement and the Defense of Rights of Malian Women (APDF)*[3] *and Institute for Human Rights and Development in Africa (IHRDA) v. the Malian Republic* (no. 046/2016), declared that the new family law did not conform to the international legal standards to which the Malian state had subscribed by signing several international conventions, most notably the Convention on the Eradication of All Forms of Discrimination against Women (CEDAW, ratified in 1985).

The contested process of reforming the Malian family law and the ACHPR's rejection of the code show how effective the "symbolic language of Islam" (Eickelman 2000) has become in mobilizing a popular support basis for Muslim activists and their increasing political influence in Mali. Even if these activists' efforts to align state law with (their interpretation of) "Islamic precepts" were halted by the ACHPR's 2018 ruling, it is important to understand to what extent these so-called Islamic precepts were historically realized in people's actual practices of matrimony and divorce. It also leaves us with the question of how ordinary people conceive of the relationship between Islam and what they refer to as "traditional culture."

In this chapter, we map the heterogeneous institutions and practices of Muslim divorce in Mali through a two-pronged analytical approach. First, based on a historical reconstruction of legal and normative pluralism in Mali, we identify systematic differences in the ways in which divorce is practiced in southern Mali and in the northern regions of Gao, Timbuktu, and Kidal. By acknowledging regional differences, especially with respect to the application of Islamic norms, the chapter expands the perspective of much existing scholarship on Mali, which focuses on "traditional" or "customary" (read "non-Islamic") matrimonial practices among the different peoples of southern Mali and tends to overlook the long-standing history of Islamic practice in the North (but see Lydon 2018; Rodet 2018; see also Schulz and Diallo 2016).

Following this analysis, we return to the discursive framing of Islam as a means to slow the divorce rate. We interpret this discourse with reference to changing household economies since the 1980s, particularly in urban areas. Here our main argument is that historically, people integrated Islamic norms into what they considered to be traditional practices of matrimony and divorce. With the Islamic awakening gaining in political strength since the late 1980s, many people—particularly in urban areas, where divorce rates have been on the rise—now debate divorce and its regulation as a matter of "applying Islamic law" to regulate family life.

## Mali's Legal-Normative Pluralism in Historical Perspective

Inconsistencies within Mali's current positive legal system, some of which the family-law reform sought to eliminate, reveal the legacy of a dual colonial administration and an autocratic postcolonial state and political system. Throughout the colonial and postcolonial history of the Malian legal system, Islamic norms were incorporated as customary regulations, not as a separate legal domain.[4] Moreover, after the country gained independence in 1960, shari'a-based law never constituted a distinct domain of Mali's positive law system.[5]

Prior to French colonial occupation in the 1880s, different politico-juridical formations existed side by side in the area of present-day Mali. Centralized polities in southern and Central Mali were based on alliances between ruling clans and Muslim scholars and traders, and the majority of the populations were not Muslim. In other areas of central and southern Mali, conglomerations of relatively autonomous village communities prevailed. Here, too, small urban communities of Muslims were surrounded by non-Islamized populations (Levtzion 2000). During the colonial period, Islam gradually gained a stronghold in the rural South, and some clans of Muslim religious specialists, whom the French regarded as representing a "traditional, African Islam," were backed by colonial administrators who were keen on containing what they considered the dangerous influence of "Arab Islam" (Harrison 1988; Triaud 1997). Colonial jurisdiction treated Islamic regulations as "customary" law, and they relied on *qadis*, specialists in Muslim law, to encourage the correct application of Islamic law concerning family matters in settings in which different normative orders intermingled (Roberts 1991, 2010; Sarr & Roberts 1991).

The situation was different in the northern regions of Gao and Timbuktu, where political power was based on alliances between dominant clans and Muslim scribes and traders. This meant that Islamic jurisprudence had been more thoroughly established for centuries and had merged more thoroughly with non-Islamic, customary practices. The majority of the population was Muslim and Maliki law was applied by Islamic judges (Christelow 2000).

In the 1890s, the French colonial administration established a dual legal system with two distinct bodies of law and spheres of application.[6] French positive law (Code Napoléon) regulated the affairs of French citizens and *assimilés*, that is, non-African foreigners and those Africans who had acquired French citizenship (*citoyens*). The rest of the colonized population, the so-called French subjects (*sujets Français*), were subject to Justice Indigène, which accommodated various "indigenous" or "customary" laws, including the Maliki legal school, for which qadis were asked to act as experts and advisers (*assesseurs*) (Hazard 1972; Sall 1986; Lydon 2018).[7] Regardless of the formal colonial distinction between Islamic and customary law, differences gradually became blurred at the local level as increasing numbers of people converted to Islam and henceforth considered Islamic regulations to be part of their "customs" (see, e.g., De Langen 2001, cited in Rodet 2018, 19, 23).

Although colonial administrators held full nominal control over legal matters, their jurisdiction remained limited to the administrative centers and their surroundings. For example, the decrees known as Décret Mendel (1939), which set a standard minimum age for marriage, and Décret Jacquinot (1951), which limited the amount of the bride-price (not to be confounded with the *mahr*, the dower that is part of an Islamic marriage contract[8]) were rarely enforced.[9] Beyond the French administrators' sphere of influence, the regulation of marriage and inheritance remained largely in the hands of male family elders (Rodet 2018, 24–25).

Since the advent of independence in 1960, Mali's governments have been reluctant to interfere in the realm of family matters. This was probably because they feared that legislating this domain of patriarchal control would meet considerable opposition from family elders, traditional political leaders, and Muslim religious authorities, thus threatening the governments' shaky foundations of political legitimacy (Schulz 2003, 2021, ch.2; Rodet 2018; Rodet and County 2018).

In continuity with the French principle of laicité, the first constitution of independent Mali of September 22, 1960, asserted the secular character of the Malian Republic in Article 1 and omitted any mention of Islam or any other religion.[10] Still, Islamic and customary norms regarding family matters did leave an imprint on codified law, as will be discussed later in the chapter. The colonial legal legacy showed in the enduring discrepancy between state law and local legal norms, with regard to inheritance, for instance, and in the limited ability of the state judiciary system to enforce court rulings and ensure access to courts.

In line with the first government's socialist economic policy, the new family law (Code de Mariage et de Tutelle, 1962) aimed to break up the extended family as the unit of agricultural production and improve the legal status of women. It laid down the full civil capacities of married women (Art. 36), set the minimum marriage age at sixteen for women and eighteen for men, and stipulated the necessity of the wife's consent to the marriage. In granting women certain rights and protections and in its modernist ambition and national scope, the code sought to overrule the often ethnically specific, local regulations concerning family matters (Schulz 2003, 2010c; Rodet 2018, 14). At the same time, the code fixed certain patriarchal prerogatives in the extended family by ensuring the husband's absolute decision-making authority and his position as the head and guarantor of order within the family. By standardizing regulations justified by reference to "tradition" or "Islam," such as bride-price and polygyny, male lawmakers, whose own views were likely informed by customary and religious norms, legally enshrined patriarchal family power and privilege (Schulz 2003; Rillon 2013, chaps. 3–5).

The aspects of the family law granting women new rights and protections prompted resentment among family elders, who felt it meddled with their control over their wives and daughters and the productivity of young males (Prats and Le Roy 1979, 171–173). Outside the urban administrative centers, where the state could enforce family law, elders retained much of their authority over marriage and divorce matters, as illustrated, for instance, by their disregard of the legal requirements of marriage registration and capping of the bride-price (Schulz 2003; Rodet and County 2018, 358). Arranged marriage, often of minors, remained a common practice. Women had few chances to oppose arranged marriages, to leave their husband without their own families' consent, or to access the court system. At the same time, kin-controlled marriage enhanced wives' material security insofar as it pressured husbands not to repudiate their wives because divorce amounted to breaking up an alliance between two families. We return to this issue later in the chapter, when we discuss increasing divorce rates. In urban areas today, the stability of marriages and wives' negotiating position vis-à-vis their husbands depends on women's abilities to mobilize familial support.

Following a military putsch in November 1968, Mali's constitution was suspended and full executive and legal powers were transferred to a junta, the Military Committee of National Liberation (CMLN).[11] A new constitution, which again established Mali as a secular state, was approved in 1974 and became effective in 1979, when the country returned to civilian rule under President Moussa Traoré and his UDPM party.[12] President Traoré sought a rapprochement with influential religious clans and cultivated relationships with a younger generation of successful Muslim business people and intellectuals with ties to the Arabic-speaking world. He integrated diverse Muslim interest groups in a Muslim umbrella organization, the Association Malienne pour le Progrès et le Salut de l'Islam (AMUPI), and gave their interests special consideration, by allocating them extra time on state media, for instance. Traoré's co-optation of Muslim groups strengthened their informal political influence, and partly because of this influence, Traoré's government was unable to obtain approval for a new family and personal-status draft law that was intended to align national legislation with international law.[13] Supported by progressive forces within the government, the proposed law aimed to achieve equal treatment of women and men in inheritance matters, which would have constituted a departure from both Islamic and non-Islamic customary conventions (the latter prohibited women from inheriting any share of family property and often treated them as part of the inheritance).[14] At that time, even some politicians and lawmakers were reluctant to adopt the new family law because they feared that Muslim religious and traditional political authorities would oppose this form of state interference with patriarchal control over women and family property.[15] Since that time, legislating matters pertaining to marriage and inheritance has remained a highly sensitive matter.

## Family Law Reform since 1991: A Tug-of-War between Muslim Interest Groups and the Secular State

After the toppling of President Traoré's single-party rule in a military coup in March 1991, a new, again strictly secular, constitution was adopted, along with a multiparty democratic system (Pimont 1993, 462). Under the democratically elected President Alpha Oumar Konaré and his party, ADEMA (1992–2002),[16] Muslim interest groups lost some of their influence. However, various Muslim leaders and interest groups capitalized on the new freedoms granted under multiparty democracy and a mushrooming infrastructure of private media outlets to call for a greater consideration of Islamic provisions in state legislation (Schulz 2012, chap.1).

President Konaré's government launched another reform of family law in the framework of a broader judiciary reform program, the Programme Décennal de Développement de la Justice (PRODEJ), which was established in 1999 with the substantial financial and logistical support of Western donor organizations. The reform sought to eliminate inconsistencies between the Constitution, the Family Code (Code de Mariage et de Tutelle), and the Code of Civil, Commercial, and Social Procedure (Code de Procédure Civile, Commerciale et Sociale) (Schulz 2003, 2012, chap.1). State officials and women's rights organizations that supported reform sought to reduce what they considered to be an undue influence of Islamic norms in previous family law, for instance, in women's and men's unequal opportunities to initiate divorce and in men's option to marry a second wife without spousal consent.[17] They argued that these regulations directly violated the equal rights of men and women stipulated in Mali's constitution and needed to be brought into conformity with international legal standards, as outlined in the Convention on the Elimination of All Forms of Discrimination against Women (CEDAW, ratified in 1985), the African Charter of the Rights and Welfare of the Child (ratified in 1998), and the Protocol to the African Charter on Human and Peoples' Rights on the Rights of Women in Africa (the so-called Maputo Protocol, ratified in 2005). The reform efforts were ultimately doomed because they met with vocal opposition from Muslim activists, represented by AMUP and by the Haut Conseil Islamique du Mali (HCIM). The political influence of these Muslim activists continued to grow under President Konaré's successor, President Amadou Toumani Touré (2002–2012), who avoided antagonizing Muslim activists because he recognized their potential to mobilize the public. When a revised family-law draft was finally submitted in 2009, the spokesmen of the HCIM mobilized popular support to block its adoption. Imam Mahmoud Dicko, who was initially the spokesman of AMUPI and then president of HCIM (2008–2019), and Mamadou Diamoutani, then general secretary of HCIM, framed their opposition to the family-law draft as an effort to protect what they referred to as the "Islamic foundations of Malian tradition." During public debates on the draft law, the Muslim activists called for more integration of Islamic precepts in codified law. Yet as we detail elsewhere in the chapter, they rarely spelled out what Islamic precepts they were referring to and their main effort appeared to be directed toward protecting patriarchal privilege (Schulz 2003).[18] A key cause of disagreement was the question of how much the state should interfere in matters that were previously under the control of family elders and religious authorities, such as marriage and inheritance (Schulz 2012, chap. 1).

Under the enormous pressure of Muslim activists mobilized by Imam Mahmoud Dicko, lawmakers were obliged to submit a revised draft law that integrated what the activists identified as "local socio-political realities" and "Islamic legal provisions" (Schulz 2003; Lydon 2018). The form in which the family law was finally adopted in 2011 maintained important patriarchal prerogatives, and it expanded Muslim privileges to handle marriage and divorce at the expense of state control over these matters. Legislating marriage, divorce, and inheritance has become a tug-of-war over influence, between the state on one side and family elders and religious authorities on the other. The latter tend to advocate for the preservation of "Islamic norms" in family law without specifying their exact legal foundations, as we discuss later in the chapter.

The success of these defenders of "Islamic norms" shows in legal inequities fixed in articles 281, 316, 319, 366, and 373, which preserve the marriage age for girls at sixteen years and at eighteen years for boys (281), stipulate a woman's obligation to "obey her husband" (316), give the husband exclusive determination over the choice of residence (319, 366), and articulate that a woman may enter into a new marriage only three months after her divorce or four months after her husband's death (373). Grounds for divorce remain gender-specific: a wife's refusal to submit to her husband's authority constitutes legal ground to divorce her, as does her proven adultery. A woman might rightfully ask for a divorce in case of her husband's prolonged absence and lack of material support or his proven adultery (Rodet 2018, 19–20).

Another critical amendment to the earlier draft law was the transfer of authority to officiate the marriage from the state administration to religious personnel associated with the mosques. Already in the late 1990s this issue had been very contentious in debates between Muslim activists on one side and state officials and women's rights organizations on the other.[19] At stake was the question of whether the state or another kind of authority should have decision-making power over family matters. Ultimately, Muslim religious personnel were granted the authority to officiate marriage ceremonies. For a religious marriage to gain legal validity, it must be registered at the Ministry of Religious Affairs. In practice, however, few religious marriages are registered. This leaves control over marital matters in the hands of religious specialists, opening up an opportunity for elders and husbands to neglect their financial responsibilities. As before, if their former husbands deny that they were legally married, women have few chances to request material support for their children in case of a marital breakup. Granting religious specialists the power to officiate the marriage ceremony also potentially takes away girls' protection against forced marriage because Article 283 requires a woman's consent only for the civil marriages.

The new family law of 2011 thus maintains juridical-legal plurality because it does not give the state full regulative power over marriage and divorce matters. It also does not grant women and men equal legal standing with regard to marriage and divorce. This directly contradicts women's constitutionally granted rights and the international legal standards endorsed by the Malian state. This was confirmed in 2018, when the ACHPR reprimanded Mali for its failure to conform to the CEDAW, the African Charter of the Rights and Welfare of the Child, and the Maputo Protocol.[20] The tug-of-war between the Malian state and Muslim interest groups has not been settled and is unlikely to be settled in the near future.

In March 2012, a group of disgruntled army officers deposed President Touré. A period of political turmoil in the capital, Bamako, followed the coup, and several Muslim militant groups temporarily occupied Mali's northern territories. The new president, Ibrahim Boubacar Keita, who took office in September 2013, maintained the secular character of the constitution and the political parties. Nevertheless, the creation of a Ministry of Religious Affairs in 2013 illustrates that the political weight of Muslim leaders and interest groups has been steadily growing. In Bamako and other towns of southern Mali, which is the nation's primary political arena, "the symbolic language of Islam" has become the dominant idiom of moral critique and of challenges to Keita's government. Even employees of the secular state administration, such as judges, now justify their decisions with reference to Islam.

In Mali's northern triangle, the growing presence of militant Muslim groups since the 2000s has altered local practices of establishing public order, as the militants have imposed a stricter application of so-called Islamic legal rules. Following the (temporary) occupation of vast areas of northern Mali in 2012, militant groups implemented what they referred to as "shari'a rules" that affected the regulation of marriage and divorce.[21] In spite of the presence of international peacekeeping forces in Gao and Timbuktu, these Muslim forces still maintain considerable influence in various areas of the North. In and around the towns of Kidal and Menaka in the far Northeast of the country, several groups including Ansar Dine, led by Iyad Ag Aghaly; Coordination des Mouvements de l'Azawad (CMA);[22] and Islamic State in the Greater Sahara (ISGS);[23] established a system to monitor local qadis. A special committee now ensures the qadis' compliance with CMA's demands for the rigorous application of so-called shari'a rules by scrutinizing all cases. The effects of monitoring shari'a rules have been twofold. First, the authority of the qadis has been formalized as an element of the new institutional infrastructure created by CMA. And second, local judiciary practices have been aligned with the novel standards of these Islamic rules.

## Regulating Family Matters: Different Regional Trajectories

In this section, we turn to social and legal practices of marriage and divorce. In our intersectional analytical view (see Crenshaw 1991) of how these practices differently affect women and men, we point to considerable regional variation in the application of "customary" and Islamic rules and in their use in intrafamilial power relations. We contrast the juridical situation for rural and urban populations of southern Mali with those in Kidal and Menaka in the country's Northeast.[24]

Many Malians throughout the country, in particular those living in remote rural areas, consider the judicial system incapable of handling legal cases in a timely and cost-efficient manner. Most urbanites, especially those with lower educational backgrounds, also experience the state judicial system as inefficient and corrupt. For people in Mali's northern triangle, the situation is aggravated by the limited road and communicative infrastructure. Large geographical distances to administrative centers and the scarcity of judicial personnel make it almost impossible for ordinary citizens to present their cases in court. For women throughout Mali, gaining access to the judicial system is particularly challenging, in part because they lack the financial and social support of male in-laws, which is necessary to file a case in court.[25]

In more remote rural areas in Mali's southern triangle, conflicts within the family are still primarily resolved by family elders, imams, and other religious specialists, and members of professional status categories (such as people of *nyamakala* social origin; see Conrad and Frank 1995) who are traditionally in charge of mediation and conflict resolution. In practice, this means that family affairs such as marriage and inheritance are dealt with within and between families and male family elders are still in charge of negotiating marriage and divorce.

The situation in the areas of Kidal and Menaka in Mali's North has both similarities and differences. The historically matrilineal Tuareg social organization granted women some economic independence and rights, both in the selection of a marriage partner and on the question of whether they wish to quit a marriage. They also had a right to own personal property and a say in family decisions. Men were subject to a moral code of honor (*eshik*) requiring them to respect women and their decisions, protect them, and refrain from insulting or physically punishing them. Women's most common reason for divorce was the husband's failure to provide for them (Nicolaisen and Nicolaisen 1997, 726–727). However, it was commonly accepted that a woman could leave an arranged marriage based simply on her "dislike" of her husband.[26] To do so, a woman would ask a male relative to solicit the intervention of a qadi on her behalf. The qadi would hear the wife and her (male) relatives and also her husband and his relatives. The qadi would subsequently make his own inquiries to confirm the depositions (which could take up to twelve months), after which he would give his verdict on the matter. While justifying his verdict by reference to the Qur'an, a qadi would generally not specify the exact textual sources.

A woman's male relatives may have objected to her divorce, perhaps because they resented returning the bride-price paid to them.[27] Still, a woman had a good chance to obtain a divorce, mainly because her husband would make it a point of honor not to ask for the restitution of the bride-price. Accordingly, divorce initiated by women in the Kidal and Menaka regions used to be more common and more accepted by both families than in southern Mali. As Nicolaisen and Nicolaisen maintain (1997, 726), an important cause of the high rate of divorces initiated by free-born Tuareg women was the custom of arranged marriages, which implied that girls were married at young ages when they were reluctant to oppose their parents. At a more mature age, a woman might divorce her husband so that she could live with a man of her own choosing; a woman might justify the divorce by arguing that her husband failed to provide for her. Nicolaisen and Nicolaisen also noted cases in which a husband and wife, having grown up together, would seek divorce on grounds that there was no mutual attraction and they just felt "like brother and sister" (1997, 726–727).

Since Mali gained independence, Tuareg women's options in divorce have been undercut by massive transformations in livelihoods in Mali's northern regions prompted by recurrent cycles of drought and by forced sedentarization and political persecution by the Malian state. In the Kidal and Menaka areas, new job opportunities created after the national pact of 1992 and political decentralization have encouraged an expanding urban settlement.[28] These changes in livelihood radically transformed power relations within families and power hierarchies between different status groups.

These developments have had varying effects on women depending on their socioeconomic standing and access to education. Women from well-to-do families have benefited from new educational opportunities for girls and, in some cases, from their families' connections to the central state in Bamako. However, for the majority of freeborn Tuareg women from the Kidal and Menaka rural areas, their obligation to take on greater economic responsibility for their families has not been matched by greater decision-making power (Bouman 2010).

Matters of marriage and divorce remain in the hands of the families, which means that young men and women must ask senior relatives for permission to marry and the bride-price must be paid. In marital conflicts, relatives from both sides are called to dissuade the conflicting partners from breaking up for good. According to prevalent norms, women still rely on male relatives to approach the qadi on their behalf because a woman is not supposed to address the qadi on her own. Educated women with access to formal employment and greater economic independence have a better chance to leave an unwanted marriage than women who are economically dependent on their relatives. However, the new restrictions imposed by Muslim militants make leaving a marriage difficult even for women who are more economically independent.

## A Situation of Legitimacy Deficiency

Throughout Mali today, local practices of marriage and divorce are informed by a disjuncture between state regulations and lived sociopolitical realities (Le Roy 1995;

Rodet 2018, 8–14; Schulz 2021, chap. 4). This is exacerbated by the state's inability to enforce laws regarding men's financial responsibility for their children in case of divorce. The state has also failed to enable citizens, particularly women, to access legal support or the judiciary system. Moreover, the state judiciary system also engages in malpractice.[29] The state's failure to ensure access to justice, legal security, and conflict resolution is perceived by many Malians as a sign of an absent state and irresponsible politicians who fail to take care of those who voted them into office (Bleck 2015; Schulz 2021, chap. 3; see Schatzberg 2001). As with other domains of the Malian state, the judiciary suffers from a "deficiency" of legitimacy (Beetham 1991, chap.1) because of its inability to satisfy people's need for material, social, and physical security (Schulz 2021).

However, it is important to note that many Malians are ambivalent about the role of the state as an arbiter of conflicts. Many Malians strongly denounce the state's failure to ensure justice. As illustrated by the controversial drafting of the personal-status and family law, many people resent state interference into the regulation of intrafamilial matters such as marriage and divorce (Schulz 2021, chap. 4). There are also regional discrepancies in how the state's failure is perceived. In southern Mali, many people frame their limited chances to access the juridical infrastructure and their criticism of its dysfunctional nature as indices of corrupt political leadership and a negligent state that fails to provide for its citizens. To people in northern and Central Mali (with the exception of the areas around Gao), the de facto absence of the state only perpetuates a long-standing historical situation characterized by a barely existing and malfunctioning state judiciary infrastructure and has reinforced their sense of political-economic marginality within the state.

## The Stakes of Muslim Divorce in Southern Mali

If, according to Muslim activists, judicial personnel, and other critical observers, the number of divorce cases has been skyrocketing over the last decades, what factors do people identify as leading to more divorce?[30] Moreover, does the apparent increase in divorce rates affect both urban and rural populations?

In southern Mali, there is a clear discrepancy between rural and urban areas with regard to the occurrence of divorce and who has a say in settling divorce. In rural areas, divorce remains the subject of family negotiations.[31] A woman may ask for a divorce because of her husband's long absence (as a migrant worker); frequent disagreements with her husband, in-laws, or co-wives; or the groom's or his family's failure pay the bride-price. Elders view the latter as the most compelling reason for divorce. A woman's family may be reluctant to accept marital disagreements as a valid reason for divorce and instead blame the woman herself for being cantankerous and insubordinate. In some cases, a woman's family is unable to return the bride-price because it has been reinvested into obtaining a bride for a son. Therefore, the key stake in negotiating divorce between families bonded in matrimony is the bride-price and its return.

For example, in 2009, in a village in the district of Bafoulabé, approximately 240 miles west of the capital Bamako, a woman we call Kadiatou decided to quit her marital homestead after months-long quarrels with several wives of her husband's brothers. Kadiatou packed up her belongings and moved back to her native village (at a distance of about 12 miles), where she declared her wish to divorce her husband. Kadiatou said she wanted a divorce because her husband did not treat her properly; for example, she said he did not side with her against her sisters-in-law. Kadiatou's father convened a family meeting and, in the presence of his wives, sons, and daughters-in-law, denounced his daughter's "irreverent" behavior and disregard for the "traditional" ideals of female submissiveness and endurance. No mention of Islam was made during his speech, which lasted for more than forty minutes. In the end, Kadiatou's father ordered her to return to her husband's home and threatened to sever all ties with her if she disobeyed his orders. Cases such as this illustrate women's limited possibilities for obtaining a divorce in Mali's rural South unless they are able to secure their families' support. Patriarchal family authority and bride-price are the main factors ensuring marital continuity and impeding marital breakups. Kadiatou's case is also typical in that the female behavioral standards were not framed as Islamic norms.

Rising divorce rates in Bamako and other southern towns reflect changing social arrangements of urban family life (Brand 2001; Schulz 2012, chap. 2). To avoid overcrowding, extended families no longer reside in one compound but instead tend to break up into individual household units. Within these nuclear family units, tensions always inherent in marital relationships, in particular in polygynous marriages, gain in explosive potential (Schulz 2012, chap. 2).[32] Rampant unemployment and lack of income-generating opportunities put a heavy strain on these domestic units. Since the late 1980s, a consequence of the neoliberal restructuring of urban economies and limited employment opportunities has been that many men are no longer able to provide for their family, and ability that had formed the cornerstone of their socially sanctioned (and legally enshrined) authority over their wives and in decision making. These financial difficulties do not keep some men from taking another wife, a decision that increases pressure on the entire household economy. When faced with penury, women assume greater financial responsibility for themselves and their children by engaging in various income-generating activities (Brand 2001; Schulz 2012; Chant 1999). Many family elders lose their control over the actions and decisions of women and children, in particular with regard to marital arrangements.[33] In many cases sons are on their own when it comes to covering the bride-price. Fathers can no longer impose their choice of marriage partner; nor can they ensure the stability of marriage by negotiating directly with the bride's parents. For daughters, increased numbers of educational opportunities grant them some room for maneuvering vis-à-vis their parents with regard to their professional and marital choices. However, as the following example illustrates, girls' greater options to influence the choice of marriage partners makes them more vulnerable to social isolation and moral disapproval.

In the southeastern town of San, Fanta, a twenty-five-year-old woman with a secondary school education, wanted to break up with her husband of more than five years, with whom she had two children. When Dorothea Schulz met her for the first time in 2006, Fanta had just quit her husband's residence (in San) and moved back to her parental courtyard, in spite of her invalid father's protest. Fanta asserted that after years of enduring her husband's failure to provide for her and their children, his decision to take another wife without consulting with her was the ultimate sign of his "disrespect" for her. Fanta also declared her intention to find a job as a nurse. Her mother, Aminata, whose petty-trade activities were the only source of family income, strongly opposed her daughter's marital breakup. When Fanta argued that her husband had not even paid the bride-price in full, Aminata, according to her own recollection, admonished her daughter "to stop thinking of money and start behaving like a proper Muslim woman." To overcome what she considered Fanta's "obstinacy," Aminata solicited the support of female friends to pressure her daughter to return to her husband and "heed his commands." When Fanta resisted, she suffered serious community repercussions. Neighbors and peers avoided socializing with her and rumors circulated that accused Fanta of "lacking compassion" for her husband, who had simply acted on his prerogative to take another wife. After three months, Fanta ceded to the pressure and rejoined her husband, who had promised Fanta's parents to transfer the remaining portion of the bride-price. After three years, however, Fanta moved back to her parents' place, this time for good. In response to her mother's strong objections, Fanta retorted that she could not stay with a husband who was not "a good Muslim husband" because he failed to treat Fanta and her co-wife equitably.

Fanta's example illuminates divorce dynamics in a situation of weakened patriarchal family authority and concomitant normative pressure to conform to so-called Islamic behavioral standards. Men's loss in authority and control over family matters is a direct outcome of their reduced employment opportunities and ability to provide for their families. Fanta's invalid father had lost a say in the matter because of his reduced economic role. Fanta's husband's failure to ensure his family's well-being and to transfer the bride-price had weakened his negotiation position. Both Fanta and her mother were obliged to assume greater financial responsibility.

The return of the bride-price is an important reason why the bride's relatives will object to divorce. Still, cases such as Fanta's, in which the husband never paid the full bride-price, are common, and this makes it easier for women to leave a marriage, even against their parents' will. Fanta's case also suggests that educated women have more leverage to make decisions on their own and greater ability to move out and build up an independent household for themselves and their children. They also have more leverage in asking for a divorce. Fanta's high school diploma increased her chances of finding salaried employment and earning an independent income. Still, her attempts to capitalize on her economic independence were dampened by peer pressure to conform to the ideal of a submissive and patient wife, an ideal represented in her community as an Islamic norm. In the end, Fanta obtained her divorce through a civil court, without soliciting an imam or other religious authority, yet all the while justifying it with reference to the obligation of a Muslim husband to treat his wives equally. In this sense, Fanta's case represents a growing tendency among men and women to criticize yet also defend divorce by reference to (however vaguely defined) "Islamic norms."

## Divorce in the Northern Triangle: Local Understandings and "Shari'a Rules"

In northern Mali, divorce has been common among the Tuareg of Menaka and Kidal and a woman can obtain a divorce against her family's will (Bouman 2010; Nicolaisen and Nicolaisen 1997, 720–727). Moreover, transformations of local modes of livelihood and power hierarchies within the family and new educational opportunities for girls have impacted women's decision-making powers. How can we relate these social transformations to the increasing divorce rate in and around Kidal and Menaka?

In conversations with Souleymane Diallo in 2019, older men and women in the region explained widespread divorce as the direct outcome of urban migration and urbanization. They identified women's enhanced employment opportunities and greater economic self-sufficiency as the main reason for their "readiness to divorce," and thus the main driver of divorce. Sidi ag Mohamed from the town of Kidal, a sixty-two-year-old man, posited a direct link between girls' education, women's formal employment, and decision-making power, maintaining that "marital mobility has always been frequent among us, the Tuareg. But nowadays the divorce rate is escalating. The difference between the past, for instance when I was born, and now is that many Tuareg are settled in towns where they work as civil servants or for NGOs. Most of these educated women working for NGOs and civil servants have their own wealth and therefore don't depend on men's incomes anymore. They are always ready to divorce."[34]

According to Sidi ag Mohamed, whereas women of relatively privileged social background benefit from schooling by finding employment in the state administration or sprawling nongovernmental organization (NGO) infrastructure, many men in the area cannot find regular work to support their wives and families. He adds nuance to his account by recognizing that educated men also drive up divorce numbers by marrying multiple wives:

> When I was in born 1958, it was rare to see a Tuareg man marrying two wives in Kidal and Menaka. At least from my childhood, I don't remember any name right now. But nowadays, many men from these areas who settle in town from rural surroundings of Menaka and Kidal marry two wives or even more! Even young men do this. Everywhere now, you meet men as young as 35 or 40 years who have two or more wives. [Another reason for the rise in divorce rates is that] . . . for those who wish to get a divorce, it

has become easier to obtain a divorce from state judges, who are corruptible, rather than from a qadi, as it used to be done at the time of my youth.

As Sidi ag Mohamed intimates, the rise in polygynous marriage arrangements and women's ability to divorce are primarily urban phenomena. He also points to how women's family, education, and socioeconomic standing inform their capabilities and decisions. That women's education increases their options in divorce matters is exemplified by the (pending) divorce proceedings involving Mohamed Ag Itily and his wife, Anna Walet Mossa.

Mohamed Ag Itily earned his MA degree in environmental sciences in Algeria in 2015. Soon after returning to Mali, he found employment as the coordinator of a nongovernmental organization (NGO) in Kidal. A few months later he married Anna Walet Mossa and settled with her in Kidal, an arrangement in which his family had played a prominent role. Anna was twelve years old at the time of the wedding and was the daughter of a police officer from southern Mali. In 2019, at the age of thirty years, Mohamed decided to marry a second wife, which prompted Anna to move back to her parental home in southern Mali and file for divorce. At the time of writing this chapter, the divorce proceedings were not yet completed. But Anna, who preferred to bring her case before the state-appointed judge in her father's town instead of presenting it to the qadi in Kidal, was confident that she would be successful. While Mohamed represents young (highly educated) men who opt for polygynous marriages, Anna exemplifies how women in the town capitalize on their parents' support and social standing to file for divorce in protest of their husband's decision to take another wife.

As noted, the political control by Muslim militant groups in Mali's northern territories since the 2000s has led to stricter application of "Islamic" regulations in the realm of family and criminal law. In Kidal and Menaka, this has affected both the role of qadis and the substance of their legal reasoning.[35] Faced with Muslim militants' monitoring activities and the threat of physical punishment, qadis feel considerable pressure to promote stricter readings of Islamic regulations and apply them in ways that discourage people from asking for divorce. Other rules forbid extramarital sexual relations, which pressures unmarried women and men to marry. The restrictions imposed by Muslim militants curtails the opportunities women gain through greater economic independence and can therefore be interpreted as an effort to contain the social transformations detailed earlier and limit educated women's new options in marriage and divorce.

Under the new shari'a rules, husband and wife still have the right to file for divorce, but they are now expected to frame the reasons for divorce in Islamic terms. This justification does not require the exact specification of legal sources and rules. For instance, it may suffice for women or men to advocate their case to family elders by arguing that "Islam" does not force someone to stay in a marital union against his or her explicit wish. In the towns of Menaka and Kidal, the most frequent reason given by men for divorcing is the wife's refusal to submit to his authority, a refusal that is often coterminous with women's greater opportunities to make an independent living. Another reason frequently cited by men is the wife's opposition to the husband's marriage to another woman. Women also mention a husband's decision to marry a second wife as a reason for divorce. Women may also ask for a divorce because of the husband's (proven) adultery. Still, to a greater extent than before, requesting a divorce means referencing what Muslim militants have defined and standardized as "shari'a rules" to justify the request.

The example of Fadi walet Hachim, a twenty-six-year-old woman residing in Bamako, illustrates the tension between Fadi's own interpretation of "Islamic divorce principles," which reflect established Tuareg conventions, and the perception of Muslim militants in Kidal that conventional understandings of Islamic divorce rules need to be corrected through stricter adherence to "the shari'a." Fadi decided to leave a marriage arranged by her family in Kidal two years earlier. She left her husband and asked her family to dissolve the marriage, maintaining that Islam's "democratic nature" allowed spouses who were unwilling to stay in a marriage to file for divorce and remarry. On her behest, male relatives presented her request to a qadi in Kidal, who at the time of writing this chapter was inspecting her case. Fadi expected the qadi's argument to center on the restitution of the brideprice, assigning responsibility for the marital breakup, and fixing a penalty according to the new "shari'a rules" imposed by Muslim militants. Fadi also expected the qadi to issue a strong reprimand to her husband and a recommendation for her to remarry soon.

Even if Fadi and the qadi, who is supervised by a committee founded by Muslim militants, differ in their interpretation of "Islamic" divorce requirements, their arguments are alike insofar as they do not ground their legal arguments in the Maliki or any other Islamic textual tradition but merely maintain that this is the "Islamic rule." Fadi's case also points out that women's demands for divorce must be presented to the qadi by intermediaries, preferably by senior male relatives. In the overwhelmingly divorce-adverse atmosphere of regions such as Kidal and Menaka today, this dependence on male relatives often constitutes another impediment for women. Men who are against the dissolution of a marriage feel emboldened to dissuade couples from breaking up. Thus, even if couples can legally end their marriage, they face greater social opposition in doing so. In addition, many qadis discourage family members from supporting divorced women. Sidi ag Mohamed recounted, "I still remember one case in Adielhoc [Kidal region] and another one in Bourem between 2012 and 2013. The Jihadists forced male relatives of two divorced women to justify why they had actively supported their sisters' decisions to divorce. When it was discovered that the two men had given false information to the qadi about their sisters' husbands, the jihadists obliged them to pay a fee for their misdeeds."[36]

Qadis also make divorce more difficult by scrutinizing the religious justifications offered in divorce requests and imposing fines on the spouse who was found responsible for the marital breakup. The new regulations set by Muslim militants reflect an effort to replace conventional interpretations of Islam with stricter "shari'a rules" and an attempt to reestablish parental authority and formalize the qadi's jurisdictional authority, which has never been granted by the Malian state. In addition, the new shari'a regulations support long-standing trends in Mali toward establishing Islam as the main normative reference point for the justification of regulations concerning marriage, divorce, and inheritance matters. We argue here that local Muslim authorities have moved into the institutional and jurisdictional void left by an absent central state, which is aggravated by the gap between state legislation and local practices.

## Conclusion

Our chapter started out with two observations. First, apprehension about the allegedly alarming rise in divorce rates is a matter of public debate in Mali. These debates play out on national media and privately owned radio stations and also in discussions among peers. Second, we observed that older women and men of different ages and educational backgrounds believe that women are mostly to blame for marital problems and divorce. This perception reflects a general criticism of changing gender relations, shifts in gender-specific household responsibilities, and new opportunities for women's decision making. As part of these broader social transformations, elders' authority and patriarchal control over young people and women is weakening, particularly in urban areas. The increasing access to Western schooling and new income opportunities for young people allows them to generate independent income and expand their decision-making options vis-à-vis their parents. All these developments encourage individual initiative and simultaneously undermine the stability of marriage, whose longevity is no longer ensured by seniors.

In Mali, socio-legal practices of divorce take place in an environment of legal pluralism that is marked by an ineffective and dysfunctional judicial infrastructure. This prompts citizens to question the legitimacy of the state and doubt the claims of transparency and the rule of law articulated by politicians. The institutional and moral vacuum left by a state that is unable to ensure basic rights and provide basic services forms the backdrop of the growing success of Muslim activists who, since the 1990s, have called for a reordering of public and family life according to—however broadly defined—Islamic principles. Since the toppling of former president Touré in 2012, political instability and the presence of Muslim militant groups in Mali's North have invigorated these calls for an Islamically grounded reform of public order. As a corollary, Mali's population has contributed to the reconfiguration of the normative-legal registers of legal pluralism, in part by engaging in "forum shopping" (Benda-Beckmann 2013).

Since the late 1990s, militants have targeted family-law reform to pressure Mali's subsequent governments to regulate public and family life according to what they call "Islamic rules." The outcome of the process of reframing has been threefold. First, under the pressure of the movement for Islamic moral renewal, people increasingly subsume "customary" conventions under the label of "Islamic" precepts, without, however, specifying from what Islamic texts or legal traditions these precepts are derived. Second, and paradoxically, Muslim activists have gained additional strength from mobilizing opposition to the project of family-law reform project, which they reject as emblematic of global discourse on human rights and gender equality. Third, although the attempts of Muslim militants in the North to impose stricter divorce rules by standardizing Islamic regulations as "shari'a rules," these rules are not grounded in elaborate doctrinal or legal argument. Third, although Muslim militants in the North justify their imposition of stricter divorce rules and standardization of Islamic regulations as a matter of enforcing shari'a rules, these rules are not grounded in elaborate doctrinal or legal arguments. This development mirrors a global standardization of Muslim activist discourse and forms of intervention.

Throughout Mali, people respond to a dysfunctional state judicial structure by falling back on religious institutions and actors invested with the authority and capacity to settle their affairs and render justice. The decades-long controversy over family-law reform illustrates the attempts by Muslim activists and religious authorities to expand their influence over a domain of social life that has been at least nominally controlled by the state judicial system. In the northern triangle, this is not a new phenomenon. Here, matters of marriage and divorce have always been in the hands of qadis, whom people have considered more effective in rendering justice than the institutional apparatus of the central state. Yet at least in the far northeast, these qadis now operate under close surveillance by Muslim militants. In the national political arena, which is centered in the urban South, the hold of religious authorities over family matters has expanded only in the last few decades. During the law-reform controversy of the 2000s, Muslim interest groups and state representatives clashed over the degree of autonomy that religious authorities should have in regulating internal affairs of Muslims without state interference. The shift in judicial authority at the national level was illustrated by the transfer of state prerogatives in officiating marriage to Muslim authorities, which allowed them to expand their control over community and intrafamilial affairs.

There is yet another dimension to Muslim authorities' expanding control over marriage and divorce. Especially in urban areas, where the elders' authority is increasingly eroding, the growing control of religious authorities over marriage and divorce helps preserve patriarchal control over women. Given the current political instability, which in 2020 manifested first in the growing challenge by Muslim activists to then president Keita and his RPM government and, in August 2020, in the overthrow of President Keita, it is far from evident that the secular state system and its representatives will hold against the onslaught by conservative Muslim forces.

### *Acknowledgments*

The chapter draws on research conducted by Souleymane Diallo and Dorothea Schulz in San, Bamako, Kidal, Menaka, and Niamey in the years 2001–2006,

2011–2016, and 2019–2020 (altogether more than thirty months). Research methods included participant observation among and semistructured interviews with members of urban and rural households, judges, legal experts, representatives of Muslim organizations and Muslim activist networks, faculty members of the University of Mali, and members of the state administration. Dorothea Schulz acknowledges the crucial import of additional data gathered by Souleymane Diallo in May 2020, after the outbreak of the COVID-19 pandemic

## NOTES

1. According to statistics from the six communal districts of the capital Bamako, more than 1,500 divorce cases are concluded in Bamako's courts every year (Diallo, personal communication, August 2019).
2. A separate Islamic judicial sector has never existed in Mali.
3. Association pour le Progrès et la Défense des Droits des Femmes Maliennes (Association for the Advancement and the Defense of Rights of Malian Women).
4. By "customary" regulations, we refer to an array of noncodified rules and procedures that regulate social, political, and property relations and mediate conflicts.
5. Mali gained independence as part of the Mali Federation, together with Senegal, on June 20, 1960. After the breakup of the federation, Mali was declared an independent republic on September 22, 1960, with a constitution adopted on that date.
6. Colonial jurisdiction took place at the district (*cercle*) and province levels and in the Court of Appeal in St. Louis, Senegal.
7. Similar to the process described by Chanock (1998), the (male) local experts played an instrumental role in fixing certain rules (usually those favorable to the interests of male elders and husbands) as "customary law" (Chanock 1998; see also Ginio 2006; Schulz 2010b; Rodet 2018, 12).
8. The mahr and Islamic marriage contracts are not commonly used in Mali today.
9. Similar to many other African societies, the bride-price (*dot* in French; *furunafòlò* in Bamanakan, the lingua franca of southern Mali), a key element of traditional matrimonial alliances, is still considered valid by most Malians, regardless of the civil or religious (Christian or Muslim) marriage ceremony they opt for. The bride-price consists of money and/or property paid by a groom and his family to the bride's family. As a token of recognition of the allocation of the bride's procreative capacities to the groom's patriclan, the bride-price, which is often paid in installments, renders a marriage valid. Failure to pay the bride-price serves as grounds for the bride or her family to revoke the marriage. There is considerable regional variation in the amount of bride-price.

   The bride-price is different from dowry (*trousseau de marriage*, in French, *kognominè*, in *Bamanakan*, the lingua franca of southern Mali), which in Mali is wealth provided by the bride's family (or the bride, increasingly) to the bride and thus to the groom's family. Bride-price in Mali contrasts with dower (nonexistent in Mali) in that the bride-price is transferred to the bride's family, whereas dower is property settled (by the groom and his family) on the bride at the time of marriage and intended to remain under her control (see Tambiah 1989). Malians do not equate these transactions with the Islamic mahr, which is a legally required transfer of wealth by the groom to the bride.
10. The new constitution included the Code of Civil, Commercial, and Social Procedure (August 1961, modified in 1972) and a Code Penal (August 1962, modified in 1967 and 1972),

which established that men, too, received punishment for adultery, abandonment of spouses and children, and refusal to provide financial support (Sall 1986, 387).

11. Comité Militaire de la Libération Nationale
12. Union Démocratique du Peuple du Mali.
13. Such as the UN Convention of the Rights of Women and of Children (Hazard 1972: 20, 22–24).
14. Also proposed was a clause to put illegitimate and adoptive children on equal legal standing with legitimate children with regard to inheritance and the obligation to support aging parents, a move that similarly broke with "customary" law and Islamic regulations.
15. Schulz, interviews with former members of the Ministry of Justice, March 1999 and April 2000.
16. Alliance pour la Démocratie au Mali.
17. In 1994, Mali's signing of the Platform of Beijing marked the starting point for a politicization of certain legislative changes and governmental measures, such as the campaign to eradicate practices of female circumcision. Whereas women's rights activists declared the practice a violation of women's right to bodily integrity, its defendants declared it to be an "Islamic" or "authentic" cultural practice.
18. In their public interventions, Muslim activists cast the efforts of government and NGO's working for women's rights to improve women's standing in divorce legislation as an attack on Mali's "traditional" cultural values.
19. Representatives of Muslim women's organizations endorsed granting full legal status to religious marriages, arguing that this protected the interests of lower-class women, many of whom were never "officially" married and therefore had fewer rights in divorce (Schulz 2003).
20. Djeugoue 2018.
21. These measures were not written down but rather were promulgated in oral form via radio broadcasts and public statements.
22. The Coordination des Mouvements de l'Azawad comprises former members of the organization Ansar Dine led by Iyad Ag Aghaly.
23. The Islamic State in the Greater Sahara operates in the area of Menaka.
24. We do not assume a neat boundary between the two "triangles," yet we argue that the peoples living in these regions have historically belonged to social and political formations and have been exposed to colonial and postcolonial state administration in distinctive ways (see Diallo 2016). Because of space limitation, we do not discuss contemporary socio-legal practices in the (Fulani-dominated) vast geographical zone north of Mopti and Douentza (to which some scholars refer as "Central Mali," e.g., Rodet 2018). In terms of sociopolitical organization and history, these societies form part of Mali's northern triangle.
25. Ethnographic findings from field research conducted by Schulz (1994–1996, 1998–2001, 2006) and by Diallo (2009–2011, 2012–2014).
26. During Diallo's research in the area, neither the qadi nor those soliciting his intervention ever referred to khulʿ as a relevant (or known) regulation.
27. This is not described as khulʿ.
28. The national pact was concluded between the Malian government and Tuareg oppositional forces in an attempt to contain the second Tuareg rebellion, which was launched in June 1990. It provided the framework for the state to undertake development actions (with

the help of international donors) in the three northern regions of Mali (Timbuktu, Gao and Kidal). This new institutional context created job opportunities for local residents.

29. All these deficiencies of the state judiciary system were mentioned as reasons for launching the 1999 law reform project PRODEJ (Programme Décennal de Développement de la Justice) under President Konaré (https://www.justicemali.org, last accessed April 2020).
30. We maintain that the divorce rate has been rising steadily in recent decades. However, in the absence of statistical data for this assertion, we draw on the statements of observers and the (scant) empirical data, such as the number of officially filed divorces (refer back to note 1).
31. This observation does not apply to the immediate rural surroundings of the capital Bamako and other towns in southern Mali.
32. Marital conflicts may result, for instance, from a husband's failure to treat his wives equally and related competition among co-wives over material resources.
33. For a detailed analysis of marital and family dynamics in town, see Schulz 2012, chap. 2.
34. Interview by Diallo in Bamako, March 2019.
35. These decisions are not specifically referred to as *hukm* but rather more broadly as "shari'a rules."
36. Interview by Diallo, Bamako, March 2019.

## REFERENCES

Beetham, David. 1991. *The Legitimation of Power.* New York: Palgrave Macmillan.

Bleck, Jamie. 2015. *Education and Empowered Citizenship in Mali.* Baltimore: Johns Hopkins University Press.

Bouman, Annemarie. 2010. "The Price of Marriage: Shifting Boundaries, Compromised Agency and the Effects of Globalization on Iklan Marriages." In *Tuareg Society within a Globalized World*, edited by Anja Fischer and Ines Kohl, 109–124. London: Tauris.

Brand, Saskia. 2001. *Mediating Means and Fate: A Socio-Political Analysis of Fertility and Demographic Change in Bamako, Mali.* Leiden: Brill.

Chanock, Martin. 1998. *Law, Custom and Social Order: The Colonial Experience in Malawi and Zambia.* Portsmouth: Heinemann.

Chant, Sylvia. 1999. "Women-Headed Households: Global Orthodoxies and Grassroots Realities." In *Women, Globalization and Fragmentation of the Developing World*, edited by Haleh Afsar and Stephanie Barientos, 91–130. Hampshire: Palgrave Macmillan.

Christelow, Allan. 2000. "Islamic Law in Africa." In *The History of Islam in Africa,* edited by Nehemia Levtzion and Randall L. Pouwels, 373–396. Athens: Ohio University Press.

Conrad, David. and Barbara Frank, eds. 1995. *Status and Identity in West Africa: The Nyamakalaw of Mande.* Bloomington: Indiana University Press.

Crenshaw, Kimberle. 1991. "Mapping the Margins: Intersectionality, Identity Politics and Violence against Women of Color." *Stanford Law Review* 43 (6):1241–1299.

Djeugoue, Brice Martiel. 2018. "IHRDA, APDF Obtain Favourable Judgment against Mali in First Case before the African Court Applying Provisions of Maputo Protocol." Press release. IHRDA. https://www.ihrda.org/2018/05/press-release-ihrda-apdf-obtain-favourable-judgment-against-mali-in-first-case-before-the-african-court-applying-provisions-of-maputo-protocol/.

De Langen, Maike. 2001. "Les assesseurs et la justice: Configurations du droit et de la coutume dans les conflits fonciers à Douentza, Mali," *Coopération juridique malienne néerlandaise*, octobre.

Diallo, Souleymane. 2016. "The Truth about the Desert: Exile, Memory, and the Making of Communities among Malian Tuareg Refugees in Niger." PhD Thesis, Dept. of Anthropology, University of Cologne

Eickelman, Dale. 2000. "The Coming Transformation of the Muslim World," *Current History* 99 (633):16–20.

Ginio, Ruth. 2006. "Negotiating Legal Authority in French West Africa: The Colonial Administration and the African Assessors, 1903–1918." In *Intermediaries, Interpreters, and Clerks: African Employees in the Making of Colonial Africa*, edited by Benjamin Lawrance, Emily Osborn, and Richard Roberts, 115–138. Madison: University of Wisconsin Press.

Harrison, Christopher. 1988. *France and Islam in West Africa, 1860–1960*. Cambridge: Cambridge University Press.

Hazard, J. 1972. "Implementing Law in Post-Keita Mali's Retreat from 'Scientific Socialism,'" *African Law Studies* 7:1–26.

Hock, Carsten. 1998. "Muslimische Reform und staatliche Autorität in der Republik Mali seit 1960." PhD diss., University of Bayreuth.

Holder, Giles. 2018. "Essai de lecture d'une democratisation malienne hors champ." In *Les Politiques de l'Islam en Afrique: Mémoires, reveil, et populismes islamiques*, edited by Jean-Pierre Dozon and Gilles Holder, 216–246. Paris: Karthala.

Konaré, A. 1982. *Les constitutions du Mali*. Bamako: Ministère des Relations Extérieures.

Le Roy, Emmanuelle. 1986. "L'introduction du modèle de l'Etat en Afrique francophone: Logiques et mythologies du discours juridique." In *Decolonisations et nouvelles dépendances*, ed. Catherine Coquéry-Vidrovitch and Alain Forest, 81–122. Lille: Presses universitaires de Lille.

———. 1995. "Thirty Years of Legal Practice in the Shadow of the State: The Taming of Leviathan." In *State and Society in Francophone Africa since Independence*, edited by D. Kirk-Greene and Daniel Bach, 34–45. Oxford: St. Martin's Press.

Levtzion, Nehemia. 2000. "Islam in the Bilad al-Sudan to 1800." In *The History of Islam in Africa*, edited by Nehemia Levtzion and Randall L. Pouwels, 63–91. Athens: Ohio University Press.

Lydon, Ghislaine. 2018. "Inventions and Reinventions of Sharia in African History and the Recent Experiences of Nigeria, Somalia and Mali." *Ufahamu: A Journal of African Studies* 40 (1):67–107.

Nicolaisen, Johannes, and Ida Nicolaisen. 1997. *The Pastoral Tuareg, Ecology, Culture, and Society*. Vols. 1–2. Copenhagen: Carsberg Foundation and Rhodos.

Pimont, Y. 1993. "La constitution de la république du Mali." *Revue Juridique et Politique. Indépendance et Coopération* 3:462–474.

Prats, Y., and E. Le Roy. 1979. "Les législations contemporaines: Mali." In *Les institutions administratives des états Francophones d'Afrique Noire*, edited by G. Conac, 170–173. Paris: Economica.

Rillon, Ophélie. 2013. "Féminités et masculinités à l'épreuve de la contestation: Le genre des luttes sociales et politiques au Mali (1954–1993)." PhD diss., Université Paris 1.

Roberts, R. 1991. "The Case of Faama Mademba Sy and the Ambiguities of Legal Jurisdiction in Early Colonial French Sudan." In *Law in Colonial Africa*, edited by K. R. Mann and R. Roberts, 185–204. London: James Currey.

———. 2010. "Custom and Muslim Family Law in the Native Courts of the French Soudan, 1905–1912." In *Muslim Family Law in Sub-Saharan Africa: Colonial Legacies and Post-Colonial Challenges*, edited by S. Jeppie, E. Moosa, and R. Roberts, 85–108. Amsterdam: Amsterdam University Press.

Rodet, Marie. 2018. Harmoniser justice traditionelle et justice étatique au Mali: Pourquoi une perspective de genre est essentielle. Report shared by the author.

Rodet, Marie, and Brandon County. 2018. "Genre, génération et contrôle de la circulation des personnes entre le Mali et le Sénégal à l'heure de Modibo Keita (1959–1968)." In *Femmes d'Afrique et emancipation: Entre normes sociales contraignantes et nouveaux possible*, edited by Muriel Gomez-Perez, 343–369. Paris: Karthala.

Sall, Y. 1986. "La codification et l'évolution de droit au Mali." *Revue Juridique et Politique. Indépendance et Coopération* 3–4:376–390.

Sarr, D., and R. Roberts. 1991. "The Jurisdiction of Muslim Tribunals in Colonial Senegal, 1857–1932." In *Law in Colonial Africa*, edited by K. R. Mann and R. Roberts, 131–145. London: James Currey.

Schatzberg, Michael. 2001. *Political Legitimacy in Middle Africa: Father, Family, Food*. Bloomington: Indiana University Press.

Schulz, Dorothea. 2003. "Political Factions, Ideological Fictions: The Controversy over the Reform of Family Law in Democratic Mali." *Islamic Law and Society* 10 (1):132–164.

———. 2008. "(Re)Turning to Proper Muslim Practice: Islamic Moral Renewal and Women's Conflicting Constructions of Sunni Identity in Urban Mali." *Africa Today* 54 (4):21–43.

———. 2010a. "May God Let Me Share Paradise with My Fellow Believers: Islam's 'Female Face' and the Politics of Religious Devotion in Mali." In *Hard Times, Hard Work: Perspectives on the Politics of Agency in Africa*, edited by Beth A. Buggenhagen, Stephen Jackson, and Anne-Marie Makhulu, 113–129. Berkeley: University of California Press.

———. 2010b. "Remaking Society from Within: Extraversion and the Social Forms of Female Muslim Activism in Urban Mali." In *Development and Politics from Below: Exploring Religious Spaces in the African State*, edited by Barbara Bompani and M. Frahm-Arp, 74–96. New York: Palgrave Macmillan.

———. 2012. *Muslims and New Media in West Africa: Pathways to God*. Bloomington: Indiana University Press.

———. 2021. *Political Legitimacy in Postcolonial Mali*. Oxford: James Currey.

Schulz, Dorothea, and Souleymane Diallo. 2016. "Competing Assertions of Muslim Masculinity in Mali." *Journal of Religion in Africa* 46:219–250.

Tambiah, Stanley J. 1989. "Bridewealth and Dowry Revisited. The Position of Women in Sub-Saharan Africa and North India." *Current Anthropology* 30 (4):413–435.

Triaud, Jean-Louis. 1997. "Introduction." In *Le temps des marabouts: Itinéraires et strategies islamiques en Afrique occidentale francaise, v. 1880–1960*, edited by David Robinson and Jean-Louis Triaud, 11–29. Paris: Éditions Karthala.

# 8

# A "Much-Married Woman" Revisited

## Kinship Perspectives on the High Frequency of Divorce among Uyghurs in Southern Xinjiang, China

RUNE STEENBERG

Uyghurs in southern Xinjiang have by far the highest divorce rates across China and Central Asia. As in most other parts of this region, the rates in Xinjiang rose in the first decades of the twenty-first century, but unlike elsewhere they had previously fallen between 1982 and 2000. Uyghur divorce rates have been high at least since the early nineteenth century. This was demonstrated in Linda Benson's influential article, "A Much-Married Woman" (1993) and confirmed in Ildikó Bellér-Hann's seminal study on Uyghur social structure in the nineteenth and early twentieth centuries, *Community Matters in Xinjiang* (2008a). Both these works present important historical evidence on the relative ease of divorce and remarriage for Uyghur men and women, which Bellér-Hann (2008a) aptly refers to as "serial monogamy." Benson focuses on gender inequality and influences of Shi'i traditions of temporary marriage, but she does not approach the basic logic of family and kinship organization that makes frequent divorce possible. Bellér-Hann treats the kinship organization in much detail including frequent divorce, but she does not analyze it within a kinship theory framework. The same is true for other discussions of Uyghur kinship and divorce (Hoppe 1998; Rudelson 1997; Abdukérim Rehman et al. 2008; Enwer Semet Qorghan 2007). This is the void the present chapter intends to fill. I aim to place frequent divorce and serial monogamy within an analysis of Uyghur kinship practice in southern Xinjiang to examine the structural connections and logics that have enabled high divorce rates here for at least two hundred years. The chapter draws on my extensive fieldwork on Uyghur kinship in southern Xinjiang between 2010–2016, on recent statistical data, and on local contemporary and historical publications.[1] It focuses on the 2000s and 2010s but also traces the logics of serial monogamy back to the nineteenth century.

## High Uyghur Divorce Rates

According to Wang Qingbin and Zhou Qin (2010), at the end of the 2000s, Xinjiang had the highest divorce rates in China.[2] After looking at Chinese divorce and remarriage trends over time and across regions, they concluded that divorce rates had risen by more than 200 percent (2010, 258, 266) since the 1980s. In what they call an "econometric analysis," they related this rise to the rise in gross domestic product (GDP) and levels of education, which they take as main indicators of development and modernization and which they conclude led to a rise in divorces. However, the numbers from Xinjiang contradict this model. The region scored highest in all divorce-related categories used in the study (crude divorce rate, refined divorce rate, and remarriage rate), in spite of its comparatively low GDP and levels of education. Indeed, the numbers fall so significantly outside the Wang and Zhou's model's predictions that Xinjiang is excluded from the analysis (7). The region continued to have the country's highest divorce rates until 2014, when some of the northeastern and western provinces caught up.[3] The numbers for Xinjiang dropped significantly in 2015, when the regional government introduced a state of emergency that resulted in increased policing, surveillance, and militarization (Roberts 2020; Klimeš 2018; Byler and Zolin 2017).[4] Divorce rates dropped further after mass internments of minorities were begun in 2017 (Zenz 2020a); the reasons for these drops are provided at the end of this chapter. The chapter's primary focus is the general social logic behind the high Uyghur divorce rate before 2015 and its historical and cultural roots. In an earlier study, Zeng Yi and Wu Deqing (2000) analyzed regional divorce data in China between 1982 and 1990. Like Wang and Zhou, they documented a significant countrywide increase in divorce following economic development. Again, Xinjiang posed an exception. Here the crude divorce rate did not rise but rather dropped 13 percent while remaining six times the national average and three times that of the second-highest region (Zeng and Wu 2000, 216–217).[5] Unlike Wang and Zhou's argument, Zeng and Wu saw lack of development as a factor contributing to frequent divorce, as they posited that the prevalent early-age and arranged marriages are less stable. Both research teams invoked ethnicity, tradition, religion, and culture to explain Xinjiang's exceptional position (Wang and Zhou 2010, 264; Zeng and Wu 2000, 218) and both attributed the high divorce rates to the region's Muslim minorities. They pointed to the relative ease of divorce in Islamic law while stressing the low tolerance of divorce in Han-Chinese traditions. Premchand Dommaraju and Gavin Jones (2011, 734–735) confirmed a relatively high rate of divorce in Muslim-majority countries in Asia. They also noted a decline in the divorce rates of some areas in Southeast Asia with increasing modernization, economic development, and individualization. Moreover, they found some of the highest rates of divorce among the least economically developed population groups, such as the Malay Muslim populations in Southeast Asia. Here, economic development, state regulation, modern education, and individualization may have changed family strategies and kinship patterns, resulting in divorce rates dropping closer to a modern, industrial average. However, neither modernization, lack of development, nor Islam alone generally explain high divorce rates. Xinjiang is and has always been one of the least developed regions of the People's Republic of China (PRC), but in other parts of the country, low development and sustained traditions of early and arranged marriages have not resulted in higher divorce rates. Nor does Islam in itself produce frequent divorce: according to Matthew Erie, most Muslim areas in China have very low divorce rates even by Chinese standards (2016, 242–243), and Zeng and Wu (2000) remarked that Xinjiang's high divorce rates are found solely among the Uyghurs. None of the other Turko-Muslim minorities in Xinjiang or post-Soviet Central Asia that are widely recognized as being closest to the Uyghurs in language, culture, and religious observance have high divorce rates, and even across Uyghur communities in Xinjiang we find marked variations, with particularly high rates in the South.[6] This suggests even higher de facto rates among Uyghurs in southern Xinjiang, as the region's other ethnic groups (40 percent Han and 5 percent other ethnic groups) and Uyghurs living in the North and East all have significantly lower rates. Zeng and Wu (2000), Wang and Zhou (2010), and other studies have invoked the generic idea of "cultural traditions" as a way to explain such variations. What does this actually mean? What type of cultural traditions are responsible for high divorce rates? I suggest that the answer is to be found in those cultural traditions that influence family structure and household strategies and that inform the way in which people conceive of their closest social relations, within which marriages and divorces take place.[7] To understand the factors that facilitate high divorce rates among Uyghurs in southern Xinjiang, we need to examine local kinship organization in its complex, varied, and historically constructed specifics (Pfeffer 2016; Barnard and Good 1984).

## Ethnographic Evidence from Kashgar

During my fieldwork in Kashgar between 2010 and 2016, more than half of the Uyghur adults I interacted with regularly had divorced and remarried at least once and many of them had done so several times. The majority of men and women remarry after divorce and very few of my acquaintances were not presently married, as marriage is seen as a good and necessary part of adult life.[8] The highest number of marriages by a single person I came across was a man who had been married seven times. His reason for marrying this often was a common one: the inability to have children, which many Uyghurs in Kashgar ascribe to the incompatibility of the partners (Bellér-Hann 1999, 127–129). Other frequently mentioned reasons for divorce were quarrels with the mother-in-law, rows over gifts between the families, and debates about whether the wife should be allowed to work outside the home. All these issues are linked to household strategies. Like marriage, divorce is not a purely individual affair but rather a part of family considerations.

As marriage is central to social relations and, for most Uyghur families, social relations are central to the household economy and long-term livelihood sustainability, decisions involving marriage and divorce are more often than not influenced by considerations that go beyond the desires and sentiments of any particular individual. In Kashgar, legally binding divorce is instigated only through the state court, though some men still invoke *ṭalāq*. Unlike in many Muslim-majority countries where Islamic family law is recognized by the modern state, marriage, divorce, and inheritance in China have been "aggressively" reformed by the Chinese Communist Party (CCP) (Erie 2016, 23, 32, 40). While the Party has accepted the continuation of religious customs as a means to organize certain areas of Muslim community life—though more so in the Hui communities than among Uyghurs—"control over the family and over property is [seen as] foundational to state power" (23). This includes fixing a legal minimum age for marriage, forbidding arranged marriages and polygamy, and requiring the registration and legal execution of all marriages and divorces. Still, most of the negotiations surrounding divorce take place in community or family forums. Uyghur men are particularly wary of leaving decisions to the courts as they feel that they favor women.[9] State authorities and some Uyghur intellectuals (Memetimin Yaqup 2009, 2, 112–118; Abdushükür Muhemmet'imin 2002, 113–115) identify divorce as a social problem, but general attitudes among Uyghurs vary. Although many of my interlocutors in 2010–2014 believed that divorce damages families and the lives of individuals, most also saw it as a necessary course of action if the marriage is not happy—for example, if the partners are not compatible or if the families do not get along. Divorce is regrettable to all, but hardly anyone in southern Xinjiang dismisses it categorically. Both Uyghur men and women discuss it as an option in difficult family situations and acknowledge its respective advantages and drawbacks. In other words, divorce is an unwanted but tolerated part of normal life.

## "A Much-Married Woman"

Frequent divorce among Uyghurs in southern Xinjiang has been prevalent for more than a century.[10] In her 1993 article, Benson examined divorce in order to shed light on women's position in Uyghur society in the late nineteenth and early twentieth centuries. Benson noted a high frequency but extremely uneven distribution of divorce: in that era, some men and women married three to five times during a lifetime while others reportedly married up to forty times (233). Benson connected the frequent divorces to the Shi'a institution of temporary (*mut'a*) marriage (236, 244).[11] However, a close reading of the material suggests that this only applies to a minority of cases. Benson mentions repeated divorces of women from all classes, including the wealthy (232; Bellér-Hann 2008a, 260). Eric Schluessel similarly documents frequent divorces in Turpan in the late nineteenth century, citing the story of a man who married four times between 1870 and 1909 (2020, 119). Although the cases of poor women who divorced up to forty times could be the result of repeated mut'a-type marriages, many of the other known cases in Benson's, Bellér-Hann's, and Schluessel's descriptions clearly are not. Temporary marriages are still found today in Kashgar and Hotan although they are not called mut'a but rather *waqitliq toy* (time-limited marriage). These marriages are stigmatizing for women as they are viewed in the community as a type of prostitution practiced by women from poor families who are in need of economic or personal security. No wealthy woman in contemporary Kashgar would enter into a temporary marriage, nor would any high-status family allow their daughter to do so. Though divorce and remarriage carry no social stigma in Kashgar, temporary marriage does, as in high-status families the practice is in conflict with long-established values of modesty and shame (Bellér-Hann 2008a, 191–194). Of the many divorces I encountered during my time in Kashgar, none was the predetermined result of a temporary marriage. Rather, they were all described to me as the unfortunate outcome of incompatibility, emotional distress, and family conflicts.

However, not all these divorces were unintended or without calculated motives. Benson described marriage as an accepted strategy for upward mobility, highlighting the strategies of privileged women who used divorce and remarriage to enhance their social position (1993, 233). Similar strategies can be found in Kashgar today. This is parodized in the 2010 comedic sketch *Kona Ayagh* (Old Shoes) by Abdukérim Abliz (2011, 49–56). The sketch depicts a modern Uyghur "much-married woman" as a marriage swindler who manipulates marriage and divorce to her own advantage. She seduces men into marriage in order to subsequently divorce them and run off with their possessions. This sort of strategizing is not common practice today, and it was rare but not unheard of in the nineteenth century (Benson 1993, 234–236).[12] Still, the idea that individuals can use divorce to their personal advantage is clearly something to which a Uyghur audience can relate. This presupposes that the negative sentiments and possible stigma around divorce are less severe than the strategic, economic, or status advantages one may gain from it or from subsequent marriages. This was confirmed by several young men and women whom I met in Kashgar and Ürümchi between 2010 and 2014, who told me that they had used divorce as a strategy for escaping the pressure of their families. In an effort to please their parents, they had married early but then quickly divorced, after which they were free to pursue their own goals. Tursunjan, a blacksmith in his early forties, had married his maternal cousin under pressure from his mother when he was not yet twenty years of age. His father had died a few years earlier and his mother had been eager to consolidate the household relations with her own natal family. Tursunjan told me that he had doubted the durability of the marriage from the outset but had agreed to try it for his mother's sake, as he did not fear the consequences of a possible divorce. The couple divorced a mere six months after the wedding, and his mother and her sister did not speak for years thereafter. However, by 2011 the relations between them had normalized and Tursunjan, who was now the father of two children from his second wife, even visited his former mother-in-law occasionally.

Another example is Anargül, a female university student in Ürümchi who was originally from Kashgar. Her mother would not let her attend university unmarried. She had therefore married a high school classmate and gone to university while leaving her husband in the village. The physical distance between them and her lukewarm commitment saw the marriage dissolved after two years. She continued her studies and was now dating someone at her university. The divorce had been emotionally challenging, and it had provoked much gossip in the village and driven a wedge between the two families. Still, she did not feel disadvantaged by her experience but rather strengthened and emancipated, and she hoped to marry her new boyfriend after graduating. As with Benson's "much-married women" in the nineteenth century, Anargül's strategy worked because divorce is not socially stigmatized and also because a woman's loss of virginity is not seen as a hindrance to marriage. Only the unlawful (*ḥarām*) loss of virginity—outside the *ḥalāl* sanction of the *nikāḥ* marriage ceremony—poses a problem and renders a woman "broken" (*buzuk*). According to Bellér-Hann, this was also the case in nineteenth- and early twentieth-century Kashgar, when attractive women who had been married and given birth, thus proving their fertility, were highly valued on the marriage market (2008a, 260).

## Models of Muslim Marriage

Looking at the ethnographic evidence of temporary marriages, strategic weddings, and the various degrees of mediated marriages encountered in southern Xinjiang, we seem to be dealing with different marriage practices that each imply different kinds of divorce.[13] The primary "condition of possibility" (Bourdieu 1977, 3–4, 233) for these variations is the general acceptance of divorce in Uyghur society. This does not mean that divorces go unnoticed or are encouraged. Second and third marriages are celebrated less lavishly and, as seen in the cases of Tursunjan and Anargül, divorce connotes failure and strife, although not beyond the accepted ups and downs of ordinary life. Divorce, though regrettable, can sometimes be a reasonable choice. This acceptance is unlikely to have emerged from low-status women engaging in temporary marriage or individuals using divorce for personal benefit. To believe this would be to make or commit a functionalist fallacy of inverting cause and effect. Both temporary marriage and the strategic utilization of divorce and remarriage require (rather than create) such a tolerance and lack of stigma, which in turn must be in accord with the wider social and moral organization of society. If this "condition of possibility" is not created by an individual's strategies, what then does it derive from? Benson (1993), Wang and Zhou (2010), Zeng and Wu (2000) and others have remarked that Islamic legal traditions treat marriage not as a sacrament, but rather as a contract between two individuals that can be dissolved with legitimate reason. In the legal framework of the Sunni Ḥanafī legal school, which is generally accepted by Uyghurs, both husband and wife can initiate divorce and remarriage is permissible, though both are easier for men than women (Burhān al-Dīn 1957; Enwer Semet Qorghan 2007). Thus, there is no religious barrier to divorce. However, other Ḥanafī Muslim communities in China and Central Asia do not have high divorce rates. Nancy Tapper even describes Ḥanafī Muslim groups in the wider region where "divorce is almost unknown," such as among the Swat Pathans and the Durrani of northern Afghanistan (1991, 17).

Tapper contrasts the marriage practices of Muslim groups with low and high divorce rates. She identifies significant distinguishing features in these groups' social organization, particularly in the social roles of married women. She establishes two general models of what she terms "Muslim Middle Eastern Marriage" (1991).[14] Model A social contexts have very low divorce rates. Here a bride is transferred from her natal family to her marriage family almost completely: besides her physical movement, her rights and duties also transfer into her husband's family. By contrast, Model B contexts have much higher divorce rates. Here the bride keeps many of her rights and duties in her natal family and often returns to them in the case of conflict. Her natal family—and not her husband's kin—are responsible for punishing her for bad behavior, and she maintains close ties to her parental household for a long time after marriage. In Model A marriages, the bride may not see her natal kin for years—or even a lifetime—whereas in Model B contexts the bride tends to bridge and unite the two families. Therefore, Model A is generally connected to a high bridewealth and low dowry. The bridewealth functions as a form of compensation to the bride's natal family for the loss of a daughter, while dowry represents her family's contribution to the new conjugal unit.[15] Model B contexts balance dowry and bridewealth to initiate continued gift exchange and visitation between the two families after the wedding. This means that in Model B contexts (1) filiation (the tie between parents and children) is strong, as married women retain significant ties to their parents and siblings; and (2) affines play an important role in daily life, as exchange relations between in-laws remain extensive; but (3) transgenerational descent is weak and less important. Cognatic and affinal links constitute the core of kinship and household strategies. Model A contexts show the reverse pattern: (1) descent is important for daily life and social organization; (2) agnatic links are central while the contact to maternal relatives and affines is limited; and (3) for women, ties of filiation and siblingship are weakened after marriage. According to Tapper, Model A contexts feature much more stable marriages than Model B contexts, which tend to have high rates of divorce. Tapper described the Durrani and the Swat Pathans in Afghanistan as Model A contexts (cf. Anderson 1982; Lindholm 1982; Berrenberg 2002). In post-Soviet Central Asia and Xinjiang, most Kyrgyz and Kazakh groups also practice marriage along Model A patterns (Ismailbekova 2017; Gullette 2010; Hardenberg 2009; Schatz 2005; Svanberg 1999; Benson and Svanberg 1988). They display strong descent, dominant agnatic rather than cognatic relations, and weak affinal ties. The kinship system of the Uyghurs of southern Xinjiang entails pronounced Model B characteristics, which corresponds to unstable marriages and high divorce rates. Such general models are merely abstract sketches of systems of marriage and kinship that ignore many important details and variations and do not account for the transforming powers of the modern state and economic development. Nonetheless, the model is useful because it accurately describes the situation in southern Xinjiang and thus holds a key to understanding the conditions of possibility for the high divorce rates.

## Uyghur Kinship

Uyghur kinship practice in southern Xinjiang is structured around the cognatic family, marriage, and gift-giving relations. Descent is rendered agnatically but plays only a limited role and relatives on the mother's side remain important for both men and women throughout life.[16] Unlike in most other Central Asian contexts, no sociocentric groups formed around descent (like lineages, tribes, or clans) play any role in social organization. Instead, the cognatic family is the central unit built around the parental household also called the "big house" (*chong öy*) and the sibling group, including married sisters and all spouses. As is typical of Tapper's Model B marriage contexts, filiation is important while descent is not. No family names are used (Sulayman 2007), and while nicknames (*leqem*) are sometimes passed on from father to son, they are personal and rarely sustained for more than one generation. Genealogical links are not considered closer than nongenealogical links. Rather, gift exchange, mutual labor assistance, and sharing of funds define the family. The closest relatives (*yéqin tughqan*) are not genealogically proscribed, but rather they are defined and confirmed through exchange. This basic pattern has been described going back to at least the mid-nineteenth century by Bellér-Hann (2008a), and despite many changes and transformations in detail and concrete practice, I found that it still held true to a large degree during my research in Kashgar in 2010–2014. In poor urban neighborhoods and in rural villages around Kashgar, the neighborhood community and marriage relations are two of the most important institutions in which kinship is constructed. Tursunjan, who lived on the outskirts of Kashgar, would always participate in weddings in the neighborhood (*mehelle*) and contribute labor support. He and the other men met regularly at life-cycle rituals and in the mosque and many were engaged in business together. He described some of his neighbors as "real relatives" (*resmiy tughqan*) or "close relatives" (*yéqin tughqan*). Marriage within these categories was popular and several marriages had taken place between Tursunjan's neighbors.

## "Close Marriage"

Since the communist takeover in 1949, the state has discouraged or forbidden cousin marriage and other types of close-kin marriage.[17] Nonetheless, such marriages have remained common among Uyghurs, especially in the South.[18] Thomas Hoppe observed a marriage preference for first cousins (*bir-newre*) in Turpan in the 1990s but saw no categorical distinction made between paternal and maternal cousins (1998, 135–137). Bellér-Hann, drawing most of her material from southern Xinjiang, saw no distinction between types of cousins. She stated that in Kashgar, "the combination of propinquity and kinship generated the trust which underpinned the desirability of this type of marriage" (2008a, 256). According to my observations in Kashgar, no preference is given to any particular category of relative. Within a family from Shamalbagh on the outskirts of Kashgar, whose members I often interviewed and joined for weddings between 2010 and 2013, no fewer than four first-cousin marriages and ten close-kin marriages had taken place over the past two generations. In several other families I found a similar pattern. However, in Tursunjan's neighborhood and in the neighborhood where I lived in Kashgar's inner city in 2011, there was a higher frequency of marriage within the neighborhood than with kin living elsewhere. I agree with Bellér-Hann (2008a, 257) that trust is a primary criterion for "closeness" and the desirability of marriage. The reasons given for marrying close varied. Two cousins in the family from Shamalbagh had fallen in love and initiated the marriage themselves in 2013. The parents were thrilled and everybody felt safe concerning this union. In another case, a woman and a man from the same neighborhood had studied together in mainland China and decided to marry because, as they said, this would enable both to stay close to their families and the affines (*quda*) in order to give good support to each other. In Tursunjan's neighborhood, many marriages have taken place among neighbors over the last few generations and parents encourage their children to marry "close." Several parents said they felt reluctant to let a daughter marry too far away. An older woman from the Shamalbagh family confirmed this as she told me that a mother desires close affines because she would not want her daughter to have a difficult life among strangers, but also because the in-laws should support the family.

Marriage creates and confirms important bonds of close kinship. These bonds are not merely emotionally supportive but also materially essential for many households' livelihoods. Especially for poor Uyghur families, household strategies focus on social networks and institutions more than on state education and employment in the formal sector. Both in Tursunjan's neighborhood and with the family in Shamalbagh, mutual labor assistance and business support by close social relations are crucial. To marry outside such circles risks diverting resources to places that are not productive for household sustainability and bypasses opportunities to consolidate important commitments. After the divorce from his cousin, Tursunjan married a woman who had been the tailor apprentice of a friend. Her parents live in another town forty kilometers away. The communication between the two families was therefore infrequent, and they did not help each other in the fields and only rarely did so at life-cycle events. This has made Tursunjan's household more isolated than if he had married closer. Tursunjan compensates for this by being very extroverted and highly engaged in the neighborhood. Well-connected individuals and households with a state salary are less economically dependent on their social networks, and so close marriage is less necessary.

However, for the family in Shamalbagh and for many of Tursunjan's neighbors, the affines are crucial for the household economy and close marriage is a safe choice. Like Tursunjan, many of these families have no stable income and draw most of their business, resources, and labor from their social circles rather than from anonymous markets. Labor help is often needed for childcare, house construction, or to till supplementary plots of wheat or rice on which the household food security depends. For such households, social networks and communities are crucial. As descent is of little relevance, there is no larger kin group with whom close cooperation is prescribed. Instead, all relations beyond siblings are subject to zealous upkeep through gift giving (including money lending and labor support) and mutual visitation. Marriage is the strongest and most effective form of forging and maintaining such connections. Seeking affines among those who are socially close raises the probability that they will fulfill this role and the expectations it entails.

## The Importance of Affines

The genealogical memory of most Uyghurs in Kashgar does not extend many generations back. Adults can rarely trace their family back beyond their own grandparents. In contrast, the knowledge of living relatives is extensive. It includes relatives connected by several degrees of affinity, such as the siblings of the husband of one's wife's sister. At childbirth, circumcisions, marriages, and funerals it is common to take part in events held by affines of affines. At weddings, affinal relatives from earlier marriages, like a groom's sister's husband, are performatively integrated as close relatives through being assigned important tasks such as waiting on the guests, cooking, and serving food. At several weddings I attended in rural Atush, some thirty-five kilometers north of Kashgar, the spouses of the groom's siblings were all included in the traditional dance session for his closest relatives. Especially in the first years of a marriage, much effort is invested in building good and stable affinal relations. Ritual gift exchanges and mutual hospitality are expected at religious holidays and life-cycle events. In Kashgar, a special series of events called *öy körsitish* (showing the house) are held at which the close female relatives of a woman who has recently married into the family are invited to the homes of all the important relatives of the groom's family in order to establish relations of mutual guesting and gift giving between them. In rural Atush, all of a household's quda (parents of children's spouses) must be present when the bridewealth for a new marriage is transferred. The rationale is that they must give their consent, since the marriage choice of their affines affects their social networks. The so-called *baja*-relation between the husbands of two sisters is both economically important and emotionally tense (cf. Rudelson 1997, 107–108; Dautcher 2009, 65). Tursunjan did not have much contact with his wife's relatives because they lived far away and were not involved with his other social circles, but he did interact with his baja—his wife's sisters' husbands. He occasionally borrowed money from them, helped one of them set up a stall at a market in Kashgar, and helped another register his motorcycle. Similarly, several of the traders from rural Atush whom I accompanied on their trading endeavors to Kyrgyzstan (Steenberg 2016) cooperated with their baja in business.

## The Bridging Role of the Bride

The baja-relation between sisters' husbands revolves around the sibling group, in which sisters and their husbands are as central as brothers and their wives. This illustrates the continued central role of married women in their sibling group. As in Tapper's Model B contexts, the bride never fully transfers into her husband's family. She remains close to her parents' house, called the "big house" (*chong öy*), where she retains extensive rights and duties. In important ways, a bride bridges the gap between the two families. She is not given from one to the other, but rather connects them, ideally uniting them into one family.[19] Meryem, a woman in her early forties from rural Kashgar, married into the family of the neighbors. Although she and her husband had moved into an apartment in the city, her husband was often away trading in mainland China, so she and their four children spent much time in the village. They usually stayed with her parents-in-law, but she saw her widowed father every day and often cooked for him, toiled in his fields with him, and looked out for her brother's children. She was also involved in all celebrations and major decisions at her parental home and in her siblings' families. At her brother's marriage, she danced in the dance session of the central relatives along with her two eldest daughters. Similarly, the four of eight married siblings (two sisters and two brothers) of the Shamalbagh family who lived close by met to have dinner on a weekly basis and celebrated the religious holidays together. The oldest brother and one sister had married within the neighborhood and therefore lived very close to their parental home.

In the marriage process, several rituals symbolize and effect the uniting of the two families as the initially clear distinction between bride's side (*qiz terep*) and groom's side (*oghul terep*) is gradually blurred. During the first meetings and negotiations, the two sides remain distinctly apart to the point of all guests being assigned to one side or the other even when they are friends or relatives of both. At subsequent meetings the division lessens, and on the evening before the wedding day, the groom's relatives arrive at the house of the bride's parents carrying all the ingredients for the early-morning wedding meal (*ashsüyi*). They spend the night preparing a morning rice meal for guests of both sides and thus act as hosts along with the bride's parents.[20] This symbolic integration of the two sides continues throughout the wedding celebrations. On the second day of the wedding, the bride's mother and her female relatives (including neighbors and friends) are invited to the groom's place. Here, the women transgress the distinction between the two sides through blurring the roles of guest and host and overruling the initially divided seating arrangements. They explicitly stress that such divisions are obsolete "now that we have become relatives." In the evening of the same day, the groom and his friends enter the courtyard in a ritual called *tartishmaq* (literally, to pull each other). They call for the bride's mother to come out to meet her son-in-law. In this process, the groom's friends keep calling her "his mother," adding flattering adjectives and using the most intimate word for "mother" (cf. Cesàro 2002, 130).[21] The bride is also encouraged to say "mother" to her mother-in-law in another ritual. After the bride has arrived at the groom's parents' place, his mother fakes a headache and falls to the ground in front of her new daughter-in-law. The bride is now expected to gently encourage her to rise, addressing her as "mother." I attended several of these ceremonies. In Shamalbagh, the tartishmaq was particularly wild, with the groom's friends taunting his "new mother" while her relatives ridiculed the groom. The purpose is to force them closer to each other—both spatially in the ritual (as the groom and the bride's mother meet and exchange gifts over the threshold of a door) and socially (as the mutual ritual teasing breaks up the strong modesty constraints of etiquette between these two groups, who are now relatives). In some families, the groom's mother fakes a toothache rather than a headache, and in rural Atush there is no tartishmaq but the groom must call his mother-in-law "mother" before she opens the door of her home to him at his first visit after the wedding. The details of the rituals vary, but they all function to bridge the two families by making the new conjugal unit an integral part of both families. The whole marriage process can be seen as a process of securing the affines as close relatives who are essential to the family's economic, ritual, and social engagements.

## A Fragile Process

Much effort is invested into merging the two families. Because the process is so important and complex, it is also tense and fragile: the affines carry much potential but also pose the risk of grave disappointment. Riswangül from Kashgar was the daughter of government workers but married a man from a trader family. They divorced some years later due to tensions between Riswangül and her mother-in-law. Riswangül's mother explained that the source of the tension had been the mother-in-law's dissatisfaction with their gifts and contributions to family events. Riswangül's mother accepted a part of the blame, as she and her husband had little free time and had therefore not been able to perform all the etiquette expected by the husband's mother who—as she delicately put it—paid more attention to traditions. This was a euphemism for being "backward." Both Riswangül and her mother saw her failed marriage as evidence for the wisdom of marrying someone similar to oneself, without significant differences in expectations and ability. In the case of a young man called Memetjan, the tension that eventually led to divorce was the disappointment that the gifts from the groom's side were too few and too cheap. I learned that this was a common cause of tension between affines that continues beyond the wedding gifts and includes expectations about lending money for the building of a house or shouldering the financial burden of sending children to university. Abdukérim Abliz (2011) illustrated this in his comedic sketch *Besh Miliyonluq Xiyal* (Dreaming of five million), where the main character's brother-in-law walks off in rage after not having received 40,000 yuan for his new house.[22] As Riswangül's case shows, the etiquette surrounding affines is complicated. Affines are treated respectfully and with reverence,[23] but when they do not meet expectations, they are judged harshly. Dissatisfaction breeds tension and concern over commitment, obligation, trust, face, and honor. A local joke captures this tension well. The Uyghur word for "mother-in-law" is *qéyin'ana*. Jokingly, by only slightly changing the pronunciation from *é* to *i*, she can be referred to as *qiyin'ana*—the "difficult mother." As a young man explained, "She is the mother [that is] so difficult to make a mother." It is clearly the ideal for a mother-in-law to be like a mother. If she cannot, it means that the affines cannot fulfill their role as close relatives and an important part of the marriage has failed. Often the result is the discontinuation of the marriage process. This can happen at any time before or after the wedding and the Muslim marriage ceremony (nikāḥ). If it happens after the nikāḥ and the state registration, it is termed "divorce" (*ajrishish*), but this distinction is less important than it may seem.[24]

The process of marriage is long and complex, full of gifts and celebrations before and after the wedding. Even before the nikāḥ, much has been invested and many people have been involved. The nikāḥ itself adds to the stakes, but they are already very high. More significant is whether a child has been born. When Tursunjan told me of his first marriage to his cousin, the lack of a child was the first thing he mentioned to support his claim that the divorce had not been devastating for either of them. The more interconnected the families become, the more significant the consequences of a divorce will be. It is often uncomplicated for a young couple to divorce within the first year of marriage. Once the families have gotten to know each other, the visits of *öy körsitish* and mutual visits of the in-laws at *qurban héyit* (Arabic, ʿĪd al-'Aḍḥā, the feast of sacrifice) have taken place, and perhaps even business relations have been established, the cut becomes more painful and consequential.

## Remarriage and Repeated Marriage

Almost all divorced people remarry. People in Kashgar see marriage as a value in itself and consider it as the natural and healthy state for all adults. Only under exceptional circumstances do widowed and divorced people remain unmarried. This is also true for older people. In Atush, a friend of mine and his siblings put much effort into getting their aging father remarried following the divorce from his third wife. One of the elder men in Shamalbagh married a divorced woman with grown children in 2010 and they divorced five years later citing conflicts between the children, although the elderly spouses were still fond of each other. A divorced shoemaker from Kashgar old city was strongly encouraged by the members of his mosque to marry a young, divorced woman from a poor background. He did so during my stay in the city in 2015, but the marriage did not even last a year.

Two years earlier, in late summer 2013, I came across another instructive case of remarriage. While on a bus traveling from Kashgar to Hotan, I entered into conversation with Feidullah, a young man who was dressed in a tuxedo and accompanied by his cousin and a close friend. He told me that he was going to a village for *qiz sorash* ("to ask for the girl"). Qiz sorash is a part of the marriage negotiations that is usually done by elder relatives of the groom in a visit to the bride's parents. It seemed odd that the groom would go himself and travel so unceremoniously. Feidullah explained that he knew the bride's parents well as the couple had already been married for several years and had a child together. Following a dispute, he had divorced her some months earlier, but they had reconciled and were now going to remarry. He was bringing the *toyluq* (bridewealth), which was less than that of their first marriage but still a considerable amount—more than ten thousand yuan (1,200 USD).[25] The *nikāḥ* was going to be performed and there would be a small wedding celebration. In response to my inquiry, he told me that none of the bridewealth or gifts from the first wedding had been returned when they divorced, nor did I hear of this in any other case.[26]

Feidullah's was the only remarriage to the same person that I learned about personally, though I heard of similar cases. This seems to have been more common before the start of mandatory state registration of marriages and divorces. In older sources from South Xinjiang, there are several mentions of divorced couples rejoining in marriage (Högberg 1917; Bellér-Hann 2008a; Benson 1993) following Ḥanafī legal rules (Enwer Semet Qorghan 2007; Burhān al-Dīn 1957). Such remarriages are generally celebrated in a much simpler style than first marriages or even second or third marriages with a new partner, but they entail the regular elements required for a marriage, including a new celebration and nikāḥ. They always require new gifts, bridewealth, and dowry to reactivate the severed bonds between their families.

## Conclusion: The Logic of Divorce in Southern Xinjiang

The handling of gifts in cases of divorce and remarriage illustrates an important point about Uyghur marriage and divorce in southern Xinjiang. Marriage is not a transfer of the bride from one family to the other (against which a compensation is transferred in the other direction), and thus divorce is not the reversal of this transfer, as would be the case in Tapper's Model A scenarios. Instead, as in Tapper's Model B, marriage unites two families, merging them through a process of building mutual trust and dependence. This is done through gifts being given in both directions between the families. The goal is for the two families to become close relatives and rely on each other for social safety and support, business opportunities, money lending, and regular labor support. Divorce signifies the discontinuation of this process. The gift giving and hospitality end. There is nothing to give back, but if the process resumes, as in Feidlullah's case, new gifts must be produced as proof of sincerity, to soothe the hurt feelings, and to formally resume the process.

In southern Xinjiang, mutual gifts and reliable support are the main ways to secure and consolidate long-term relationships. This is an open, active process, which is not determined by genealogical ties. Moreover, the affines play central roles in the process. The key to understanding the high frequency of divorce in Kashgar thus lies in ideas and practices pertaining to nongenealogical kinship and close marriage as a process of producing and consolidating close social relations. It is the ideal for affines to become "central relatives," who are crucial to the social and economic life of a household providing labor help and financial support.[27] Yet the marriage process is long and arduous, involving much communication and gift exchange before, during, and after the wedding. Affinal relations are at the same time laden with the ambiguities of expectation and tension. Therefore, people often seek affines among those who have the best potential for becoming close relatives by meeting the gifting, aid, and visiting expectations, such as relatives and neighbors.

If the affines do not fulfill the obligations expected of close relatives, conflict is inevitable and divorce is often the consequence. From the perspective of a Uyghur household, this is regrettable but rational, as someone else can now fill the important structural position of the affines. Even though not all marriages or divorces follow this pattern, the basic logic of nongenealogical kinship, important affines, close marriage, and acceptance of divorce as household strategies underlie Uyghur kinship practice, informing expectations, wishes, and understandings of social relations. Within this social organization, divorce—like close marriage—is an accepted strategy of a household or family to optimize its position in society and secure livelihoods for its members. Divorce is not an individual decision, just as a mismatched marriage is not an individual grievance. This is the logic that creates the conditions for the possibility of relatively easy divorces with little social stigma and the option of remarriage. As Benson and others have described, it enables a number of related phenomena, including serial monogamy, the instrumentalization of divorce and remarriage for personal gain, temporary marriage, and blaming childlessness on the failed match with the option of trying again with someone else.

## Outlook: The Modernization of Uyghur Divorce

After the Chinese government eased divorce regulations in the marriage law of 1980 (Zeng and Wu 2000, 215), divorce rates surged in all provinces of China except Xinjiang, where it dropped between 1982 and 2000. Even at the lowest point, Xinjiang's rates were still extremely high by comparison within both China and Central Asia and matched the highest rates in Europe and North America. The fall of divorce rates in Xinjiang up to 2000 can likely be attributed to the same factors that contributed to a rise elsewhere. The traditional kinship structures were weakened and a modern state-centered society was created, with a market-driven economy and modern laws, regulations, and desires. In other words, between 1982 and 2000, we may have seen a convergence of divorce rates between different historical traditions of kinship organization closing in on a similar contemporary "modern" average, with that of the Uyghurs and some other Asian Muslim groups (Dommaraju and Jones 2011, 734–735) falling rather than rising towards the mean. After 2000, this changed in Xinjiang: the regional divorce rates resurged back to above 1982 levels.[28] The reasons for this resurgence are complex and multifaceted. However, building on the argument of this chapter, I would like to suggest viewing the changing divorce rates as a meandering process within the logic of Uyghur kinship. If marriage is the institution where the central units of Uyghur society are constructed, and if affines are the most significant relatives beyond the parents and siblings, then this is where society breaks apart when under pressure. In 1999, the Chinese government introduced a massive modernization program to "Develop the Great West" (*da xibu kaifa*, 大西布开发; Lai 2002; Shan and Weng 2013), and in the same year the railroad reached Kashgar at China's westernmost extreme. The following fifteen years saw unprecedented economic growth and the integration of a majority of the region's inhabitants into the formal state and market systems. This led to a massive restructuring of society, the fragmentation and dismantling of many long-established communities, and extreme alienation and crises of identity and morality among Uyghurs (Bellér-Hann 2013; Kobi 2016; Pawan and Niyazi 2016; Steenberg and Rippa 2019). In my view, the rising divorce rates reflect this difficult transformation process in a way that accords both with the working of the historically based kinship system and the modernization and individualization of society. A similar dynamic may also account for the particularly high divorce rates in Xinjiang in 1982, as this too was a period of upheaval and rapid social transformation. It was only a few years after the conclusion of the Cultural Revolution and at the beginning of China's reform period of gradual marketization and liberalization (see Davis and Harrell 1993).

The latest development in Uyghur divorce rates is puzzling and worrying. Starting in 2015 and particularly in 2017 and 2018, we see a sharp decline in divorces and marriages in Xinjiang. The reasons for this are not clear, but it may mark the deterioration of normal social life in the region during the securitization of 2015–2016 and the following mass incarceration of Turko-Muslim minorities from spring 2017 (Byler and Zolin 2017; Zenz 2020a). Uyghurs in South Xinjiang have been harshly affected by government incarceration, which has torn apart tens of thousands of families and seemingly contributed to a massive drop in birth rates.[29] Both marriage and divorce rates in Xinjiang hit a historical low in 2018, when the mass incarceration and intimidation of the local minority population was at its highest. Rates seemed to recover slightly in 2019, when many of the detention centers and re-education camps were beginning to close.[30] Whether or not these numbers return to pre-2015 levels in the coming years may provide us with hints at the degree of social recovery from the political shocks of this state violence.

## NOTES

1. As part of my participant observation, I recorded more than twenty cases of divorce in southern Xinjiang in detail, interviewed may of those involved, and attended several marriages.
2. Compare China n.d. See also Erie 2016, 243.
3. See China n.d.
4. The state of emergency (also known as the People's War on Terror), which was introduced in Xinjiang starting in May 2014 and intensified up until 2018, had complex and multiple causes. The immediate causes cited by the government were a number of violent incidents attributed to Uyghur "terrorists" and "separatists." Underlying causes include the deterioration of trust between Uyghur communities and the government following violent clashes in 2009, the massive inflow of Chinese migrants and capital, and the preparation of the region to play a key role in Xi Jinping's Belt and Road Initiative.
5. Whereas in 1982 no other region had general divorce rates over 3.50, Xinjiang had a staggering rate of 20.92. In the 1990s the corresponding numbers were 6.00 and 17.40. A similar picture is revealed in the crude divorce rate: no other region reached 1.0 in 1982, whereas Xinjiang attained 4.20. In 1990 only six regions exceeded 1.00 but none reached 2.00, whereas Xinjiang had a rate of 3.79 (Zeng and Wu 2000, 216).
6. I have found no statistics supporting regional or ethnic differences in Xinjiang, but both anecdotal and historical evidence as well as my own observations in the region between 2010 and 2016 strongly suggest particularly high divorce rates among Uyghurs in the South.
7. The Central Asian countries have very low rates (see United Nations 2017).
8. One popular local idiom for marrying is to "set [a person]'s head straight" (*beshini ongshap qoyush*). Remaining single is viewed as unnatural and unhealthy regardless of whether one has been married before (cf. Bellér-Hann 2008a, 236; Memetimin Yaqup 2009, 149).
9. Before the enactment of the stricter policies of 2014, many marriages in rural Kashgar went unregistered and thus the divorces also did not involve the state. After 2014 this became much rarer as the penalties became more severe, even including imprisonment.
10. Cf. Cable and French 1927; Murray 1993; Macartney 1931; Skrine 1926; and see Benson 1993; Hoppe 1998, 132; Rudelson 1997, 88; Bellér-Hann 2008a, 260, 282.
11. Mut'a is a form of temporary marriage in which the marriage is automatically dissolved after a certain period of time stipulated in the contract. Almost all Uyghurs in Kashgar follow Ḥanafī Sunni traditions, and mut'a is a Shi'i practice. The word is not used in Kashgar today and I have not seen it mentioned in the older sources. However, this does not mean that a similar practice does not exist. Various Shi'a practices have been documented in Xinjang, small Shi'a communities among Uyghurs are found in Yarkant, and several Shi'a groups live in their vicinity, such as the Tajiks in Tashkurgan. If we view Islam as a discursive tradition (Asad 1996, 14–15), defined not through rigid border delineation but rather through family resemblance of its various parts and branches, then it should not surprise us to find this kind of mutual influence. Thus, the terms do not necessarily reveal the practice.
12. The Communist family laws of 1950 and 1980 granted women improved rights in divorce. However, Matthew Erie has reported that even though "a centerpiece of [PRC]

marriage law reform since the 1950s has been to empower women with the right to divorce," Hui women seeking divorce still "encounter patriarchy from multiple sources, including Chinese custom, Islamic law, and state law" (2016, 221).

13. I use the term *mediated marriage* to indicate that almost all Uyghur marriages in South Xinjiang take place with the involvement and consideration of more than just the two individuals who are marrying. In this way I seek to escape the unhelpful dichotomic conceptualization of "arranged marriage" versus "love marriage."
14. Tapper's concept of the Muslim Middle East also includes South Asia and Central Asia but not Southeast Asia.
15. Bridewealth is wealth transferred in the opposite direction of the bride as a compensatory payment for the loss of her labor and fertility, whereas dowry is wealth transferred in the same direction in regard to the bride but from the older generation to the younger. Goody and Tambiah (1973) called dowry "diverging devolution" and saw in it a type of pre-mortem inheritance for women.
16. Although inheritance follows regional and Islamic tradition in being mainly passed on agnatically, women also inherit; moreover, they are often equipped with a substantial dowry at marriage.
17. Cf. Engel 1984, 958; Chow 1992, 199; Bellér-Hann 2004, 190–191.
18. Cf. Rudelson 1997, 107–108; Hoppe 1998, 45, 135–137; Bellér-Hann 2008a, 256–258.
19. Certain idioms denoting marriage stress the transfer of the bride, while others stress the element of connection and of addition. *Qiz bermek, qiz almaq* (to give a girl, to take a girl) mean to marry off or marry a young woman and are examples of the former. *Tegmek, chaplimaq, birleshmek* (literally, to touch on, to stick onto, to unite) are examples of the latter. The former group of idioms owes much to male-biased ideology and refers to the bridewealth, while the latter group is especially relevant to the present argument.
20. This event is known as *toy neziri. Nezir,* a word used across Central Asia as a generic term for rituals commemorating death, denotes a ritual communal meal given on behalf of someone to create auspiciousness for this person. Feeding the needy is well regarded at a nezir (cf. Beller-Hann 2008b, 156; 2008a, 225).
21. "*Chirayliq anisi, bodek anisi, omaq anisi . . . chiqsun!* [His beautiful mother, his shortish, plump mother, his cute little mother . . . let her come out!]."
22. The whole sketch *Besh Milyonluq Xiyal* can be watched on youtube at https://www.youtube.com/watch?v=GJCkdozDXTU.
23. Cf. Abdukérim Rehman et al. 2009, 856–858; Weli Kérem 2010, 25–33; Abdukérim Abliz 2011, 26–29; cf. also Bellér-Hann 2008b.
24. The Uyghur term for divorce, *ajrishish,* is the gerund of a verb also signifying separation more generally. If the separation takes place before the wedding, the almost synonymous verb *ayrilish* (to part) is generally used.
25. *Toyluq* is to be understood as classical bridewealth given to the parents of the bride in compensation for their loss of a daughter. It may entail the mahr known from Islamic law, but this is usually of merely symbolic size. Today most people do not know about this custom, but before 1949 it was common (Bellér-Hann 2008a). Among Hui, *mahr* is used as a type of bridewealth similar to the Uyghur toyluq (Erie 2016, 234–238).
26. According to Matthew Erie, among Hui the bridewealth may be returned if the marriage lasted only a short period and the divorce was initiated by the wife, in order to "discourage women from marrying for material gain" (2016, 248).
27. "'Central relatives"' would be part of the local category of *yéqin tughqan* (close relatives) and *resmiy tughqan* (real relatives), but they make up an even smaller core within it on

whom the household depends for labor help, accessing funds, and emotional support, among other things. Cf. Enwer Semet Qorghan 2010, 2–3, 10; Yarmuhemmet Tahir Tughluq 2009, 213, 161; Abdushükür Muhemmet'imin 2002, 155.

28. See China n.d. These comparisons are difficult to make and rely on estimates as no constant, standardized numbers exist for the entire period and statistical methods have changed several times between 1982 and 2020.

29. Unlike what Adrian Zenz (who works for the conservative, Washington, DC–based, anticommunist group, Victims of Communism Memorial Foundation) suggested in his report (2020b), I see no evidence to attribute the fall in fertility among Uyghurs in Xinjiang between 2016 and 2019 to systematic sterilizations and forced abortions by the Chinese government. Instead, it is very likely that the massive securitization of the region along with the mass incarcerations have been a major cause of this decline.

30. See China n.d.

## REFERENCES

Abdukérim Abliz. 2011. *Abdukérim Abliz Étutliri.* Ürümchi: Shinjang Yashlar-ösmüler Neshriyati.

Abdukérim Rehman, Shirin Qurban, Esed Sulayman, Qurban Muhemmettursun, Erkin Idris, Sawutjan Abduxaliq, Nusret Turdi, and Muhemmetursun Ibrahim. 2009. *Ezizane Qeshger: Shinjang qeshgerning gheyriy maddiy medeniyet miraslirini qoghdash.* Kashgar: Qeshqer Uyghur Neshriyati.

Abdushükür Muhemmet'imin. 2002. *A'ile.* Ürümchi: Shinjang Unívérsitéti Neshriyati.

Anderson, Jon W. 1982. "Cousin Marriage in Context: Constructing Social Relations in Afghanistan." *Folk. Dansk Ethnografsk Tidsskrift København* 24:7–28.

Asad, Talal. 1996. *The Idea of an Anthropology of Islam.* Washington, DC: Georgetown University, Center for Contemporary Arab Studies.

Barnard, Alan, and Anthony Good. 1984. *Research Practices in the Study of Kinship.* London: Academic Press.

Bellér-Hann, Ildikó. 1999. "Women, Work and Procreation Beliefs in Two Muslim Communities." In *Conceiving Persons: Ethnographies of Procreation and Fertility, and Growth*, edited by Patrick Heady and Peter Loizos, 113–138. London: Athlone Press.

———. 2004. "Law and Custom among the Uyghur in Xinjiang." In *Central Asian Law: An Historical Overview: A Festschrift for the Ninetieth Birthday of Herbert Franke Topeka*, edited by Irina Popova and Wallace Johnson, 173–194. Kansas City: University of Kansas, Society for Asian Legal History.

———. 2008a. *Community Matters in Xinjiang, 1880–1949: Towards a Historical Anthropology of the Uyghurs.* Leiden: Brill.

———. 2008b. "Strangers, Guests and Beggars in Xinjiang: The Ambiguities of Hospitality among the Uyghurs." *Etudes Orientales* 25 (1):145–164.

———. 2013. "The Bulldozer State: Chinese Socialist Development in Xinjiang." In *Performing Politics in Central Asia: Ethnographies of the State*, edited by Judith Beyer, Madeleine Reeves, and Johan Rasanayagam, 262–289. Bloomington: Indiana University Press.

Benson, Linda. 1993. "A Much-Married Woman: Marriage and Divorce in Xinjiang, 1850–1950," *Muslim World* 83 (3–4):227–247.

Benson, Linda, and Ingvar Svanberg. 1988. *The Kazaks of China: Essays on an Ethnic Minority.* Uppsala: Almqvist and Wiksell.

Berrenberg, Jeanne. 2002. *Eine Sache der Ehre: Über die Grundlagen sozialer Prozesse bei den Pashtunen Pakistans und Afghanistans anhand ihrer Heiratsformen.* Frankfurt: Peter Lang.

Bourdieu, Pierre. 1977. *Outline of a Theory of Practice.* Cambridge: Cambridge University Press.

Burhān al-Dīn ʻAlī ibn Abī Bakr al-Marghīnānī. 1957. *The Hedaya, or Guide: A Commentary on the Mussulman Laws.* Translated by C. Hamilton. Lahore: New Book.

Byler, Darren, and Nicola Zolin. 2017. "Uyghur Migrant Life in the City during the People's War on Terror." *Youth Circulations Online*, October 17. Http://www.youthcirculations.com/blog/2017/10/22/uyghur-migrant-life-in-the-city-during-the-peoples-war.

Cable, Mildred, and Francesca French. 1927. *Through the Jade Gate.* London: Constable.

Cesàro, Maria Cristiná. 2002. "Consuming Identities: The Culture and Politics of Food among the Uyghur in Contemporary Xinjiang." Unpublished PhD thesis, University of Kent.

China, Government of. n.d. Accessed March 3, 2020. Http://data.stats.gov.cn/english/easyquery.htm?cn=E0103.

Chow, Ju-Chin. 1992. *Verlobung und Eheschließung in China: Das Eherecht im IV. Buch des Nankinger BGB Familienrecht vom 26.12. 1930 (in der Fassung vom 3.6. 1985) und das Pekinger Ehegesetz vom 10.9. 1980.* Frankfurt: Lang.

Dautcher, Jay. 2009. *Down a Narrow Road: Identity and Masculinity in a Uyghur Community in Xinjiang, China.* Boston: Harvard University, Asia Center.

Davis, Deborah S., and Steven Harrell. 1993. *Chinese Families in the Post-Mao Era.* Berkeley: University of California Press.

Dommaraju, Premchand, and Gavin Jones. 2011. "Divorce Trends in Asia." *Asian Journal of Social Science* 39 (6):725–750.

Engel, John W. 1984. "Marriage in the People's Republic of China: Analysis of a New Law." *Journal of Marriage and the Family* 46 (4):955–961.

Enwer Semet Qorghan. 2007. *Uyghurlarda Perhiz.* Ürümchi: Shinjang Xelq Neshriyiti.

——. 2010. *Uyghurlarda Nesebname.* Ürümchi: Shinjang Xelq Neshriyiti.

Erie, Matthews. 2016. *China and Islam: The Prophet, the Party, and Law.* Cambridge: Cambridge University Press.

Gullette, David. 2010. *The Genealogical Construction of the Kyrgyz Republic: Kinship, State and "Tribalism."* Kent: Global Oriental.

Hardenberg, Roland. 2009. "Reconsidering 'Tribe.' 'Clan' and 'Relatedness': A Comparison of Social Categorization in Central and South Asia." *Scrutiny: A Journal of International and Pakistan Studies* 1 (1):37–62.

Högberg, Lars E. 1917. "Et bröllup." In *På obnade stigar: Tjugofem år i Ost-Turkestan*, edited by J. E. Lundahl, 107–113. Stockholm: Trykkeri Aktiebolget Ferm.

Hoppe, Thomas. 1998. *Die ethnischen Gruppen Xinjiangs: Kulturunterschiede und interethnische Beziehungen.* Hamburg: Institut für Asienkunde Hamburg.

Ismailbekova, Aksana. 2017. *Blood Ties and the Native Son: Poetics of Patronage in Kyrgyzstan.* Bloomington: Indiana University Press.

Klimeš, Ondrej. 2018. "Advancing 'Ethnic Unity' and 'De-Extremization': Ideational Governance in Xinjiang under 'New Circumstances' (2012–2017)." *Journal of Chinese Political Science* 23 (3):413–436.

Kobi, Madlen. 2016. *Constructing, Creating, and Contesting Cityscapes: A Socio-Anthropological Approach to Urban Transformation in Southern Xinjiang, People's Republic of China.* Wiesbaden: Harrassowitz Verlag.

Lai, Hongyi. 2002. "China's Western Development Program: Its Rationale, Implementation, and Prospects." *Modern China* 28 (4):432–466.

Lindholm, Charles. 1982. *Generosity and Jealousy: The Swat Pukhtun of Northern Pakistan.* New York: Columbia University Press.

Macartney, Catherina. 1931. *An English Lady in Chinese Turkestan.* London: E. Benn.

Memetimin Yaqub. 2009. *Nikahtin ajrishish we uning ziyini.* Ürümchi: Shinjang Xelq Sehiye Neshriyati.

Murray, Charles A. 1993. *The Pamirs Being a Narrative of a Year's Expedition on Horseback and on Foot through Kashmir, Western Tibet, Chinese Tartary and Russian Central Asia.* New Delhi: Vintage Books.

Pawan, Sawut, and Abiguli Niyazi. 2016. "From Mahalla to Xiaoqu." *Inner Asia* 18 (1):12–34.

Pfeffer, Georg. 2016. *Verwandtschaft als verfassung: Unbürokratische muster öffentlicher ordnung.* Baden-Baden: Nomos Verlag.

Roberts, Sean. 2020. *The War on the Uyghurs: China's Campaign against Xinjiang's Muslims.* Princeton: Princeton University Press.

Rudelson, Justin. 1997. *Oasis Identities: Uyghur Nationalism along China's Silk Road.* New York: Columbia University Press.

Schatz, Edward. 2005. "Reconceptualizing Clans: Kinship Networks and Statehood in Kazakhstan." *Nationalities Papers* 33 (2):231–254.

Schluessel, Eric. 2020. *Land of Strangers: The Civilizing Project in Qing Central Asia.* New York: Columbia University Press.

Schrode, Paula. 2008. "The Dynamics of Orthodoxy and Heterodoxy in Uyghur Religious Practice." *Die Welt des Islams* 48 (3–4):394–433.

Shan, Wei, and Weng Cuifen. 2013. "China's 'New Deal' in Xinjiang and Its Challenges." In *China: Development and Governance,* edited by Gungwu Wang and Yong-Nian Zheng, 71–80. Singapore: World Scientific Publishing.

Skrine, Clairmont P. 1926. *Chinese Central Asia: An Account of Travels in Northern Kashmir and Chinese Turkestan.* London: Methuen.

Steenberg, Rune. 2016. "Embedded Rubber Sandals: Trade and Gifts across the Sino–Kyrgyz Border." *Central Asian Survey* 35 (3):405–420.

Steenberg, Rune, and Alessandro Rippa. 2019. "Development for All? State Schemes, Security, and Marginalization in Kashgar, Xinjiang." *Critical Asian Studies* 51 (2):274–295.

Sulayman, Esed. 2007. "Hybrid Naming Culture in Xinjiang. Problems Surrounding Uyghur Name/Surname Practices and Their Reform." In *Situating the Uyghurs between China and Central Asia,* edited by Ildikó Bellér-Hann, Rachel Harris, Cristina Cesàro, and Joanne Smith Finley, 109–130. Hampshire: Ashgate.

Svanberg, Ingvar. 1999. *Contemporary Kazakhs: Cultural and Social Perspectives.* London: Routledge.

Tapper, Nancy. 1991. *Bartered Brides: Politics, Gender, and Marriage in an Afghan Tribal Society.* Cambridge: Cambridge University Press.

United Nations. 2017. *Demographic Yearbook.* Https://unstats.un.org/unsd/demographic/products/dyb/dyb2011/Table25.pdf.

Wang, Qingbin, and Zhou Qin. 2010. "China's Divorce and Remarriage Rates: Trends and Regional Disparities." *Journal of Divorce & Remarriage* 51 (4):257–267.

Weli, Kérem. 2010. *Méhmandostluq terbiyesi.* Ürümchi: Shinjang Éléktron Ün-Sin Neshriyati.

Yarmuhemmet Tahir Tughluq. 2009. *Qa'ide yosunlirimiz.* Kashgar, Ürümchi: Qeshqer Uyghur Neshriyati; Shinjang Güzel Sen'et-foto Süret Neshriyati.

Zeng, Yi, and Wu Deqing. 2000. "Regional Analysis of Divorce in China since 1980." *Demography* 37 (2):215–219.

Zenz, Adrian. 2020a. "The Karakax List: Dissecting the Anatomy of Beijing's Internment Drive in Xinjiang." *Journal of Political Risk* 8 (2). Https://www.jpolrisk.com/karakax/.

———. 2020b. *Sterilizations, Forced Abortions, and Mandatory Birth Control: The CCP's Campaign to Suppress Uyghur Birthrates in Xinjiang.* Washington, DC: Jamestown Foundation. Https://jamestown.org/wp-content/uploads/2020/06/Zenz-Internment-Sterilizations-and-IUDs-UPDATED-July-21-Rev2.pdf?x90091.

# 9

# The Ends of Divorce

## Marital Dispute as a Locus of Social Change in India

KATHERINE LEMONS WITH NADIA HUSSAIN

On a cold day in January 2019 a woman in her late twenties carrying a four-month-old baby wrapped in a blanket entered the offices of the *dar ul-qaza* (Arabic, *dār al-qaḍā'*, or shari'a court) in Patna, Bihar, shouting and crying. She directed her fury at the *qazis* (Arabic, *qāḍī*, or Islamic judges) of the court, who had recently granted her a divorce, and at her now ex-husband. She appeared to be stunned that the qazi had granted the divorce and accused him of bias against women. "He has enabled my husband to marry a young and beautiful girl," she fumed, "and to leave me with his four children." We had been following this woman's case, and Nadia Hussain, who was there that day, was surprised by her fury. After all, we had first met this woman, whom we call Ruksana, a year and a half earlier, in May 2017, when her husband, Iqbal, had summoned her to the dar ul-qaza.[1] The case was for *rukhsati*: a request that she return to her marital home. At the time, Ruksana had been living in the Persian Gulf for the better part of seven years, working two different jobs and sending remittances to her parents, who were caring for her children. The rukhsati case became a platform for renegotiating the household economy following the changes effected by Ruksana's migration, and it ended with a short-lived reconciliation. However, several months later, in September 2018, Ruksana requested a divorce by *khula* (Arabic, *khul'*, which is a divorce at the wife's initiative) at the dar ul-qaza on the ground that her husband beat her and that she could no longer bear living in the marriage. She told the qazi that she would rather commit suicide than live with Iqbal. In December Iqbal divorced her, thereby granting the khula that motivated her to storm into the dar ul-qaza in protest.

Two unexpected elements of Rukhsana's story demand analysis. First, the case for rukhsati—a demand for an unhappy wife to return to her marital home—proved to be a site for discussing radical changes to the household economy. And second, Ruksana was disappointed that her suit for khula was successful, as a difficult personal struggle for social change ended along with her marriage. The expectations created by the first court case, the rukhsati, along with common knowledge that divorce processes in state courts can take years to resolve, created the conditions for Ruksana's surprise and anger at receiving the divorce for which she had filed.

The change Ruksana sought was located within her household and entailed radically shifting household economies, which gave it broad social implications. During the rukhsati case, Ruksana negotiated for changes necessary for her to pursue what she called *dhang ki zindigi*, a "decent life." Specifically, a decent life required upsetting the "male breadwinner ideal," which assumes a male head of household and a wife engaged solely in household-based reproductive labor. Such changes, in turn, presupposed family relationships that resemble the ethical life of the bourgeois family, what Hegel has called *Sittlichkeit* (2015, 163). As we explain in this chapter, the changes Ruksana sought thus disrupted the existing household economy: the circulation of remunerated and unremunerated labor, money, and relationships (between spouses, in-laws, children, and others sharing the household) within and between households and the management of that circulation. Attending to Ruksana's anger provides a view of the difficult and intimate labor of social change, in which marital dispute processes play an important role.

## Ruksana

We followed Ruksana's case from May 2017 until several months after her divorce in December 2018. Nadia interviewed Ruksana, her husband, and her mother-in-law numerous times, thus learning more about her life, her family, and her cases at the Imarat-e-Sharia, a nonstate Islamic legal institution. The Imarat-e-Sharia was founded in 1921 by anticolonial Muslim leaders including Maulana Azad and Maulana Sajjad (Ghosh 2008, Sajjad 2019). The institution's headquarters, at which we conducted our research, is on the outskirts of Patna, Bihar. The Patna compound contains a charitable hospital, an information technology (IT) training center, a dar ul-ifta where Muslims come to request *fatwas* (authoritative legal opinions), and a dar ul-qaza complete with a marriage registration office, waiting rooms, an extensive case archive, five judge's chambers, a bookstore, a prayer room, and a qazi-training school where students with advanced training in Islamic law learn to be judges. The dar ul-qaza is the center of a network of sixty-five courts located in Bihar and the neighboring states of Orissa and Jharkhand, for which it also serves as an appellate court. Although the dar ul-qaza is technically an extralegal institution, it is an important resource for poor Muslim women in Bihar, Orissa, and Jharkhand who seek a divorce.[2] Ruksana cut an unusual figure at the Imarat-e-Sharia, not because of her clearly articulated desires nor because she migrated to the Gulf for work several times during the course of her marriage but because of her straightforward demands and biting criticism, which she made no attempt to soften in court or in interviews.

Ruksana was the second of five children born to a family that struggled to make ends meet. Her father worked as a mechanic and could only afford to house his family in a *kaccha basti*—a settlement of temporary housing resembling tents made of plastic tarps—in the outskirts of Patna. According to Ruksana, the determination we observed during her case at the dar ul-qaza was not new but rather a quality she had always had. Perhaps the most important evidence of her determination was that as a child she had convinced her reluctant parents to send her to school like her brothers. She therefore studied at an Urdu-language government (public) school through the eighth grade, which she completed around the age of fourteen.[3] She took significant pride in this achievement and often cited it as a key difference between herself and her illiterate mother-in-law, whom she described as ignorant (*jaahil*). She told Nadia that although she did not think she fit local standards of beauty, her education gave her confidence and enabled her to provide for her children both by earning money and by ensuring that they in turn received decent educations.

In October 2007, when she was nineteen years old, Ruksana married Iqbal and, as is common, moved in with her husband, his parents, and his younger brother.[4] The couple loved each other and continued to do so, even at the time of their divorce eleven years later. However, from the beginning of their marriage, Ruksana and her mother-in-law disliked one another, an antipathy that both women expressed independently to the qazi and to us. In this way, Ruksana's situation was typical: animosity and tension between mothers-in-law and their daughters-in-law is one of the major tropes in scholarship, literature, and film about Indian kinship. In an interview with Nadia in 2018, Ruksana said that following her marriage she tried to perform the role of the good wife by participating in the reproductive labor of the household, in particular cooking and cleaning. She also gave birth to two children in the first two years of her marriage, first a daughter and then a son. None of this assuaged the tensions between Ruksana and her mother-in-law, however.

In addition to household conflicts, Ruksana agonized about her marital family's poverty, a condition shared with many Bihari Muslims. As with many men whose cases appeared in the dar ul-qaza, Iqbal was chronically underemployed. His employment history has been difficult to ascertain: when we first met him, he claimed that he worked as a driver, though later, during the divorce case, he stated instead that he worked as an informal laborer on construction sites and sometimes pulled a rickshaw to earn extra money.[5] During his first years of marriage, Iqbal and his brother were the only wage earners in the household, and their underemployment meant that the family was poor. Ruksana was not willing to accept this poverty and aspired to dhang ki zindigi (a decent life). Ruksana describes this period of her life as agonizing, characterized by crushing poverty and by fights and abuse instigated by her mother-in-law and carried out by Iqbal.

When Ruksana was given the opportunity to move to Oman in 2010 to work as a maid for an Indian family there, she decided to take it. The decision to migrate to Oman marks Ruksana as unusual. She was the only woman we encountered at the Imarat-e-Sharia who migrated abroad for labor, and according to national statistics, male migrants far outnumber women migrants to the Gulf Cooperation Countries (GCC).[6] Ruksana's account of her time in Oman is also surprising from the perspective of literature on domestic migrant labor. Whereas Ruksana refers to working in the Gulf as the best time of her life, a substantial body of scholarship on what Rhacel Parreñas (2015) has called the "international division of reproductive labor" demonstrates that often such women migrants end up carrying out the same reproductive labor that they did at home but for abusive employers (see, for example, the introduction of Friedman and Mahdavi 2015). Parreñas defines the international division of reproductive labor as "a transnational division of labor . . . shaped simultaneously by global capitalism and systems of gender inequality in both sending and receiving countries of migration" (2015, 40). Not only does this division of labor perpetuate gendered hierarchies of labor, moving women from one patriarchal family to another to carry out devalorized household labor, it also augments relations of domination and hierarchies between rich and poor (sending and receiving) countries. Wealthier women in receiving countries can afford more expensive domestic labor, while their employees have relatively less ability to pay for care for their own families, leaving overworked women in sending countries to reproduce the households of women working abroad. In this way, such analyses show that in spite of the improvement that working in the Gulf represented for Ruksana, such migration exacerbates the global economic disparities that also contributed to her family's initial condition of dire poverty.

On the other hand, as C. Y. Thangarajah (2003) has shown, migration can grant women a kind of social capital that alters their status in their home communities. In Ruksana's case, working in the Gulf hurt her reputation at home, as we discuss below, while shaping her concrete view of and aspirations to secure dhang ki zindigi. While she was in the Gulf, from 2010 to 2014, she earned sufficient income to live comfortably there—dressing nicely and eating well—and to send substantial remittances to her family. For four years she sent remittances of 8,000 Indian rupees (112 USD) per month to her parents, with whom she had left her two children.[7] She directed her family to use some of this money to pay for a ritual sacrifice, called *aqeeqah*, to celebrate the birth of her son and for boarding-school tuition for her daughter. She also found the time and inspiration to develop a religious practice, in particular a regular practice of prayer, which she emphasized in the dar ul-qaza.

Iqbal found Ruksana's departure to the Gulf and all it entailed unbearable, and over the course of the next several years, he initiated acts that twice brought Ruksana back to Patna. First, Iqbal was distraught that his children lived with his in-laws and he accused Ruksana's brother-in-law of behaving inappropriately toward his eldest daughter. In 2014, he attempted suicide by taking an overdose of blood pressure medication. At the urging of her employer, Ruksana returned to India and to her marital home, where she gave birth to her third child, a girl, the same year. Family life quickly deteriorated, and Ruksana became literally sleepless with worry about their lack of resources. When sleep medication stopped helping, Ruksana regularly left the house in the middle of the night to wander the neighborhood as she agonized over her family's future, her husband's inability to earn an income, and the way her mother-in-law ran the household. Her husband and especially her mother-in-law thought this roaming was not suitable for a woman and her mother-in-law accused Ruksana of taking a lover.

Fed up with the suspicion and the worry, Ruksana took another job in 2015, this time as a nanny for an Indian family in Jeddah, Saudi Arabia.[8] Again she left her children with her parents, again she was happy with her employers and with her ability to live well in the Gulf, and again she sent remittances of 8,000 rupees per month to support her children. However, after a year, she began to receive summonses from the dar ul-qaza at the Imarat-e-Sharia to respond to a case of rukhsati that Iqbal had filed against her. In 2017, after receiving her third summons to appear, the family for whom she worked sent her back to India to appear in court.

## The Dar ul-Qaza as a Platform for Negotiation

For Ruksana, Iqbal, and her mother-in-law, the rukhsati case *peshis* (hearings) offered a place to formally renegotiate the terms of the household economy that her migration had unsettled. A case of rukhsati is initiated by a husband to request that his estranged wife return to the marital home. The qazis who hear such cases understand their primary aim to be helping couples to reconcile.[9] Cases for rukhsati are common at the dar ul-qaza. According to our analysis of the court's case register, which includes information about the grounds for each case registered in a given year, the year that Iqbal filed for rukhsati (1438/2017), he was one of 129 husbands.[10] Rukhsati cases in that year comprised 34.5 percent of the 374 cases registered at the Imarat-e-Sharia.

Rukhsati cases require the qazi to help the couples and families involved negotiate whether and under what conditions the wife will return to her marital home. This can be a difficult project, given that women who have left their marital homes, often for months or years, can be loath to return. Qazis accepted that in certain cases reconciliation was not possible. They explained to us that when a woman does not want to remain in a marriage, there is no point in forcing the issue. They cannot compel someone to live with a spouse they despise, the qazis have told us. When reconciliation was not possible, which was the case in about a third of the rukhsati cases we encountered, the qazi instead helped the couples negotiate the terms of a khula divorce.[11] Since, from the qazi's perspective, reconciliation is an aim but not a foregone conclusion, rukhsati cases can provide the space for negotiation about how a household should be organized and what the duties of marriage ought and ought not entail, as happened in Ruksana and Iqbal's case.

The qazi's skill helped make the rukhsati case into an opportunity for dispute and renegotiation. This particular qazi, whom we call Aabid, impressed us with his equanimity and respectful attitude toward the litigants. Qazi Aabid's approach to the peshi exemplified the prescribed *adab* (disciplined comportment) discussed in the *Adab al-Qazi* literature that is part of the curriculum for qazis-in-training at the Imarate Sharia. According to the *Fatawa-i-Alamghiri*, which forms a part of this literature, "Adab for a qadi is to abide by what the Law has ordained in promoting justice, removing injustice, showing impartiality, protecting the limits of Law, and following the sunna" (translated in Masud 1984, 146).[12] Adab here entails both good character—being moral and virtuous in dealings with others—and conformity with shari'a. Ruksana and Iqbal's rukhsati case provided Qazi Aabid with ample opportunities to demonstrate his adab, and his attentiveness to Ruksana's demands shaped the judgment in which the case culminated.

Throughout the peshis we observed, Ruksana laughed, belittled her in-laws, fought with her mother-in-law, and joked acerbically and persistently, inciting Qazi Aabid to tell her that her predicament was no laughing matter and to exhort her to treat both her family and the court process with more respect. In spite of Ruksana's irreverence, however, the qazi treated all parties respectfully, using his position to lecture them about the duties of marriage but not to chastise or mock them, as some qazis do.

Qazi Aabid's persistent questioning and respectful but direct discussions with Ruksana, her husband, and her mother-in-law revealed that Ruksana had very specific ideas about the household economy. As Ruksana told Qazi Aabid, she thought that both she and Iqbal should work, especially because her literacy in Urdu qualified her to earn a decent wage, and that only one of them should manage the household's money. Iqbal was reticent about Ruksana working outside the household, however, and insisted that she was needed to perform reproductive labor at home. Ruksana resented this view of women's work, which Iqbal's mother shared. Ruksana referred to their opinion as *jaahil*—ignorant, illiterate, and uncultured. She nonetheless recognized that Iqbal would not budge on this point and appeared prepared to negotiate, concretely, to regain the right at least to manage the household income, if not to contribute to it. She presented a household budget according to which Iqbal would earn an income of 8,000 rupees a month, of which he would give her 5,000 rupees to manage and his mother 2,000 rupees. The remaining 1,000 rupees would be for Iqbal to spend as he wished.

After listening to the parties discuss this proposal and intervening when the argument became too heated, Qazi Aabid brokered an agreement: Ruksana would return to her marital home, after which Iqbal would pay her the 5,000 rupees per month that she requested for household expenses and she would be an obedient wife. In doing so, the qazi proposed an approach to household budgeting that sociologist Shalini Grover, following Whitehead, refers to as a "whole wage system" (2018, 39). Grover's study found whole wage systems to be common in poor household in Delhi. The whole wage system contrasts with a system in which the wage-earning husband simply takes care of household expenses himself, leaving the wife without access to money. As Grover points out, it is usual for the whole wage system to be one facet of a marital bargain characterized by a firm gendered division of labor: it requires men to earn and women to respect their husbands' authority.

Before he adjourned the peshi, Qazi Aabid turned to Ruksana's in-laws and addressed a different part of the household economy: the circulation of care. He asked Iqbal's family to confirm that they were ready for Ruksana to come back and he enjoined them to attend to the relationship between husband and wife. "If someone from the family has an injured relationship, it is just like a physical illness [*jism ki bimari*]," he told them. "It obliges the family to help them to heal. You need to remind each other to do this work," he concluded. Ruksana, for her part, agreed to limit the time she spent with her natal kin. With this understanding, Qazi Aabid wrote up his decision specifying when Ruksana would return to her marital household, the agreement about the budget, and the exigencies her return placed on her and on Iqbal and his family. Ruksana thereby returned to the normative role of unremunerated household manager and reproductive laborer but with a formal mandate to manage most of the household income.

In the context of the rich literature on marital disputes across the world, it is not surprising that the dar ul-qaza can provide the opportunity for women to articulate their wishes. In locations as diverse as coastal Kenya (Hirsch 1998), Zanzibar (Stiles 2009), Iran (Mir-Hosseini 1993), Malaysia (Peletz 2002 and 2020), and India (Lemons 2019), scholars have observed that qazi courts are viewed by the public as "women's courts" because women approach them readily and with great success. What is interesting about this case is that the dar ul-qaza proved helpful not because Ruksana won her case (though women very often do) but because it created a space to explore the conflict about how her household ought to be organized and her marriage ought to be lived. The dar ul-qaza and the qazi's adab enabled the couple to have a discussion about the household economy that could not take place within the household itself. So although Ruksana's departure enacted a challenge to that economy, the qazi's intervention allowed her to articulate this departure as part of an effort to secure a decent life. Implicitly, Ruksana also argued that the decent life necessitated refusing dominant ideals about the household and its economies and remaking the quality of family relationships. However, the dar ul-qaza decision only partially achieved these aims even as the process itself revealed them.

## Against the Male Breadwinner Ideal

Ruksana's focus on the household budget during the rukhsati case drew attention to one of the primary reasons for her migration: Iqbal's underemployment. The discussion of the budget during the rukhsati case further suggests that the reason Ruksana's departure had such a deeply unsettling effect on Iqbal and his mother was that it constituted a practical critique of the ideal of the male breadwinner. This ideal captures the dominant view of how households should be organized in modern-day North India, which is that a household ought to be headed by a man who earns sufficient income to support his wife and children as well as his parents while the woman performs unremunerated reproductive labor within the household. Historians argue that this division of labor emerged with industrial capitalism in nineteenth-century Europe (Laslett and Brenner 1989). Although only skilled and unionized workers were able to earn a wage high enough to support their families, Barbara Laslett and Johanna Brenner noted that the ideal itself was also pervasive, if unrealizable, among the working poor, especially as women were pushed out of factory work (Laslett and Brenner 1989, 391). The male breadwinner ideal has, in certain contexts, served as the basis for welfare policies such as the erstwhile and exclusionary Fordist family wage in the United States (see Cooper 2017). The ideal has also proven pervasive in poor and working-class, as well as middle-class, households in India (Grover 2018). Ruksana's decision to flout the household economy required by the male breadwinner ideal therefore seemed to her marital family to be a betrayal of a conjugal agreement.

In India, the male breadwinner ideal is powerful even where people like Ruksana and Iqbal live in conditions of poverty and chronic underemployment that make it impossible to achieve. Indeed, this impossibility produces conflicts forceful enough to compel families to approach the dar ul-qaza. In thirteen of the thirty-four marital cases that we were able to follow until they reached a judgment, poverty was the central cause of conflict. In ten of these cases, members of the family blamed the husband for the family's difficulties because he was unemployed or underemployed. In these cases, it was not always the wife who called the marriage into question. For example, one woman we met had filed for khula because her parents were dismayed that their son-in-law did not earn sufficient money. The wife proclaimed her love for her husband continuously and made it clear that she had no interest in divorce. However, for her parents, his inability to earn was unacceptable and a breach of the marital bargain.[13] In such cases, the impossible ideal led to marital disputes centered on the husband's failure to earn.

Yet other cases reflected a different approach. We followed four cases in which the central dispute was about whether the wife should be allowed to complete her studies after marriage and/or to work outside the home. In one of these cases, the wife wished to work to support her natal kin, and in another, she wanted to contribute to the earnings of her marital home. The cases represent a shared predicament: women who wish to work outside the home presented a problem in light of the male breadwinner ideal and the divisions of labor it requires. Marriage, according to this ideal, both places responsibility to earn on husbands and equally places responsibility for reproductive labor on wives. This in turn makes working outside the household pragmatically difficult and morally suspect. In the first type of case, the husbands' failure to live up to these expectations produced friction, while in the latter type, it was the wives' wishes to deviate from their expected roles that proved to be a problem. Ruksana was among those wives who sought to play an unorthodox role in the household. In this, her aspirations and actions resemble those discussed in Michelle Gamburd's research in Sri Lanka, which showed that many women migrate for work in response to their husbands' chronic underemployment, a decision that at once responds to and makes visible men's inability to act as sole breadwinners (2003).[14]

The male breadwinner ideal rendered Ruksana's aspirations unacceptable. In contrast to scholarly work that shows how women's earnings (Sen 1990) or their access to landed property (Agarwal 1994) enable them to bargain more effectively, Ruksana's migration instead elicited disdain. Iqbal and his mother could only see her migration for work as evidence that Ruksana was money-hungry and perhaps unfaithful. In this way, their reaction at once resonates with the ambivalence about migrants from the Indian state of Kerala to the Gulf that Filippo Osella (2015) identified, and perhaps exacerbates it: not only was Ruksana far from the oversight of family when she was abroad, as in the cases Osella studied, she also refused to abide by the economic order that the male breadwinner ideal necessitates. Yet for Ruksana, this migration meant something quite different.

Ruksana sought dhang ki zindigi, a decent life: a proper or acceptable but not lavish life in which she and her family would have sufficient resources to eat and dress well and she could send her children to good schools. Such a life would also be conducive to regular religious practice, in particular, prayer. In 2018, Ruksana told Nadia that she had learned over the years that "to lead a decent life requires money." As the necessary condition for a decent life, she understood money (and perhaps the labor through which it is earned) to be a moral and pragmatic necessity. Furthermore, she understood earning to be among her responsibilities to her family to such an extent that about a year following the rukhsati decision she took three jobs as a maid in Patna, defying both the qazi's decision in her case and Iqbal and her mother-in-law's wishes.[15]

## Sittlichkeit: Of Marriage and Motherhood

For Ruksana, the male breadwinner ideal was part and parcel of a household economy that prevented her from pursuing the life she wanted for herself and her children. The household economy she instantiated by migrating also entailed a particular quality of family relationships. Like other women who migrate for work, Ruksana went to the Gulf for economic reasons but also because "migration is a covert strategy to relieve women of their unequal division of labor with men in the family" (Parreñas 2015, 32). Here, global capitalism, and specifically the international division of reproductive labor, appears to have offered Ruksana a way to dodge the long-standing tensions that comprised married life, in particular in a multigenerational household, by giving her the "freedom" to sell her reproductive labor.[16]

Ruksana's decision to undertake remunerated labor reflects an alternative approach to family life. Rather than pursuing the male breadwinner ideal, her ethic of relating to her husband, her children, and her mother-in-law is effectively captured by Hegel's concept of Sittlichkeit, or ethical life. Although the family form that Ruksana sought to forge does not exactly fit the nineteenth-century model of the bourgeois family of Hegel's *Philosophy of Right* and the objective conditions of her life made such a family form unrealizable, the quality of the relationships that she desires are akin to Sittlichkeit. The Hegelian family is, as Rahel Jaeggi puts it, "*a specifically modern family ideal* whose central moment is the idea of the autonomy of its members, which is directed against the patriarchal family. This idea of autonomy includes the voluntariness of the relationships that are entered into here and the self-sufficiency of the new family that is established through marriage vis-à-vis the family of origin" (2018, 147, emphasis in original).[17] The Hegelian family is centered on a married couple living independently from extended families—natal and marital (Hegel 2015, 172). It is, in other words, a nuclear rather than a joint family, in which several generations live in the same household. The independence of the nuclear family is, according to Hegel, distinctive because rather than comprised of natural (blood) relations it is forged around the ethical-legal (*rechtlich sittliche*) relation of a couple. In this way the couple is the center of a new, modern family structure; the married couple is united neither just by romance nor just by contract but instead by a mutual desire for unity and a "love, trust, and common sharing of their entire existence as individuals" (Hegel 2015, 163). In other words, a Hegelian bourgeois marriage is one that supersedes both fleeting carnal attraction and romantic love as well as an initial marriage contract and therefore allows the spouses to become free in and through one another (Jaeggi 2018, 147–151). This is what makes marriage an ethical relation. Jaeggi persuasively argues that because of his emphasis on the nuclear family and on the companionate marriage at its core, Hegel's depiction of the family aptly describes the ideal bourgeois family even in contemporary Europe and North America. Catachrestic though it may seem, we turn to Hegel in a discussion of an Indian joint family because the quality of the family relationships that he understands to be ideal help to capture at least some of Ruksana's aspirations for her own family life. Moreover, Hegel's theory of the family must address the problem of "combining dependence and independence, of living a life of independence in dependence and of dependence in independence" (Jaeggi 2018, 152). For Ruksana, Sittlichkeit is the ground, not for escaping kinship, but for living well in it.

The family form that Ruksana desires and the family form that she lives diverge in significant ways from the historically specific form of the family that Hegel describes. Hegel, for example, writes against a different type of "patriarchal" family from the family that Ruksana resists. Hegel criticizes the Roman law according to which women remained members of their natal homes and were therefore unable to participate in the independent nuclear family (2015, 172n.109). Rather than aspiring to gain full independence from her natal kin, Ruksana lives in a joint family with her husband's kin while maintaining strong relations of care and dependency with her natal family, which disturbs her mother-in-law. In this way, Ruksana's situation is similar to that of other poor, urban, North Indian women, in particular Muslims, who commonly marry relatives and remain in close contact with their natal kin, often living relatively nearby (Vatuk 2017; Grover 2018). As in Ruksana's case, mother-daughter relationships often remain strong following the daughter's marriage and are the source of important emotional and material support (Grover 2018; Palriwala and Uberoi 2008). Ruksana seeks to reform her relationship with her parents-in-law but does not aspire to a nuclear family strongly separated from her natal kin. Yet the relations she seeks to cultivate with her kin are ethical in Hegel's sense.

Three key relationships demonstrate Ruksana's aspirations for kinship: with her mother-in-law, with Iqbal, and with her children. We have already discussed Ruksana's wish for independence from her mother-in-law and, when she is working locally, for a nuclear household. Her criticisms of Iqbal, whom she accused of failing as a husband and a father, indicate that she would like him to assume the position of head of household on the one hand, and to affirm her independence on the other. She blamed his failure as a husband and father on her mother-in-law and, until the divorce came through, she thought that their marriage could be reconfigured. Indeed, her belief in this possibility appears to be one reason she was so dismayed, and so surprised, by the outcome of the divorce case. Iqbal, for his part, clearly and regularly articulated a regard for Ruksana that rose above the romantic and the contractual and recognized her independent character. After the divorce, for example, he told Nadia that he had always liked Ruksana's nature (that she laughed and told jokes) and that he admired her forceful character.

Perhaps the most important way in which Ruksana sought a life of ethical relations is implied by her approach to motherhood. Her decision to migrate produced what scholars call a *transnational family*: a family in which one or both parents live far from their children, usually because of migration.[18] Ruksana's approach to being separated from her children shows us what it means to enact motherhood not according to an ideal of fusion but as a form of ethical relation whose centerpiece lies in providing for one's children. Ruksana usually talked about her children with an eye to her responsibility to provide for them. Among her primary concerns on returning to India from the Gulf was that she was no longer able to send her daughter to a good boarding school. The children's education was central to her struggle with her mother-in-law: sometimes they accused one another of failing to take the children to school; sometimes her mother-in-law accused Ruksana of taking the children to school as an excuse to evade housework. Affection and love were also at issue. Ruksana's mother-in-law voiced anger that both Ruksana's remittances and her children's affection were directed toward her natal family. And finally, during the divorce case, Ruksana made a strong argument for retaining custody of her children. To counter her mother-in-law's claims that she was not raising the children well, she asked her oldest daughter, who was eleven at the time, to testify. The girl tearfully argued that she and her siblings were neglected and hungry when with their father and pleaded to stay with their mother.

With her aspirations to establish a family that offered her the independence to work and to manage the household budget, recognizing such work as a form of care for her husband, her children, and their collective future, Ruksana sought to enact kinship as a web of ethical relations. In seeking this kind of change, Ruksana is far from alone: a robust scholarship discusses changing marital arrangements in India and, in particular, a shift to family structures where the relationship between spouses takes precedence over the relation between extended families, even when the couple lives in a joint family household (Raheja and Gold 1994; Majumdar 2009; Uberoi 1993). Yet her story gives us a sense both of the intimate struggle of which such social change is made and the relationship between renegotiating gendered divisions of labor and the qualitative relationships between family members.

## The Unexpected Divorce

In the months following the rukhsati case, after Ruksana had returned to her marital home and given birth to her fourth child, relations remained tense. Ruksana's mother-in-law refused to believe that Ruksana had been faithful to her husband while she was in the Gulf and she would not recognize Ruksana's fourth child, a son, as her grandchild. The unpleasant atmosphere was augmented by the family's poverty: Iqbal was not earning a living at the time, leaving his parents to support the household financially, yet he continued to refuse Ruksana's wish to work and insisted that her job was to be in the home. Ruksana disobeyed him and took three jobs as a maid; she earned a small income but aggravated the tensions in the household. Ruksana was unwilling or unable to live this way and in September 2018, less than a year later, she filed for divorce by khula at the dar ul-qaza.

The khula process was quick, and Ruksana's appearance in the dar ul-qaza was irregular. Following three hearings, only the first of which Ruksana attended, she was granted an ex-parte khula in December 2018. The husband gives the khula by stating in writing that he has given "one ṭalāq bā'in," after which the couple are divorced. In the dar ul-qaza, the husband usually signs a statement that he has given ṭalāq and the wife signs a statement that she has accepted a khula and forgiven a certain amount of property or money in return. Technically, a husband gives a khula following a negotiation led by the qazi. The ex-parte khula was legal according to the interpretation of Hanafi law in the dar ul-qaza—a man can give a ṭalāq before the qazi without his wife present—but anomalous. The qazi who heard the divorce case based his decision on Ruksana's opening petition and on witness testimonies corroborating the difficulty of the marriage. There was no financial settlement as a part of the judgment, which was unusual; Iqbal was simply encouraged to initiate a separate case if he wanted custody of the children.

Perhaps the most unexpected turn in Ruksana's story was the surprise she articulated at receiving the divorce. In January, Ruksana was shocked to learn that she had been divorced without signing any documents or appearing in court. It seems that in filing for khula, she had sought not divorce but a different end. As she continued to protest on that January day, it became apparent that instead of hoping for a divorce, she had expected that her petition for khula would culminate in an apology from Iqbal and an agreement to live separately from her mother-in-law. She had expected, in other words, that rather than leaving her alone with her four children, the divorce suit would give her another chance to renegotiate her household economies and the quality and shape of her familial relationships. She had approached the dar ul-qaza as a space of argument, not as an efficient divorce-granting mechanism.

Two converging contexts of the divorce proceeding may have led to Ruksana's surprise. First, the sluggish pace and indeterminacy of state district and family courts that hear divorce cases is well known, not only to scholars but also to the general public (Basu 2015; Vatuk 2017). It is also common knowledge that most of the divorce cases that are initiated in these institutions do not culminate in divorce but instead end in dismissal or withdrawal. In such circumstances, it is reasonable that Ruksana might have expected her divorce suit to be more of an opening gambit than a decisive end to her marriage.

The second context was the dar ul-qaza itself. Nadia and I did not share Ruksana's surprise at the outcome of her case or the speed of the decision, as our research has found that the dar ul-qaza at the Imarat-e-Sharia typically grants divorces to women plaintiffs within several months. We also knew from our research that although it was unusual for a khula to be given ex-parte, this was entirely possible given that a khula is effected when a husband gives his wife a *ṭalāq*. But Ruksana's experience with the dar ul-qaza during her rukhsati case had shown a different aspect of this institution. During that case, the dar ul-qaza served as a forum for negotiation, involving seven meetings over the course of a number of months before the judge made a decision. The decision itself explicitly reflected an agreement between the parties and could not have been given without their participation. Ruksana seemed to expect that a divorce petition could also produce such a result. Delay, for Ruksana, would not have been an abrogation of justice but rather a means to it.

## Conclusion

With divorce, marriage ends. This is not an absolute end; divorce always leads to something else, to other configurations of kinship, for better or for worse. However, it is an end to the challenges that a particular marriage can be asked to undergo and the changes it can be asked to undertake. The institution and its ideal outlive the individual instance. The horizon of possibility following the divorce is very different for Ruksana and Iqbal: we were told that Iqbal's mother had already found him a young wife. Following this last encounter with Ruksana in January, we lost touch with her. The kaccha basti in which she lived on the banks of the Ganges River was razed to make way for "Smart City Patna," a beautification and infrastructure improvement initiative, among whose effects has been displacement and disruption for the poor. We know only that she now has four children to support with the help of her natal family, and that while remarriage is not impossible, it will likely not be easily arranged. In a context where the marriage imperative is alive and well, the loss that accompanies this divorce includes the loss of the space for argument—the loss of a struggle for reconfiguring household economies, which is an intimate and social change.[19] It seems to us that at the end of the day, part of Ruksana's sadness about the divorce was that it cut short a project that was less about getting out of a marriage than about reconfiguring it. The irony is that among prevalent laments about the difficulty Muslim women have in divorcing, in comparison to their husbands, Ruksana divorced too easily. The much-despised lethargy of the Indian courts was perhaps both what she expected and what she needed to forge the household economies of money and ethical love that she sought.

### Acknowledgments

We would like to thank our interlocutors at the Imarat-e-Sharia, and in particular, the woman we call Ruksana. Thanks also go to Daniel Chiu-Castillo for research assistance. Nada Moumtaz, Rachel Berger, and Gretchen Bakke read and commented on an earlier draft of the essay. The research was funded by the Canadian Social Sciences and Humanities Research Council.

NOTES

1. Ruksana and all the other names in this article are pseudonyms.
2. Relative to the number of Muslims living in these states, the case numbers at the Imarat-e-Sharia are low. However, according to our analysis of the Patna district court files, there are also very few Muslim cases in civil courts. Of the 572 cases for divorce, dissolution of marriage, and separation by mutual consent filed between July 5, 2016, to March 21, 2017, 6 percent (39) cases were from the Muslim community. The low number of Muslim cases is best explained by the fact that most divorces take place extrajudicially. For Muslim women seeking divorce, the dar ul-qaza is an important resource.
3. Ruksana managed in this way to prevail in spite of the odds. Although in India children are legally required to complete at least primary school—grades one through eight—poor children, and particularly girls, often fail to attain this level of education. According to the Ministry of Human Resource Development, the dropout rate before the completion of fifth grade in 2013–2014 was 18.30 percent and 21.20 percent for boys and girls, respectively. As children age, the dropout rate diverges along gender lines, so the dropout rate before completion of eighth grade was 32.9 percent and 39.2 percent for boys and girls, respectively. Among adults, the gender literacy gap is significant: according to the Census of 2011, the national female literacy rate was 65.46 percent and the male literacy rate was 82.24 percent (see India 2011). In Bihar, the census showed that literacy rates are far below national averages for both men and women, and the gender gap was pronounced, with a 51.5 percent literacy rate for women and a 71.2 percent literacy rate for men (para 3.3).
4. According to the later dar ul-qaza case, the mahr was 11,000 rupees.
5. When Nadia interviewed him again in January 2019 he had just gotten a job driving with Ola Cabs, India's Uber, indicating a significant increase in status.
6. The International Labor Organization (ILO) reported that in 2013, of 1,112,032 total migrants to Oman from India 14.4 percent (92,819) were women and 85.6 percent (551,885) were men. In Saudi Arabia, to which Ruksana later migrated for a different job, the gender ratio is slightly different, with women making up 30 percent of the migrant population. In 2013, the total number of Indian migrants in the GCC countries was 13,276,229, and 5,9000,000 of migrants were women (44 percent) (Sasikumar and Thimothy 2015).

7. Eight thousand rupees was also the amount that Iqbal said he was earning at the time, so these remittances would have doubled their income had the money gone to Ruksana's marital household.
8. Ruksana's account of where, specifically, in the Gulf she lived was inconsistent. Usually she said that the first time she left she worked in Oman as a maid and the second time she worked in Jeddah, Saudi Arabia, as a nanny, but sometimes she referred to Kuwait.
9. The qazis at the Imarat-e-Sharia insist that divorce is the most despised of permissible actions in Islam. Therefore, although they help women to separate from their husbands, they first try to help couples reconcile. Among the avenues for woman-initiated divorce, the qazis prefer khula over faskh, as khula is ultimately carried out by the husband when he pronounces a divorce and therefore implies that both parties have agreed to separate.
10. The record books are kept according to the Hijri year, which runs from Muharram to Muharram. May 2017 was in Hijri 1438.
11. Of the thirty-four cases that we were able to follow to their conclusions, ten were rukhsati cases. Of these, three ended as khula, four ended as rukhsati (including Ruksana's case), and another three were unresolved.
12. In the qazi's training course, they also study *Adab Qaza* by Hazrat Qazi Mujahid Al-Islam Qasmi, which includes chapters on the comportment of the qazi.
13. From the perspective of the spouses, this case ended happily, as the husband was able to come up with some money for Eid and they were reunited. It seemed that although they were no less poor thereafter, the family decided to accept the marriage (which they had, after all, arranged).
14. It is interesting that both Gamburd's (2003) research in Sri Lanka and Grover's (2018) research in urban India suggest that when men are underemployed, families adjust their expectations, making it acceptable for women to perform remunerated labor outside the home. In the cases we saw at the Imarat-e-Sharia, this instead seems to be a source of serious friction between women and their marital kin.
15. She took these jobs out of necessity—they were part-time, insecure labor characteristic of much domestic work in India now, rather than full time, more secure jobs (on changes in domestic labor arrangements in the neighboring state of West Bengal, see Ray and Qayum 2009).
16. Ruksana was also lucky, as she enjoyed living with the family that employed her, mitigating the frustrations that Parreñas has convincingly argued often accompany the move from one patriarchal family to another (2015).
17. See Hegel's *Philosophy of Right*, Part 3, Section 1A for his account of marriage and the family (2015). In feminist debates about Hegel's concept of the family, one important question is whether the strict gender hierarchies that are central to his analysis can be dismantled without undoing his view of bourgeois families and marriage (see, for example, Frederick Neuhouser 2000, chap. 7). I am also not claiming that Ruksana or anyone else *ought* to aspire to the bourgeois family. My claim instead is that Sittlichkeit as Hegel theorizes it offers a helpful conceptual vocabulary for the desires that Ruksana articulated.
18. On the sacrifices mothers in particular make to escape abusive marriages, see especially Parreñas 2015, chap. 3. On the pathos of maternal separation but also the many different configurations of family and intimacy that result from migration, see Boehm 2016.
19. As Srimati Basu has pointedly shown, marriage and the imperative to marry may be the problem, yet divorce is only sometimes the solution.

## REFERENCES

Agarwal, Bina. 1994. *A Field of One's Own: Gender and Land Rights in South Asia*. Cambridge: Cambridge University Press.

Basu, Srimati. 2015. *The Trouble with Marriage: Feminists Confront Law and Violence in India*. Oakland: University of California Press.

Boehm, Deborah A. 2016. *Intimate Migrations: Gender, Family, and Illegality among Transnational Mexicans*. New York: New York University Press.

Cooper, Melinda. 2017. *Family Values: Between Neoliberalism and the New Social Conservatism*. Brooklyn: Zone Books.

Friedman, Sara, and Pardis Mahdavi, eds. 2015. *Migrant Encounters: Intimate Labor, the State, and Mobility across Asia*. Philadelphia: University of Pennsylvania Press.

Gamburd, Michelle. 2003. "Breadwinners No More." In *Global Woman: Nannies, Maids, and Sex Workers in the New Economy*, edited by Barbara Ehrenreich and Arlie Russell Hochschild, 190–206. New York: Metropolitan Books.

Ghosh, Papiya. 2008. *Community and Nation: Essays on Identity and Politics in Eastern India*. New Delhi: Oxford University Press.

Grover, Shalini. 2018. *Marriage, Love, Caste, and Kinship Support: Lived Experiences of the Urban Poor in India*. Abingdon: Routledge.

Hegel, Georg Wilhelm Friedrich. 2015. *Hegel's Philosophy of Right*. Translated by T. M. Knox. Oxford: Oxford University Press.

Hirsch, Susan F. 1998. *Pronouncing and Persevering: Gender and the Discourses of Disputing in an African Islamic Court*. Chicago: University of Chicago Press.

India, Government of. 2011. Ministry of Statistics and Programme Implementation, chap. 3, para. 3.1.

Jaeggi, Rahel. 2018. *Critique of Forms of Life*. Translated by Ciaran Cronin. Cambridge, MA: Belknap Press of Harvard University Press.

Laslett, Barbara, and Johanna Brenner. 1989. "Gender and Social Reproduction: Historical Perspectives." *Annual Review of Sociology* 15:381–404.

Lemons, Katherine. 2019. *Divorcing Traditions: Islamic Marriage Law and the Making of Indian Secularism*. Ithaca: Cornell University Press.

Majumdar, Rochona. 2009. *Marriage and Modernity: Family Values in Colonial Bengal*. Durham: Duke University Press.

Masud, Muhammad Khalid. 1984. "Adab al-Muftī: The Muslim Understanding of Values, Characteristics, and Role of a Muftī." In *Moral Conduct and Authority: The Place of Adab in South Asian Islam*, edited by Barbara D. Metcalf, 124–150. Berkeley: University of California Press.

Mir-Hosseini, Ziba. 1993. *Marriage on Trial: A Study of Islamic Family Law: Iran and Morocco Compared*. London: Tauris.

Nair, Janaki. 1996. *Women and Law in Colonial India: A Social History*. New Delhi: Kali for Women in collaboration with the National Law School of India University.

Neuhouser, Frederick. 2000. *Foundations of Hegel's Social Theory: Actualizing Freedom*. Cambridge, MA: Harvard University Press.

Osella, Filippo. 2015. "Migration and the (Im)morality of Everyday Life." In *Migrant Encounters: Intimate Labor, the State, and Mobility across Asia*, edited by Sara Friedman and Pardis Mahdavi, 46–67. Philadelphia: University of Pennsylvania Press.

Palriwala, Rajni, and Patricia Uberoi. 2008. *Marriage, Migration, and Gender*. Vol. 5 of *Women and Migration in Asia*. New Delhi: SAGE Publications.

Parreñas, Rhacel Salazar. 2015. *Servants of Globalization: Migration and Domestic Work*. Stanford: Stanford University Press.

Peletz, Michael G. 2002. *Islamic Modern: Religious Courts and Cultural Politics in Malaysia*. Princeton Studies in Muslim Politics. Princeton: Princeton University Press.

Qasmi, Hazrat Qazi Mujahid Al-Islam. 2005. *Adab Qaza*. Patna: Muktaba Imarat Sharia.

Raheja, Gloria Goodwin, and Ann Grodzins Gold. 1994. *Listen to the Heron's Words*. Oakland: University of California Press.

Ray, Raka, and Seemin Qayum. 2009. *Cultures of Servitude: Modernity, Domesticity, and Class in India*. Stanford: Stanford University Press.

Sajjad, Mohammad. 2019. *Muslim Politics in Bihar: Changing Contours*. London: Routledge.

Sasikumar, S. K., and Rakkee Thimothy. 2015. "From India to the Gulf Region: Exploring Links between Labour Markets, Skills and the Migration Cycle." International Labor Organization. Https://www.ilo.org/wcmsp5/groups/public/---asia/---ro-bangkok/---sro-new_delhi/documents/publication/wcms_397363.pdf.

Sen, Amaratya. 1990. "Gender and Cooperative Conflicts." In *Persistent Inequalities: Women and World Development*, edited by Irene Tinker, 123–149. New York: Oxford University Press.

Stiles, Erin E. 2009. *An Islamic Court in Context: An Ethnographic Study of Judicial Reasoning*. New York: Palgrave Macmillan.

Thangarajah, C. Y. 2003. "Veiled Constructions: Conflict, Migration and Modernity in Eastern Sri Lanka." *Contributions to Indian Sociology* 37 (1–2):141–162.

Uberoi, Patricia, ed. 1993. *Family, Kinship, and Marriage in India*. New Delhi: Oxford University Press.

Vatuk, Sylvia. 2017. *Marriage and Its Discontents: Women, Islam, and the Law in India*. New Delhi: Women Unlimited and Kali for Women.

# Conclusion

## Islamic Divorce in Context and in Action

### Notes from the Field

ERIN E. STILES AND AYANG UTRIZA YAKIN

For many years, I (Erin Stiles) conducted ethnographic research in the *kadhi* (Swahili; Arabic, qāḍī) courts in Zanzibar, a semiautonomous island state of Tanzania. The status of Islamic law in Zanzibar differs from the other contexts described in this volume. Islamic courts are part of Zanzibar's state legal system and they have jurisdiction over personal-status matters for all Muslims, including marriage, divorce, and inheritance; the population of Zanzibar is nearly entirely Muslim. Although state law regulates procedure, there is little legislation relevant to personal-status law and the kadhis decide cases based on their training in Islamic jurisprudence (fiqh). The kadhi with whom I worked most, a man I call Shaykh Hamid, presided over the court in the fishing village of Mkokotoni, which serves the northernmost rural region of the Zanzibari island of Unguja. Shaykh Hamid would frequently refer to his court as a "hospital," in that his goal was healing relationships. He once told me, "Where do you go for *dawa* [medicine] for an illness? And if you are sick [with legal problems] you come to get your dawa at the court. You come and tell the kadhi that you are sick" (Stiles 2009, 189). In this vein, the typically mild-mannered Shaykh Hamid once angrily reprimanded a young man trying to repudiate his wife in court by telling him that the court was a "place to solve problems—*not* a place to divorce!" (190).

I attended Shaykh Hamid's daily court sessions for over fifteen months in 1999–2000, and also on subsequent shorter visits until his death in 2005. I listened closely to initial conversations about disputes and to case hearings, I interviewed litigants, and I talked for hours every day with Shaykh Hamid and his chief clerk. I have argued elsewhere that Shaykh Hamid's ardent commitment to "curing" broken marriages reflected his overall view of the work of a kadhi. He frequently characterized his approach as one of compromise and, in his gentle way, he was adamant that his job was not to apply *sheria za dini* (Swahili, religious law) in full. Indeed, he told me that such an approach would be "too heavy" for Africa and that Zanzibari laws were comparatively very "light" (193). As he saw it, his legal practice was grounded in the Qur'an, hadith, and Shāfiʿī fiqh, but it also drew on community norms and understandings of marriage, state regulations of procedure, and state and local patterns of authority in dispute processing.

WE CONCLUDE OUR VOLUME with a brief look at Zanzibar because it presents yet another type of legal landscape in which Muslims can obtain Islamic divorces—a landscape in which state-appointed kadhis preside over state-run Islamic courts but decide cases according to their understandings of Islamic law, as there is little Zanzibari legislation relevant to marriage and divorce. As the chapters in this collection show, this is only one among many ways in which Muslims can access Islamic legal remedies today. Our chapters describe the varying legal landscapes of nine countries in Africa, Asia, and the Middle East and the diverse ways in which Muslims seek out or are subject to religious divorces. Despite these differences, the chapters show similar patterns in the way legal professionals, religious experts, and laypeople engage in legal practice and reasoning. Taken together, the chapters document how twenty-first-century patterns of social mobility, economic and legal changes, and political upheaval are influencing the practices and processes of divorcing among Muslims across these legal landscapes.

In considering the collection as a whole, what emerges as one of the most obvious conclusions is that the ability to resolve marital issues and dissolve marriages according to Islamic law is very important for many Muslims today, from Ghana to India and from Lebanon to Indonesia. Muslims in vastly different cultural and political contexts similarly value the ability to end marriages in religiously appropriate ways, often regardless of whether a particular state recognizes religious law. However, how people achieve this varies significantly, and in the pages of this book, we encounter Muslims seeking out Islamic means of divorcing in myriad ways: from appealing to local religious authorities and nonstate judicial councils to bringing claims to state-supported Islamic courts or civil courts that apply religious law. Muslims seek resolution from religious experts known as malamai in Ghana, from community qāḍīs in Mali, and from Shiʿi scholars in Lebanon. Muslims seek religious divorces from nonstate Islamic judicial councils in South Africa and from the dar ul-qaza in India. In China, an "Islamic divorce" might be a simple private pronunciation of ṭalāq that has no official legal standing. In Indonesia and Lebanon, Muslims may seek divorce in state-supported religious courts. In Pakistan, Egypt, and India, Muslims may pursue divorce in state family courts where judges draw on shariʿa in some fashion, even if they are not extensively trained in fiqh.

The chapters in this collection make evident the necessity of considering twenty-first-century Muslim marriage and divorce practices in the global context and as subject to global processes. From West Africa to western China, Muslim marriages are impacted by global discourses on Islamic authority, authenticity, global discourses on gender rights and gender equity, global patterns of and approaches to secularity, and global economic inequalities and attendant patterns of urbanization and migration. The realities and practices of Islamic divorce thus illustrate the productive interplay of the global and the local (see Appadurai 1996), or what some scholars refer to as *glocalization* (Robertson 1995). In general, these interactive exchanges between global and local are linked to migration, socioeconomic and technological changes, media, and education, and in particular in this volume, we see them manifest in terms of marital expectations at the household level and in dispute processing, divorce practice, and patterns of legal reasoning at the community and institutional levels. The chapters in this volume shows how Islamic divorce practices result from and are subject to processes of adaptation, adoption, hybridization, and legal innovations within the framework of a "glocalized" world.

For example, several of the chapters show us what kinds of twenty-first-century developments and patterns of global change affect expectations for Muslim marriages and in, some cases, cause friction that can lead to divorce. Some chapters illustrate this in the way that economic changes lead to a reconfiguration of gendered household roles and to new expectations in marriage—particularly on the part of women. Schulz and Diallo find that older Muslims in Mali attribute a perceived rising divorce rate to a changing economy that has led more women to seek employment outside the home, which has in turn led to a lack of adherence to a more universalized view of "Islamic values" and declining authority of elders. Lemons and Hussain show how Indian women's participation in global labor migration can lead to changing expectations of household responsibilities and economics. Issaka-Toure's chapter, on Ghanaian marriages, also touches on the impact of labor migration. Steenberg indicates that in western China, changing economic patterns have led to a destabilizing of the affinal relationships among Uyghurs, which are critical to keeping marriages intact. The contributions also show how global discourses of gender rights and of Islamic authenticity and authority affect marital expectations at the household level. Schulz and Diallo note that in Mali, Muslims in some regions argue that greater adherence to "universal" standards of Islamic behavior would counter the perceived rising divorce rate. In Indonesia, men and women are filing increasing divorce claims on grounds of a wife's sexual dissatisfaction, and Yakin traces this trend to an increasing emphasis on and acceptance of the importance of a wife's sexual pleasure in marriage.

Many of the chapters in this volume look at legal venues, both courts and other types, as sites of negotiation, resistance, and accountability in managing both spousal relationships and the interplay of different legal ideas, norms, and institutions, and thus build on earlier work in this vein (Rosen 1989; Hirsch 1994, 1998; Osanloo 2009). In most cases, this is particularly important for Muslim women, who most frequently have fewer options for divorcing than men do—even in states that have instituted reforms intending to improve women's options in divorce. Lemons and Hussain, for instance, address this directly by showing how Ruksana specifically intended to renegotiate the terms of her marriage by bringing a divorce suit to the dar ul-qaza. In Issaka-Toure's chapter, we similarly find Ghanaian Muslim women approaching the malamai in order to negotiate ṭalāqs (known as *saki*) pronounced by their husbands. And Landry describes how in Lebanon, there are strategic steps that women will take to secure the best outcome in a difficult situation by suing for maintenance when divorce is actually the goal (this is very similar to women's strategies in Zanzibar).

What is particularly notable in the chapters is that the "doing" of Islamic law in these processes of negotiation (to reference Dupret's call for scholars to examine "what do people do when referring to Islamic law" [2007, 81]) is interactional and intersubjective. We see that legal reasoning is not simply the domain of legal professionals or religious experts but is also the purview of disputants who strategize about their best legal options and best sorts of claims. Litigant arguments can inform the reasoning of legal experts, and the chapters particularly note this in regard to women's strategies and reasoning. Together, the chapters illustrate the flexibility inherent in the twenty-first-century Islamic legal tradition, and we see that resolutions for marital disputes are sometimes generated through exchanges between disputing parties and adjudicating authorities, through the interactions of individuals and familial networks, and in both community-level and institutional practice. Issaka-Toure's chapter, for example, shows how local understandings of legitimate divorce initiated by women in Ghana, such as the action known as hijra (going home), can influence the way in which Islamic authorities interpret Islamic modes of divorce such as khulʿ and ṭalāq. And Lemons and Hussein describe how in India, a woman's arguments in favor of altered household economic arrangements significantly shaped the qazi's ruling in her case. Yakin shows that in Indonesia, litigant complaints about sexual dissatisfaction inform how judges consider grounds for divorce. By contrast, Schulz and Diallo describe tensions in northern Mali between lay understandings of Islamic divorce, which adhere to local Tuareg conventions, and the views of Muslim militants, who advocate a particular view of "shariʿa rules" that differs from local norms.

Other chapters emphasize this interactional process by showing how judicial reasoning can negotiate the relationship between different kinds of legal sources in response to cases brought forward by litigants and in light of globally circulating discourses. For example, Giunchi describes how in Pakistan, state-court judges use Islamic legal tools such as talfīq (patching together) and takhayyur (choosing between schools of legal thought) to reconceptualize legal positions in light of global discourses on human rights and gender equity (sometimes to the chagrin of the ʿulama'). Yakin shows how in Indonesia, religious-court judges expand the meaning of syiqaq (Arabic, shiqāq) in order to grant divorces brought on grounds of sexual dissatisfaction, all the while adhering to state law (which does not permit divorce on such grounds) and Islamic legal argumentation. Bernard-Maugiron similarly describes how in Egypt, state judges sometimes pointedly cite Ḥanafī fiqh in their reasoning processes as a means of legitimizing state legislation. The chapters in this volume thus not only describe situations of legal pluralism but also examine pluralism in action by considering how people—both laypeople and religious and legal experts—navigate legal options and draw on various kinds of legal resources in strategizing and decision making. Despite widely varying cultural contexts and differences in the official status of shari'a vis-à-vis the state, in everyday legal practice, Muslims develop similarly pragmatic strategies for navigating plural legal landscapes to achieve favorable outcomes in marital dissolution.

A particularly intriguing aspect of this trend is the competition that sometimes results between differing kinds of authority figures, and a number of chapters take up this issue. Landry's chapter on Lebanon describes the tension between Shi'i clerics and state-appointed judges, who typically disregard the Shi'i scholars' support of ṭalāq al-ḥākim when women bring such decision to the state courts. Landry describes this as a power struggle, in which the state wants to be the only avenue for ṭalāq al-ḥākim. The tensions revolve around who is qualified to serve as the mujtahid (interpreter of the law), and state-court judges are frequently skeptical of the claims of Shi'i scholars. Giunchi also discusses debates about who is qualified to exercise ijtihād in her chapter on Pakistan, where 'ulama' have questioned whether secular judges are qualified as mujtahids. Bernard-Maugiron describes how in Egypt, religious and political authorities compete over control of the religious sphere through debates about family law. Schulz and Diallo argue that in northern Mali, local qadis have asserted themselves as official authority figures in the absence of a strong state presence, a development that the authors propose is exacerbated by a yawning gap between state legislation and local practice. And Issaka-Toure describes tensions in Ghana that arise when malamai support divorces initiated by women but that their husbands do not acknowledge.

Of course, this book leaves many questions unanswered, and these unanswered questions suggest many fruitful lines for future research. Promising future projects might consider unregistered and religious-only marriages, such as *nikāḥ sirri*, *nikāḥ mishwar*, and *nikāḥ shar'ī*, both in Muslim-majority and -minority contexts. Other areas of research might delve more closely into the relationships between state and nonstate actors in the processing of disputes and the ways in which they collaborate and compete. Another promising avenue of research would move beyond formal marriage to consider other types of partnerships that Muslims make, such as different kinds of cohabitation and co-parenting relationships. This could include a focus on same-sex partnerships and how gender identity informs marital and other relationships in Muslim contexts. In the 1980s, for example, fatwas issued by Shaykh Muḥammad Sayyid Ṭanṭāwi at al-Azhar University in Egypt and Ayatollah Khomeini in Iran both argued for the permissibility of gender-confirmation surgery from an Islamic perspective (Alipour 2017).

The many cases and contexts described in the chapters of volume have revealed how various actors (judges, laypeople, lawyers, religious experts) contextualize Islamic law (fiqh) in their understanding and practices, and also how the interpretation of Islamic law as it exists in the scriptural sources and the jurisprudential literature can be "adjusted," so to speak. This adjustment can result from reinterpretations favorable to the dominant economic structure or political situation, through the acknowledgment of local norms and customs, or through attempts to bring shari'a into accord with international conventions, norms, and developments. We thus notice how the constraints of legal relevance and procedural correctness are exercised in context and in action and how what might be considered extralegal motivations frequently inform reasoning processes. Together, the chapters of this book present a compelling case for considering Islamic divorce not simply as something that exists on paper, in classical Islamic legal texts, in contemporary law codes, or in the records of a court case. Rather, it should be studied in practice and in context and with attention both to the internal dynamics of the family and the community and the many attendant influences emanating from elsewhere.

## REFERENCES

Alipour, M. 2017. "Islamic Shari'a Law, Neotraditionalist Muslim Scholars and Transgender Sex-Reassignment Surgery: A Case Study of Ayatollah Khomeini's and Sheikh al-Tantawi's Fatwas." *International Journal of Transgenderism* 18 (1):91–103.

Appadurai, Arjun. 1996. *Modernity at Large: Cultural Dimensions of Globalization*. Minneapolis: University of Minnesota Press.

Dupret, Baudouin. 2007. "What Is Islamic Law? A Praxiological Answer and an Egyptian Case Study." *Theory, Culture & Society* 24 (2):79–100.

Hirsch, Susan F. 1994. "Kadhi's Courts as Complex Sites of Resistance: The State, Islam and Gender in Postcolonial Kenya." In *Contested States: Law, Hegemony and Resistance*, edited by Susan F. Hirsch and M. Lazarus-Black, 207–230. New York: Routledge.

———. 1998. *Pronouncing and Persevering: Gender and Justice in an African Islamic Court*. Chicago: University of Chicago Press.

Osanloo, Arzoo. 2009. *The Politics of Women's Rights in Iran*. Princeton: Princeton University Press.

Robertson, Roland. 1995. "*Glocalisation*: Time-Space and Homogeneity-Heterogeneity." In *Global Modernities*, edited by Mike Featherstone, Scott Lash, and Roland Robertson, 25–44. Sage: London.

Rosen, Lawrence. 1989. *The Anthropology of Justice: Law as Culture in Islamic Society*. Cambridge: Cambridge University Press.

Stiles, Erin E. 2009. *An Islamic Court in Context: An Ethnographic Study of Judicial Reasoning*. London: Palgrave Macmillan.

# NOTES ON CONTRIBUTORS

**NATHALIE BERNARD-MAUGIRON** is a senior researcher at the French Institute of Research for Development (IRD). Her main fields of interest are the transition processes in Egypt and the Arab world after 2011 and personal-status law reforms and the judiciary in Egypt and in the Arab world. From 2010 to 2014 she was the codirector of the Institut d'études de l'Islam et des sociétés du monde musulman (IISMM) at Ecole des Hautes études en sciences sociales (EHESS) in Paris. She teaches courses in introduction to Middle East law courses at Paris 1 Panthéon-Sorbonne University, SciencesPo Paris, and EHESS.

**SOULEYMANE DIALLO** is a lecturer at the Department of Social Anthropology at the University of Münster, Germany. His publications include the monograph, *"The Truth about the Desert": Exile, Memory, and the Making of Communities among Malian Tuareg Refugees in Niger*; "The Truth Is That We Are Not Tuareg: Exile, Memory, and the Making of Bellah-Iklan Community in Niger," in B. S. Lecocq and A. Niang (eds.), *Identités saheliennes en temps de crise: histoires, enjeux et perspectives*; and several articles on changing social identities among Tuareg refugees in Niger.

**FATIMA ESSOP** is an advocate of the High Court of South Africa and is currently a doctoral candidate in the Law Faculty at the University of Cape Town, where she also lectures. She has practiced as an attorney in public-interest litigation at the Legal Resources Centre and Women's Legal Centre in Cape Town and as an advocate of the High Court of South Africa in various areas of law including constitutional law and Muslim family law. She is an accredited family-law mediator with extensive experience in the area of Muslim family law.

**ELISA GIUNCHI** is associate professor of the history and politics of North Africa and the Middle East at the University of Milan, Italy. She holds an M-Phil in Islamic studies and a PhD in history from the University of Cambridge and is a member of the editorial boards of various academic journals. Her research interests include the political and legal implications of shari'a discourses in Pakistan and the rewriting of Pakistani history through school textbooks.

**NADIA HUSSAIN** holds a BA in law from Jamia Millia Islamia University and an LLM in Law from the Amity Institute of Advanced Legal Studies with a focus on human rights.

**FULERA ISSAKA-TOURE** completed her postdoctoral fellowship at the University of Bayreuth and took up a lecturer position at the University of Ghana, Legon. Currently she is on study leave from the University of Ghana, Legon, and undertaking research on West African migrants in Germany with a research affiliation at the University of Bayreuth.

**JEAN-MICHEL LANDRY** is assistant professor of anthropology at Carleton University and an affiliated researcher at the Institut Français du Proche-Orient. He graduated from the University of California, Berkeley, in 2016, and in 2017 he received the award for best dissertation from the Association of Middle East Anthropology. His work focuses on Islam in the Middle East and North America as well as anthropological uses of critical theory. It has appeared in *L'Homme*, *Telos*, *Comparative Studies of South Asia, Africa and the Middle East*, and the *Immanent Frame*.

**KATHERINE LEMONS** is associate professor of anthropology at McGill University and author of *Divorcing Traditions: Islamic Marriage Law and the Making of Indian Secularism*, as well as numerous articles on Islam, law, gender, and India.

**DOROTHEA SCHULZ** is professor of social anthropology at the University of Münster, Germany. Her publications include *Political Legitimacy in Postcolonial Mali*; *Muslims and New Media in West Africa: Pathways to God*; the coedited volumes *Prayer in the City: The Making of Muslim Sacred Places and Urban Life* and *Cultural Entrepreneurship in Africa*; and numerous articles and book chapters on Islam in Mali.

**RUNE STEENBERG** is an anthropologist focusing on the Uyghurs and Xinjiang. His fields of interest are in kinship and economic anthropology as well as narrative studies and the anthropology of values and ideology. After doing research on marriage, local communities, and trading networks in Central Asia and China, in recent years he has also documented the mass incarceration, surveillance and propaganda in and about Xinjiang Uyghur Autonomous Region, PRC. He is currently a researcher at Palacky University Olomouc.

**ERIN E. STILES** is associate professor of anthropology at the University of Nevada, in Reno. She has conducted ethnographic research on marital disputing and Islamic courts in Zanzibar, Tanzania, and on religious experiences in northern Utah. She is the author of *An Islamic Court in Context: An Ethnographic Study of Judicial Reasoning* and the coeditor of *Gendered Lives in the Western Indian Ocean: Islam, Marriage, and Sexuality on the Swahili Coast*, and she has published numerous articles and book chapters on the practice of Islamic law in Zanzibar.

**AYANG UTRIZA YAKIN** is a research associate at the section of the chair of law and religion of the research institute, Religions, Spiritualities, Cultures, Societies (RSCS) at the Université Catholique de Louvain (UCLouvain), Belgium, and postdoctoral researcher at Sciences-Po Bordeaux, France. He was a visiting fellow and postdoctoral researcher in Oxford (2012), Harvard (2013), Tokyo (2016), and UCLouvain (2016–2019) and visiting professor in Arabic and Islamic Studies at the Department of Languages and Cultures, Section Middle-East, Ghent University (2019–2021). He is the co-editor of *Rethinking Halal: Genealogy, Current Trends, and New Interpretation.*

# INDEX

**Available titles in The Politics of Marriage and Gender: Global Issues in Local Contexts series:**

Joanne Payton, *Honor and the Political Economy of Marriage: Violence against Women in the Kurdistan Region of Iraq*

Rama Srinivasan, *Courting Desire: Litigating for Love in North India*

Hui Liu, Corinne Reczek, and Lindsey Wilkinson, eds., *Marriage and Health: The Well-Being of Same-Sex Couples*

Sara Smith, *Intimate Geopolitics: Love, Territory, and the Future on India's Northern Threshold*

Rebecca Joubin, *Mediating the Uprising: Narratives of Gender and Marriage in Syrian Television Drama*

Raksha Pande, *Learning to Love: Arranged Marriages and the British Indian Diaspora*

Asha L. Abeyasekera, *Making the Right Choice: Narratives of Marriage in Sri Lanka*

Natasha Carver, *Marriage, Gender, and Refugee Migration: Spousal Relationships among Muslim Somalis in the United Kingdom*

Yafa Shanneik and Annelies Moors, eds., *Global Dynamics of Shi'a Marriages: Religion, Gender, and Belonging*

Anna-Maria Walter, *Intimate Connections: Love and Marriage in Pakistan's High Mountains*

Viktoriya Kim, Nelia G. Balgoa, and Beverley Anne Yamamoto, *The Politics of International Marriage in Japan*

Anne-Marie D'Aoust, ed., *Transnational Marriage and Partner Migration: Constellations of Security, Citizenship, and Rights*

Minjeong Kim and Hyeyoung Woo, eds., *Redefining Multicultural Families in South Korea: Reflections and Future Directions*

Erin E. Stiles and Ayang Utriza Yakin, eds., *Islamic Divorce in the Twenty-First Century: A Global Perspective*